IN PRAISE OF ANTIHEROES

VICTOR BROMBERT

IN PRAISE OF

ANTIHEROES

FIGURES AND THEMES IN

MODERN EUROPEAN LITERATURE

1830–1980

THE UNIVERSITY *of* CHICAGO PRESS

CHICAGO AND LONDON

VICTOR BROMBERT is the Henry Putnam University Professor of Romance and
Comparative Literatures at Princeton University.

The University of Chicago Press, Chicago 60637
The University of Chicago Press, Ltd., London
© 1999 by The University of Chicago
All rights reserved. Published 1999
Printed in the United States of America
08 07 06 05 04 03 02 01 00 99   2 3 4 5
ISBN: 0-226-07552-4

Library of Congress Cataloging-in-Publication Data

Brombert, Victor H.
     In praise of antiheroes : figures and themes in modern European literature, 1830–1980 /
Victor Brombert.
          p.   cm.
     Includes bibliographical references and index.
     ISBN 0-226-07552-4 (cloth : alk. paper)
     1. European literature—19th century—History and criticism.   2. European literature—
20th century—History and criticism.   3. Antiheroes in literature.   I. Title.
PN761.B76   1999
     809'.93352—dc21   98-36832
                                                                                              CIP

⊗ The paper used in this publication meets the minimum requirements of the American
National Standard for Information Sciences—Permanence of Paper for Printed Library
Materials, ANSI Z39.48-1992.

for BETTINA — *as always*

for JAMES GILL — *in memoriam*

CONTENTS

ACKNOWLEDGMENTS

I owe a great deal to many friends, students, and colleagues whose intellectual and human presence stimulated and encouraged me. But my greatest debt is to my wife Beth, who has been my generous and demanding reader. Her incisive and judicious comments have been most valuable throughout the writing of this book.

Some chapters have appeared elsewhere, a few of them in a much shorter version and with a different title: "Georg Büchner: The Idiom of Anti-heroism" (chap. 2), in *Literature, Culture and Society in the Modern Age*, Stanford Slavic Studies (Stanford, 1991); "Meanings and Indeterminacy in Gogol's 'The Overcoat'" (chap. 3), *Proceedings of the American Philosophical Society* 135, no. 4 (1991); "Dostoevsky's Underground Man: Portrait of the Paradoxalist" (chap. 4), *Raritan* XV, no. 1 (Summer 1995); "Italo Svevo" (chap. 6) *The Yale Review* LXXXII, no. 1 (January 1994); "Max Frisch: The Courage of Failure" (chap. 8), *Raritan* XII, no. 2 (Fall 1993); "Primo Levi and the Canto of Ulysses" (part of chap. 10), *Revue de Littérature Comparée*, no. 3 (1996); "Svevo's Witness" (Appendix), *The American Scholar* LX, no. 3 (Summer 1991).

Two chapters appeared in French, and in a quite different form: "La chambre de Félicité: bazar ou chapelle?" (chap. 5) in *George Sand et son temps* (Geneva: Slatkine, 1994); "Chvéïk, crétin d'envergure (ou l'éloge de la roublardise)" (chap. 7), in *Pratiques d'écriture* (Paris: Klincksieck, 1996). For permission to reprint in a revised form I wish to thank the respective editors and publishers.

1

UNHEROIC MODES

"No monsters and no heroes!"
FLAUBERT

The title of this book may be surprising. To write in praise of antiheroes could seem ironic, if not downright perverse. The term "antihero," as it has come to be used, is indeed linked to a paradoxical, at times provocative stance. Dostoevsky gave that term currency in the final section of *Notes from Underground*, a seminal work that questions the idea of the hero in life as well as in art. The last pages of Dostoevsky's narrative explicitly associate the word "antihero" with the notion of paradox. The narrator, who is called a paradoxalist, explains: "A novel needs a hero, and all the traits of an antihero are *expressly* gathered together here." [1] The deliberate subversion of the literary model is associated with the voice from the underground challenging accepted opinions.

The title of my study may have been determined by Dostoevsky's self-styled antihero, but only up to a point. The plural "antiheroes" is meant to suggest that Dostoevsky's protagonist is not the only countermodel, and that my aim is not to define a single type, but rather to explore a widespread and complex trend in modern literature. Clearly, no single description or definition will do. Yet eschewing a dogmatic approach and stressing diversity and variation do not preclude a search for underlying patterns and common tendencies. Even though the term and the figure of the antihero are multifaceted, this is not a mere sampling of significant texts. The underlying issues are conceptual as well.

The antiheroic mode, as we shall see, implies the negative presence of the subverted or absent model. But it is as much a question of mood as of mode. No single theoretical formulation, however ingenious, can possibly accommodate the specific thrust and quality of a given work. Wary of pre-formatted definitions, I have preferred to be an attentive reader and inter-preter of the works under discussion, to remain flexible in my approach, and to tease the theme of "antiheroism" out of the individual texts. What mattered to me in all cases was to respect the texture and inner coherence of the works in question.

The lines of demarcation separating the heroic from the unheroic have become blurred. Raymond Giraud, some forty years ago, justly observed that the "unheroic heroes" of Stendhal, Balzac, and Flaubert were the prototypes of heroes of inaction such as Proust's Swann and Joyce's Leo-pold Bloom.[2] Nineteenth- and twentieth-century literature is moreover crowded with weak, ineffectual, pale, humiliated, self-doubting, inept, oc-casionally abject characters—often afflicted with self-conscious and para-lyzing irony, yet at times capable of unexpected resilience and fortitude. Such characters do not conform to traditional models of heroic figures; they even stand in opposition to them. But there can be great strength in that opposition. Implicitly or explicitly, they cast doubt on values that have been taken for granted, or were assumed to be unshakable.

This may indeed be the principal significance of such antimodels, of their secret strengths and hidden victories. The negative hero, more keenly perhaps than the traditional hero, challenges our assumptions, raising anew the question of how we see, or wish to see ourselves. The antihero is often a perturber and a disturber. The accompanying critique of heroic concepts involves strategies of destabilization and, in a number of works examined in this study, carries ethical and political implications.

At stake are large issues. Across the ages, the "hero" has reflected, at times determined, our moral and poetic vision as we try to cope with the meaning or lack of meaning of life—much as tragedy, or, broadly speak-ing, the tragic spirit—answers our deep need to bestow dignity and beauty on human suffering. That is why the "death of tragedy," characterized by George Steiner in a book that turns around Nietzsche's famous title, rep-resents such a momentous cultural shift.[3] One thing is clear, however. Whether it is inflated or deflated, whether exalted or minimized, we can-not do without an image of ourselves.

But what is the heroic temper, and what is this notion of the hero against which so much of modern literature seems to be in reaction? The word "hero," as Bernard Knox reminds us, seems to have had in Homer the general meaning of "nobleman," but by the fifth century B.C. the cult of heroes had developed and become something of a religious phenome-non. Heroes were honored and revered. They were associated with an age of myth, when men and gods were said to have come into close contact. Heroes were exceptional beings recorded in legend, sung in epic poetry, enacted in the tragic theater. Their characteristics, behind the multiplicity of individual types, are fairly constant: they live by a fierce personal code, they are unyielding in the face of adversity; moderation is not their forte, but rather boldness and even overboldness. Heroes are defiantly committed to honor and pride. Though capable of killing the monster, they themselves are often dreadful, even monstrous. Witnesses are appalled by the "enormity of their violent actions" and the strangeness of their destiny.[4] Whether their name be Achilles, Oedipus, Ajax, Electra, or Antigone—for the heroic concept extends to exceptional women—the hero or heroine is a unique, exemplary figure whose fate places him or her at the outpost of human experience, and virtually out of time.

One might speak of a morality of will and action. Whether the hero fights and kills the monster, rushes toward his own undoing, or proudly shoulders his role as rebel against superior forces, it is through choice and the exercise of free will that he affirms his heroic temper. Prometheus knows it, when he haughtily declares to the chorus: "Of my own will I shot the arrow that fell short, of my own will." Oedipus also knows it, when he blinds himself upon discovering the horrible truth that he himself willed to find out.[5] As Maurice Blanchot put it in an essay on the nature of the hero, heroism is a revelation of the "luminous sovereignty of the act"; he adds that the act alone is heroic. Such epiphanic glorification of action leads Blanchot to conclude that heroic authenticity or substance (he doubts that the latter exists) needs to determine itself through the verb rather than the substantive.[6] In this perspective the "moral" nature of the hero's impetus remains questionable, and the relation between bravery and ethical concepts is not altogether obvious.

The denunciation of the heroic code, a code often associated with war, violence, and the cult of manliness, is of course not new. Voltaire's *Candide* not only depicts war as ignoble carnage (a "heroic butchery" in which any number of "heroes" indulge in high deeds of disembowelments and rapes), but provides a literary critique of the heroic mode. The Venetian nobleman Pococurante explains to Candide why he so dislikes Homer's *Iliad*. The constant recital of fights and battles, the seemingly endless account of the siege of Troy, he finds nothing short of intolerable. But "mortal boredom" is not the chief reason for demoting the "hero" to the rank of arsonist, slaughterer, and rapist. Moral indignation and the hope that his own pessimism about human behavior throughout history might serve the cause of tolerance and justice are at the root of Voltaire's antiheroic stance.[7]

Primo Levi, in our own day, similarly disliked the *Iliad* and for much the same reason. "I find reading the *Iliad* almost intolerable: this orgy of battles, wounds and corpses, this stupid endless war, the childish anger of Achilles." Levi's hatred for militarism explains his admiration of Georg Büchner's *Woyzeck*, which he considered a masterpiece of world literature. Levi characteristically preferred the *Odyssey*, the epic of homecoming, to the relentlessly heroic *Iliad*.[8]

But even the figure of resourceful Odysseus, for whom Levi had a quite special fondness, tends to be treated ironically and at times with hostility in modern texts. Odysseus, known as *polymêtis* (a man of many schemes), may appear especially attractive to modern readers because he seems to be the embodiment of *mêtis*—a combination of craft, cunning, adaptability, flexibility of mind, skill in all manner of obliquities, illustrating at almost every point the priority of intelligence over sheer brawn and impulsiveness.[9] Yet it is he who in book II of the *Iliad* chastises the cowardly and abject Thersites for hurling insults at Agamemnon and for showing disrespect for the heroic code. And the slaughter of the suitors in book XXII of the *Odyssey* is arguably the goriest and most "heroic" single action in the Homeric poems. In "Penelope's Despair" (which should be read side by side with "Non-Hero"), the modern Greek poet Yannis Ritsos has imagined the fright and frigidity with which Penelope greets her returning hero-husband, appalled by this "miserable, blood-soaked" man.[10]

The moral nature of the hero has been the subject of considerable dissension. Some have held that heroism responds unselfishly to a call of high duty, to a fundamental moral law.[11] But this moral law is not evident to all. Diversity of opinion and contradictions characterize most attempts at delineating the "moral" nature of the hero. Friedrich Schiller believed that the hero embodies an ideal of moral perfection and ennoblement ("Veredlung"). Thomas Carlyle saw heroes as spiritual models guiding humanity, and thus deserving of "hero worship." And Joseph Campbell, in our own day, described the thousand-faced hero as capable of "self-achieved submission," and willing to give up life for something larger than himself.[12]

But there are less exalted views. For Johan Huizinga, the hero was only a superior example of *homo ludens*, projecting in his endeavors the human impulse to excel in competition, and illustrating the "playfully" passionate desire to master the self, to face hurdles and tests, and to be victorious. Sigmund Freud, in a less playful mode, while also stressing competition, proposed a more somber view. In *Moses and Monotheism*, he defined the hero as one who stands up to his father and "in the end victoriously overcomes him," and even less reassuringly (the notion of parricide is hardly edifying) as a man who rebels against the father "and kills him in some guise or other."[13]

A somber view seems to prevail in those works of fiction where the hero is explicitly associated with a world of darkness and transgression. Joseph Conrad's *Heart of Darkness* not only provides an exemplary title and a central figure who yields to the temptation to "step over the threshold of the invisible," but suggests that "darkness" is the privileged domain of the heroic soul.[14] The affinity between the hero and obscure zones has often been formulated. Paul Valéry maintained that whatever is "noble" or "heroic" is necessarily related to obscurity and the mystery of the incommensurable, echoing Victor Hugo's remark about the legendary darkening ("obscurcissement légendaire") that surrounds the figure of the hero. While nostalgic of heroic values associated with epic literature, Hugo repeatedly called for the demise of the traditional hero, and for liberation from hero worship.[15]

Through exaltation of will, action, and bravery, heroes were meant to be exemplary even when associated with uncontrollable darker forces. They were seen standing high above ordinary human beings, almost on a pedestal, destined to be revered as effigies or monuments for all posterity. The images of the statue and the pedestal may also, at least in part, explain the impulse to undermine and topple the exalted figure.

This study proposes to examine the sundry ways the heroic model—indeed the very notion of a model—has come to be subverted, as well as the reasons that may underlie this trend. Large areas of Western literature have been increasingly invaded by protagonists who fail, by a deliberate strategy of their authors, to live up to expectations still linked to memories of traditional literary or mythical heroes. Yet such protagonists are not necessarily "failures," nor are they devoid of heroic possibilities. They may embody different kinds of courage, perhaps better in tune with our age and our needs. Such characters can captivate our imagination, and even come to seem admirable, through the way in which they help deflate, subvert, and challenge an "ideal" image.

Primo Levi, as we shall see, praises the antihero—the "eroe a rovescio"—for his allegiance to the strictly human dimension. Levi is evidently not the only one to be suspicious of hero worship and to denounce it for fostering illusions, dishonesty, and moral inertia that come from relying on ideal and inimitable models. But this critique of vicariousness implies the diagnosis of a moral void as well as the paradoxical nostalgia for heroic values and models no longer found relevant.

A void of this sort cries out to be filled. This is one of the hypotheses of this study. The ironic memory of the absent or unattainable model acts as a steady reminder and as an incentive. The very notion of the "antihero" depends on such a memory. Herbert Lindenberger put it well when he observed that the antihero is possible only in a tradition "that has already represented real heroes." [16] The reason is that such a memory acts as more than a foil; it suggests a yearning, perhaps even a quest. In an age of skepticism and dwindling faith, an age marked by the pervasive awareness of loss and disarray, the deliberate subversion of the heroic tradition may betray an urge to salvage or reinvent meaning. The negative assessment does not prove resignation or assent. An absence can be a form of presence. To put it in other terms, some of the most characteristic works written in opposition to traditional heroic models may well reflect a moral and spiritual thrust, as well as an attempt to adjust responsibly to new contexts.

The chapters that follow will thus unavoidably deal with some of the troubling tensions of our time: conflicts between individual and collective values, thematic and historical discontinuities, resistance to conformity, radical questionings of authority, attempts at new empowerments as well as their subversion, critiques of rationalism and traditional humanism together with the emergence of less smug "humanistic" reaffirmations of the human spirit in terms of unheroic resilience and tenacity.

꿒

The authors studied all raise moral issues through the antiheroic perspective. They challenge the relevance of handed-down assumptions, induce the reader to reexamine moral categories, and deal, often disturbingly, with the survival of values. Survival and renewal, at times in a conflicting manner, are at the heart of these radical texts. Strength that takes the form of weakness, deficiency translated into strength, dignity and hidden victories achieved through what may appear as loss of worth, the courage of failure experienced as the affirmation of fundamental honesty—these are some of the paradoxes underlying not only the writings of Gogol, Flaubert, Italo Svevo, and Max Frisch, but those of the other writers under discussion.

Georg Büchner (1813–37), the first author discussed, is surprisingly modern in his willful undermining of the idiom of tragedy. Yet through his pitiful Woyzeck, who lives out a destiny of victim and loser, Büchner reaches out to universal man, and retrieves tragedy in an unheroic context. Nicolai Gogol (1809–52), in "The Overcoat," also deals with serious themes by portraying a meek and derided scapegoat protagonist, a downtrodden creature whose story raises social, moral, and even spiritual issues, but in unsettling terms, through satire, pathos, parody, narrative instabilities, and mutually canceling ironies.

Notes from Underground by Fyodor Dostoevsky (1821–81) is an altogether crucial text in the antiheroic tradition. A disparaging self-portrait of a moral cripple who blackens himself on purpose and loves his infirmities, this first-person narrative displays the relentless will to be outside of the norm and in opposition to it. Vilifying the word as well as the concept of hero, Dostoevsky's underground voice—aggressive, intransigent, self-centered, neurotic, at times strident—cries out an indictment of a "negative age" that has lost its sense of values. In denouncing materialistic rationalism, this voice takes on almost prophetic tones. The adversarial consciousness that speaks out from below is, however, that of a *sick* prophet. But, ultimately, the textual strategies that exploit the duplicitous resources of the confessional mode convert the negative into the positive, conveying the experience of intense spiritual needs.

Flaubert's simple-minded servant Félicité, a distant relative of Büchner's Woyzeck and of Gogol's Akaky Akakyevich, is even further removed, if possible, from any heroic model. In "A Simple Heart," Flaubert (1821–80) has conceived a character incapable of conceptualizing anything, unaware of her own courage, and totally unable to see herself in any "role," least of all a heroic one. Yet her self-denial, her devotion, her ability to commune in suffering, and above all the author's complex handling of irony, transform emptiness into plenitude, allowing Félicité to attain a legendary status. The latent hagiographic thrust of the story may even be understood as related to the author's own deepest yearnings.

With Italo Svevo (1861–1928), we encounter almost the opposite type of antihero—highly articulate, self-reflective, hyperconscious to the point of morbidity, suffering from the inertia of the dreamer and self-mocker. Ironic modes stress the sense of failure and marginality. The typical Svevian protagonists cultivate their inadequacies, and indulge in passivity and procrastination to the point of paralysis. *Confessions of Zeno*, Svevo's most characteristic work, is a humorous and also moving narrative about the incurable wound of consciousness. But in this fictional world in which the only tragedy seems to be the absence of tragedy, strange reversals take place. Zeno discovers that the consciousness of his weakness is his true strength, that ironic lucidity can convert defeat into victory.

The case of the good soldier Schweik seems at first glance to fall squarely in the category of caricature—though it soon becomes evident that this caricature is far from simply entertaining. The Czech writer Jaroslav Hašek (1883–1923) succeeded in giving the droll silhouette of the cunning army orderly, who serves in the Austrian Army during World War I, a legendary dimension as an unheroic yet rebellious survival artist in a jingoistic world gone mad. Disarming, resilient and resourceful, simulating submissiveness, Schweik uses his feigned feeble-mindedness in a permanent combat against authority. This feeble-mindedness must not be taken at face value. A true subversive, Schweik is a perturber energized by moral indignation who speaks and acts for the downtrodden, conveying a lesson not only in unheroic courage, but in strategies of passive resistance especially valid under oppressive political regimes.

Hostility to the heroic, in the wake of war and mass extermination, also marks the works of Max Frisch (1911–91). Conscious of the epic and tragic tradition, very much aware that heroes allow us to experience vicariously the exercise of free will and the high drama of fate and action, Frisch unwaveringly exposes the harm done by the heroic illusion. His antiheroic stance—in his plays, novels, and literary diaries—has moral as well as political implications. The concept of the hero is shown to provide lessons of false freedom and dangerous models in history. By contrast, what Frisch considers the nonheroic virtues embodied by the self-doubting, self-denying, and even humiliated figures in his works raises his characters to new levels of consciousness. Frisch's most significant texts lead to a positive revelation of the finite: the moving acceptance of failure and human limits, the value of the prison of inner life, the love of human fragility, the desperate will and courage to embrace life.

The themes of courageous lucidity and allegiance to the strictly human dimension are at the heart of the writings of Albert Camus (1913–60). Pressing home the point that heroism is not, after all, a supreme value, suspicious of heroic attitudes and heroic rhetoric, Camus shows himself from the outset more interested in how weakness can be transformed into strength, how negation can be converted into affirmation. At stake is the fragility of any victory in the context of never-ending defeat. Camus's entire work reaches out to nonheroic forms of courage and to values predicated on horror of violence, distaste for doctrinaire abstractions, and a refusal to seek absolutes. Finding both hopelessness and exhilaration in the sense of mortality, Camus resorts to the mythical metaphor of Sisyphus in order to justify a commitment to a struggle that requires relentless vigilance precisely because a definite victory can never be achieved. Camus's tragic humanism, which takes the side of victims (never of "heroes" or "saints"), implies the concept of the witness in its noblest and most engaged sense.

Primo Levi (1919–87) illustrates perhaps better than anyone else the extent to which the witness has assumed priority over the hero. One large question looms over most of Levi's work: What can heroism possibly mean in an age of totalitarian ideologies and death camps, where naked bodies are herded to the gas chambers? Heroic models and heroic expectations are shown to be illusory and misleading. Offended by any rhetoric that might present the victim as hero, Levi is interested rather in what he calls the "gray zone" of moral contamination, as well as in the difficulty and shame of survival. His main concern is not physical, but moral survival. In this attempt at salvation, writing and testifying take on a redemptive value. Heroic longings may have led Levi to write a prize-winning novel about Jewish partisans in World War II, but his guerrilla fighters, men and women alike, are tired of war and heroism. Levi's chief hope is related to the metaphor of a homecoming (hence his attachment to the figure of Ulysses), and to the search for the courage needed to face the daily struggle against despair.

The writers discussed in this study belong to several distinct cultural and linguistic traditions. In all cases, I have based my analyses on close readings in the original language. Some chapters deal with a specific work, others with a large body of writings. These chapters can be read as independent essays only insofar as they respect the specific and unique voice of each author. They all address common problems, and have all been conceived from the start as integral parts of this book. But I have been careful to avoid a definitional scheme or method of approach, preferring instead to remain attuned to individual authors and works, and to cast light on an array of complex, yet related subjects.

GEORG BÜCHNER

THE IDIOM OF ANTIHEROISM

Georg Büchner's *Woyzeck,* more than a century and a half after it was left unfinished in 1836, remains a baffling and astonishingly modern text. Even the intended sequence of the completed scenes remains uncertain. Büchner died at the age of twenty-three, without a chance to make revisions and crucial decisions about the structure and ultimate thrust of the play. *Woyzeck* was not "reconstructed" until some forty years after Büchner's death, and was not performed until another forty years had almost elapsed—in Munich, in 1913. Basic editorial and dramaturgical questions have remained unresolved. But the untimely death of the author is only a contributing factor to the unconventionality of the play. Structural discontinuities are part of Büchner's theatrical strategies.

So are the dramatic and psychological discontinuities that frustrate expectations of reassuring developments and resolutions. There is indeed much here to disturb both spectator and reader. Not only is the protagonist downtrodden, inept, and humiliated, but the techniques of fragmentation and disjointedness bring out a stark cruelty made worse by dehumanizing stylizations of human despair.

Various modern aesthetic schools have hailed Büchner as a bold precursor and an inspiring model. Historians of the theatre like to link his name to such diverse artistic manifestations as naturalism, impressionism, expressionism, or the epic and proletarian drama.[1] Such proposed affinities may be suggestive, but specific affiliations can be misleading. More significant are some of the striking features responsible for the uniqueness of Büchner's achievement: fadeouts and sudden changes in setting and pace that anticipate cinematographic techniques and communicate the abrupt transitions of nightmares; repeated emphasis on isolated moments highlighted as epiphanies of anguish and rooted in the horror of banality; language always beyond, besides, and ill attuned to needs and fears. Typical of this language is the stammer and pathetic eloquence of muteness.

Büchner unsettled and transfigured the idiom of tragedy, while undermining the traditional notion of the tragic hero. His deliberate choice of prose, instead of the time-honored verse form, represents a direct challenge to the code of tragedy. George Steiner, in some fine pages on Büchner, went to the heart of the matter when he discussed the "dissociation of tragedy from poetic form" and referred to the writer's radical break with social and linguistic conventions. For what Büchner achieved by means of ironic undermining was nothing short of a new concept of tragedy. Steiner sums it up well: "*Woyzeck* is the first tragedy of low life. It repudiates an assumption implicit in Greek, Elizabethan, and neo-classic drama: the assumption that tragic suffering is the sombre privilege of those who are in high places."[2]

It would seem that Büchner set out to disprove Hegel's contention that the death of tragedy was inevitable the day the Slave, unable to grasp the notion of fate, appeared on the tragic stage. Hegel also theorized that modern society, with its stress on functionalism and specialization (even kings had to serve!), could no longer tolerate the aristocratic notion of the hero.[3] Certainly the soldier Woyzeck is not a tragic hero by usual standards, even though he experiences within his own limited range the jealousy and destructive rage of an Othello. But this most unheroic loser, this socially and economically oppressed and disinherited little man, is somehow granted the dignity of suffering to the precise extent that Büchner, through a rhetoric that undercuts dramatic conventions, achieves the dignity of tragedy in a "prosaic" register.

Büchner's experimentation with a new aesthetic system is not limited to the subject of the poor and the downtrodden. The breadth of aperture is what gives this experimentation its deeper resonance. *The Death of Danton* deals with a powerful revolutionary figure in a momentous historical context that offers heroic possibilities. *Lenz* projects the mental and spiritual torments of an artist who confronts religious doubts and the horror of nothingness. If *The Death of Danton* has been hailed as a revolutionary text that renews the conventions of the historical play, the originality of the lesser known *Lenz* has not been sufficiently stressed. This narrative account of the gradual mental breakdown of the historical figure of the poet Lenz (Büchner drew his materials from the memoirs of Pastor Johann Friedrich Oberlin—1740–1826) is not only subversive of plot structure, but focuses on mental states and in particular on the "mighty rift" ("un-geheurer Riss") that splits the personality of the poet in two as he con-fronts, terror-stricken, his own sense of a spiritual void. Lenz's hopeless struggle against insanity and suicidal impulses is conveyed by what could be characterized as an indirect schizophrenic monologue, a style that imi-tates and mediates the mental processes of the protagonist. The objective and subjective worlds are thereby blurred, as the landscape itself, though apparently described by the narrator, in fact projects the character's vision-ary apprehension of outer reality.

The natural setting, with its ominous masses of light, ghostlike shafts of sunbeams, depths of silvery mist, shimmering bluish reflections, and mountains rising against a red sky, provides mirror images of Lenz's terror. Even more so than in *Woyzeck*, the landscape takes on otherworldly, apoca-lyptic features. Vanishing forms are suddenly revealed, the howling winds are likened to uncanny titanic music, while the violence of the setting suggests images of hell. Lenz has the impression of standing on the brink of the abyss, whose terrifying voices seem to pull him with unrelenting power. Lenz's propensity to hear voices, to perceive sunbeams as flashing swords, and to glimpse clouds like "wild neighing horses" galloping to-ward him, is clearly related to the imagery of the apocalypse, and corre-sponds to an ecstasy of horror.[4]

The notion of nothingness also informs *The Death of Danton*. "Nichts" is a recurrent word. But here the context is political, though Büchner's Danton—cynical, sensuous, and attracted to death—is hardly a hero of liberty and of patriotic action. Büchner's views of Danton and of the French Revolution, in this fundamentally antiheroic and parodistic play, are doubtless colored by his own political commitments and disappoint-ments. While a medical student in Strasbourg, he became acquainted with a conspiratorial society, and later helped found similar groups in Giessen and Darmstadt. Forced to flee (a warrant for his arrest was indeed issued), he soon turned to a scientific career, obtained his doctorate, and lectured in comparative anatomy at Zurich, while pursuing his literary ambitions. His incendiary pamphlet *The Hessian Messenger* (*Der Hessische Land-bote*) had been seized by the authorities, and his family was alarmed by his revolutionary associations. The fate of his incarcerated political friends probably cooled his ardor. Certainly his ideas about history and politics underwent considerable evolution, became more complex and even con-tradictory. All of these were reasons for appreciating the elusiveness, multi-plicity of meanings, and camouflage offered by the theatre as an essen-tially dialogical genre.

A letter to his family is revealing. Referring to the group known as "Young Germany," Büchner writes:

I'm going my own way and staying in the field of drama, which has nothing to do with all of these disputes; I draw my figures as I see fit in accordance with nature and history, and I laugh about people who want to make me responsible for the morality or immorality of these characters. I have my own ideas about that . . . [5]

Equally telling is the "antiheroic" thrust of another letter to his family. This time, Büchner refers specifically to *The Death of Danton*, which he had recently completed and sent to the writer and editor Karl Gutzkow. Defending himself against the charge of having used crude and even ob-scene language, and of having expressed immoral ideas, he protests that the dramatic poet is concerned not with a moral message, but with truth-fulness to history, and that history is not made to be suitable reading mate-rial for young ladies. "I can't make a Danton and the bandits of the Revo-lution into virtuous heroes!" [6]

More significant still, because it goes to the heart of the antiheroic con-cept, is a letter to his fiancée, Minna Jaeglé, in which he complains that studying the history of the French Revolution has thoroughly depressed him. All of history, he claims, is a gloomy lesson in determinism; he feels crushed by the horrible "Fatalismus" of events; individuals are mere foam on the waves, and genius or greatness mere chance and puppet play. As Büchner was about to begin work on *The Death of Danton*, he vowed never again to bow down before the so-called great men, or providential figures, of history.[7]

Büchner's antiheroic stance is thus related to an antihistorical bias and a growing distrust of rhetoric. His grim view of history, and specifically of ideological bloodbaths, is quite logically bound up with the noxiousness of inflated language. Such a language becomes the accomplice of brutality and injustice. Büchner's Danton seems to be allergic to speechmaking and poses. Early in the play, he makes it known that he could never look at the pompous Catos of this world without an irresistible desire to kick them in the behind (I.1).[8] Büchner's theatre of antirhetoric is thus to be understood as a reaction against the excesses of rhetorical flourish and the lofty tones of "idealistic" dramaturgy. Schiller was his *bête noire*. Danton, the well-known revolutionary orator, paradoxically questions with utmost skepti-cism what Herbert Lindenberger aptly calls "the validity of rhetoric in voicing any human ideals." [9]

The problem of rhetoric seems indeed to be at the heart of Büchner's perceptions and themes. As a pupil at the classical *Gymnasium* in Darmstadt, he had been an outstanding practitioner of the *ars rhetorica* and the *ars oratoria*. His talent for oratory was repeatedly recognized by the headmaster of the school, Carl Dilthey, who on three occasions chose him for the honor of giving a public speech, twice in German and once in Latin. The Latin speech has been lost, but we do have the two German school exercises: a speech on Cato's suicide ("Rede zur Verteidigung des Kato von Utica") which glorifies the Stoic virtues of antiquity, and an earlier speech belonging to the genre known as the *genus demonstrativum*, in commemoration of the sacrificial death of the burghers of Pforzheim ("Helden-Tod der Vierhundert Pforzheimer")—a heroic episode of the Thirty Years' War. The word "hero" (*Held*) recurs in various combinations: "Helden-Tod," "Heldenzeit," "Heldenstamm," "Heldenschläfe," together with the related lexicon of virtue ("Tugend"), courage ("Kühnheit") and magnanimity ("Seelengrösse"). In both texts, these terms are contemptuously opposed to the slavish spirit of the masses that grovel in the dust.

The speech about Cato of Utica is particularly interesting. Young Büchner was obviously conversant with all the structures and figures of rhetoric; he knew all about the order of discourse: proemium, propositio, narratio, argumentio, refutatio, peroratio. But the speech is not just a rhetorical and stylistic exercise. The political implications of a suicide conceived as an act of protest against tyranny are inescapable, especially if one takes into account that the school ceremony took place barely two months after the July 1830 revolution in Paris; that uprisings were occurring in Hessen; and that the Darmstadt bourgeoisie had good reason to be alarmed. Moreover, Büchner had already referred glowingly to the French Revolution of 1789, and to its struggle for liberty, in his oration on the heroic burghers of Pforzheim.[10]

𖧧

Rhetoric, the heroic tradition, and political action were thus from the start closely linked in Büchner's mind. The opening of his Cato speech stresses the exhilaration of witnessing the noble struggle with fate any time man dares intervene in the march of world history (". . . wenn er es wagt einzugreifen in den Gang der Weltgeschichte"). *Der Hessische Landbote*, a violent diatribe and call to arms against the ruling classes and officialdom in the State of Hessen, was surely Büchner's attempt to translate such a notion of heroic political intervention into militant practice. *The Hessian Messenger* is a most interesting document, not only for the obvious historical and political reasons, but because of what it reveals of the contradictions of Büchner's thought—contradictions nonetheless held together by an inner logic that was to give an enigmatic resonance to his literary work.

The opening statement of *Der Hessische Landbote* is a declaration of war ("War on the Palaces!") and a call to violence. In a letter to his family written a year earlier, the young Büchner had indeed asserted that the only way to fight the "eternal, brute force" inflicted on the have-nots is revolutionary *violence*. "My opinion is this: if anything can help in these times of ours, it is violence."[11] The language in which *The Hessian Messenger* is couched reflects metaphorical violence more than a precise program for violent struggle. The metaphors are earthy, rooted in vivid images of sweat and manure. On the other hand, the metaphorical language is strongly Biblical, and repeatedly inspired by the style of prophecy, especially toward the end. This Biblical vehemence is attributable in large part to the coauthor and editor of the pamphlet, Pastor Friedrich Ludwig Weidig, though there can be no doubt that Büchner himself was well versed in religion and intimately acquainted with the Bible. In any case, the experience of writing the political tract in collaboration with Weidig encouraged the overlapping of the sociopolitical and religious themes, and further complicated the link between rhetoric and heroism.

But what is distinctly new in *The Hessian Messenger* is that heroic political action is given a consistently anti-elitist character, and thus conceived in exact opposition to the rhetorical school exercises grounded in the classical humanistic tradition which extolled the "hero" as totally different in nature, and superior to, ordinary humanity. Both the "Helden-Tod der Vierhunderdt Pforzheimer" and the "Rede zur Verteidigung des Kato von Utica" refer disdainfully to the millions of slavish creatures who crawl like worms in the dust and deserve to be forgotten.[12]

The tone is altogether different in *The Hessian Messenger*, and in a letter written to his family at about the same time Büchner underlines the following words: "I have contempt for no one." Least of all, he adds, does he scorn those who did not have the benefit of an education. And he concludes that elitism ("Aristokratismus") represents "the most despicable contempt for the holy spirit in a human being." Such a denunciation of arrogant scorn for the humble and the underprivileged is in itself consonant with Biblical language. Walter Hinderer quite aptly recalls the passage from St. Matthew (18:10) that may have been on Büchner's mind when he denounced the elitism of the "gebildete Klasse": "Take heed that ye despise not one of these little ones."[13]

That Büchner's concern for unidealized, ordinary humanity became a permanent motif is made explicit in the programmatic statement of the poet Lenz: "One must love human nature in order to penetrate into the unique character of any individual; one must not consider anybody too insignificant, too ugly. Only then can one understand humankind." *Menschheit* is a notion that can have meaning only if it is rooted in understanding and love of the most ordinary human being. A similar idea appears in a different context in the romantic comedy *Leonce und Lena:* "... even the most insignificant of human beings is so important that a whole lifetime is far too short to love him." [14]

As Büchner reached literary maturity—in his case this occurred at a surprisingly early age—he tended systematically to undermine the classical rhetoric of his school exercises and polemical writings. Through parody he thematized the uses and misuses of idealistic rhetoric, while fully aware of its resources for multivalence. For it could camouflage political meanings, as in the Cato speech, or be ironic in praising an absence of ambiguity (Cato, for instance, was expressly lauded for his onesidedness, his "Einseitigkeit"). [15] But rhetoric, Büchner knew, could also be a despotic and murderous weapon, as in the case of Robespierre. And it could be a framework for vacuity, a tool for illusions and untruths about human nature, an accomplice in the most fundamental betrayal of human values. [16]

It is hardly surprising that Büchner consistently scorned literary "Idealismus," accusing it, much in the same terms as elitism, of representing the most shameful contempt ("schmählichste Verachtung") of human nature. A writer must not attempt to be a lofty teacher of morality. Büchner repeatedly takes to task those he calls "Idealdichter," who construct puppets with "sky blue noses" and "affected pathos," mere marionettes or wooden dolls, instead of creatures of flesh and blood whose failings and human passions might fill us with awe and compassion. Schiller, it would seem, was his chief target. "I think highly of Goethe and Shakespeare, but very little of Schiller," he writes to his family. Instead of seeking effects of bombast and amplification, Büchner would like to find a human idiom suited to human matters ("... für menschliche Dinge müsse man auch menschliche Ausdrücke finden"). [16]

※

The political implications of the antiheroic mode, necessarily hostile to the cult of personality, are illustrated in *The Death of Danton*. The deliberate deflation of heroic rhetoric goes hand in hand with the deflation of the political hero. But the political implications are in themselves ambiguous, since the antipolitical mood is political in nature, and serves to denounce the reign of the guillotine. In the same manner, one might say that the double ambiguity regarding both the Revolution and the traditional notion of the hero has a distinct heroic dimension.

According to revolutionary mythography, Danton's historical role blends political and personal heroic "virtues"—though Büchner's Danton makes it clear that he himself considers political courage (he calls it "Nationalkühnheit") the only true heroic virtue. Personal courage ("Privatkühnheit") as a value in itself is viewed as reprehensible. Yet on the face of it, Büchner's Danton still displays "personal" heroic attributes, and even brags about them. He refuses to go into hiding when his life is threatened, he takes pride in embodying the spirit of freedom, he sees his name in the Pantheon of history, he claims to be one of those mighty figures— "gewaltige Naturen"—who are the instruments of fate. But there is obvious contextual irony in the play's references to heroic capabilities that are so ineffectual or so unemployed. Saint-Just, while planning Danton's destruction, jokes about laying him out "in full armor" and slaughtering his horses and his slaves on his burial mound! The parodistic intention is flagrant. As for heroic suicide, which remains a distinct possibility, only the women in the play seem to be capable of it.[17]

No matter how one chooses to perform the play, there is no way of avoiding parody and demystification. The implicit debunking corresponds no doubt to the "historical" despondency Büchner mentions in the letter to his fiancée, but it is also a critique of the "noble" play in the manner of Schiller. The obscene puns, coarse language, and erotic images (women's thighs become a metaphor for the guillotine, and the *mons veneris* is compared to the Tarpeian rock) have much the same iconoclastic function.[18] But such images also suit Büchner's conception of Danton's character: his lustful yet weary nature, his basic cynicism, his flirtation with nothingness, his almost voluptuous attraction to death, his obsession with putrefaction and decomposition. Büchner's bitterness, however, is not limited to his protagonist. Danton wonders what it is in human nature that lies, steals, whores, and murders. For it is indeed human nature that corrupts the idealism claimed by the Revolution.

The unheroic perspective in *The Death of Danton* is what makes of it an essentially antirevolutionary play. Büchner's view of human lust, greed, and violence has an almost theological cast. But it is political cruelty and the unleashing of brutal political instincts that are specifically indicted. The men of the Revolution, capable of denying medicine to prisoners, are said to have the instinct of the tiger. More precisely, Büchner denounces the prostitution, plotting, and doctrinaire stance of political ideologues: their ruthlessness, their slaughterhouse mentality, their taste for bloody spectacles. But even the guillotine becomes a bore. The banality of horror soon anaesthetizes the moral sense, leading to an orgy of self-destruction. The Revolution, like Saturn, devours its own children.[19]

As Herbert Lindenberger shrewdly pointed out, Danton's stature in the play derives from his having been consciously conceived as an antihero.[20] Such a conception does indeed imply the hidden presence of the rejected heroic model, just as it provides a constant reminder of the physicality of the human animal: hair and nails that grow, painful corns on the feet, sneezing spells, perspiration due to fear. Danton's free spirit manifests itself through a resigned playfulness, largely verbal, in the face of pain, misery, and powerlessness. Life is seen as an epigram rather than an epic. "Who's got enough breath and spirit for an epic poem in fifty or sixty cantos?" Danton's friend Camille Desmoulins puts it bluntly: there is no point in affecting heroic poses.[21]

If one of the revolutionaries describes Danton as a bloodhound with dove's wings (ironically parodying a mythological trope), it is because Danton has other than heroic values. His addiction to sex symbolizes a fundamentally sensualist view of the world. He counts himself among the pleasure seekers ("die Geniessenden"). He believes that the whole world is made up of Epicureans, the coarse ones and the refined ones. Even Christ, he explains to Robespierre, was a pleasure seeker. At the level of character conception, Danton is what Flaubert later defined as an "inactive" hero. He hesitates, procrastinates, surrenders to daydreams, meditates on the futility of any decision. His Hamlet complex (does he not also wish for a death without memory?) is no doubt that of a muscular, sensuous, tempestuous Hamlet.[22] If he refuses to enter into a duel with fate, it is not for lack of energy. But he recognizes the pointlessness of all action. "We are puppets whose strings are pulled by unknown powers." At best, one can react in a playful manner. Danton almost becomes a poet of the absurd as he indulges in a spirited development on the boredom of putting one foot in front of another. There is something deeply perverse and pessimistic in such antiheroic sallies. For Danton, all of creation is a senseless wound inflicted by Nothingness on Chaos.[23]

Büchner's other antiheroes also function in a political and metaphysical context. Lenz's halfhearted, clumsy attempts at suicide do not attain any nobility; they are pathological rather than tragic. Yet this visionary poet of the inner rift, who experiences religious torments and ecstasies of terror, develops aesthetic theories with unmistakable sociopolitical undertones— theories that call for an anti-idealistic mimesis of reality, sympathy for the common people, and a program of anti-elitism. As for Leonce, whose *mal du siècle* and *ennui* (he compares his head to an empty ballroom) make him a brother to Musset, he wallows in self-pity, self-denigration, and melancholy. The shade of Hamlet looms once again; Leonce even quotes from Shakespeare's play. His values are explicitly antiheroic. "Heroism stinks of liquor," he replies to his friend Valerio, who teases him into action. "Away with your Napoleonic romanticism!" Such unhealthy illusions only becloud moral responsibility. For behind the lighthearted opera buffa or commedia dell'arte ambience of the comedy, behind the wistful playing with language and the farcical unmasking of king and court, there once again lurk serious moral and political motifs: denunciation of militarism, compassion for the lower classes, contempt for the total arbitrariness and emptiness of political power.[24]

꿈

It is in *Woyzeck*, his incompleted masterpiece, that Büchner was able to realize most fully the antirhetorical techniques and antiheroic themes tried out in his earlier works. It is as though he set out to illustrate Lenz's concern for prosaic creatures and his anti-elitist belief that nobody, however insignificant or ugly, should be despised. Writing a play about an insignificant or even repulsive character is no doubt what Büchner had in mind when he referred to his "Ferkeldramen."[25]

The story of the demented soldier Woyzeck, who killed his woman in a fit of jealousy, is surely a depressingly banal subject. Yet this victim of dehumanizing circumstances, this human being more sinned against than sinning, achieves the stature of one who willingly rushes toward his fate, running "like an open razor blade" through the world.[26] The allusion to Shakespeare is not out of order, for Shakespeare was very much on Büchner's mind. The epigraph to the first act of *Leonce und Lena* is a quotation from *As You Like It*, and *Hamlet*, as we have seen, is also quoted in that play. In *Woyzeck*, the oblique textual reference seems to be *Othello*. Woyzeck is a miserable, downtrodden private, not a glorious general. But his passion, in every sense of the word, also leads to murder and to his undoing. Already in the early draft of Büchner's play, in which Woyzeck was still named Louis, there are echoes of Othello's famous "the pity of it." As for Woyzeck's desire for another kiss when he is about to stab the woman he loves, the parallel with Othello is inescapable.[27] But Lear also looms in the background, whether in the figure of the Fool or the symbolic stripping bare of the "forked animal." The King, who now scorns his regal robes ("Off you lendings!"), and the common soldier, who quite literally "divests" himself of his pitiful belongings, both participate in a genuinely human confrontation with mortality.

What counts, however, more than sources, influences, parallels, and models is the eloquent uses of other texts in a play devoted to the least eloquent of protagonists. Speechlessness is here full of resonances. The scene in which Woyzeck shaves the Captain is exemplary. This scene, which is frequently used as the opening scene of the play, is almost entirely based on the sharp contrast between the Captain's self-indulgent verbosity and the private's laconic exclamations of obedience and acquiescence: "Ja wohl Herr Hauptmann" ("Yes, Captain, sir"). The Captain, like others in the play who wield power and oppress (the Doctor, the Drum Major), is deprived of the dignity of a name and reduced to a pure "function." The intent is not merely comical. Much of the scene may appear onesided. The Captain's flow of words is smug and rings patently false, as he refers to metaphysical concepts of time and eternity. It is also cruel, for he takes perverse pleasure in verbally tripping Woyzeck.

The result is a multiple discrediting. The Captain's pompous talk points up the noxiousness of all inflated language. By contrast, Woyzeck's linguistic inadequacy seems almost a virtue. Words such as "morals" and "virtue" ("Moral" and "Tugend") as used by the Captain are empty clichés— words and nothing else. "Morals, that means when a man is moral. It is a fine word," explains the Captain. And, as though to confirm the inauthenticity of the socioethical discourse, he hides behind an institutionalized moral judgment, quoting the garrison chaplain. "You have a child without the blessing of the Church," he says reproachfully to Woyzeck, making sure to attribute the statement to the army chaplain, the Right Reverend Garnisonsprediger. The displaced judgment is meant to come as fully authoritative, irrefutable. But the effect is different. The quoted religious reprobation becomes arbitrary, formalistic, intolerant: words in the service of a conventional and inhuman morality.

And here the extraordinary happens. Woyzeck, silent and submissive until this point, suddenly finds the words to reply. Only this reply is also a quotation. Referring to his child born out of wedlock, he suggests that God, in his mercy, will not ask whether Amen was said before his making. "Our Lord said, suffer the little children to come unto me." The effect of the double quote is clear, though complex. Behind the surface babble of the scene, a deeper dialogue has been engaged. The two "religious" quotes confront each other, and they remain irreconcilable. On the one hand, institutionalized religion, associated with the State and the Army, places itself in the name of Christ at the service of a hypocritical and repressive social order; on the other hand, Christ's own words carry his message of love and compassion.

The gap between the two discourses explains the discomfort felt by the Captain toward the end of the scene. He brings the conversation to an abrupt end. "You think too much. . . . Our chat has quite unnerved me." But the gap is not merely psychological and dramatic in the immediate context; it illustrates a fundamental principle of the play. The real dialogue is always elsewhere, in the intertextual articulations and ironies of which the protagonists are not even dimly aware.

It is true that Marie also refers to Woyzeck's "thinking" too much. ("He'll crack up with all that thinking.") But she finds a better word for the haunted ways of the man who is to murder her: "vergeistert"—"demented." The word is particularly apt since it contains the word *Geist* (mind, but also spirit) and thus corresponds to Woyzeck's visionary tendencies: his apocalyptic perceptions of bright streaks in the landscape, sweeping fires in the sky, sounds of trombones, terrible voices as the world goes up in flames. Büchner did not forget that the historical soldier Johan Christian Woyzeck, who was executed on the Market Square in Leipzig on August 27, 1824, had claimed to hear voices, and that his case gave rise to a medical and legal controversy focusing on the relation between insanity and legal responsibility.

This medico-legal controversy raises a question that lies at the heart of all dramaturgy: the relation between free choice and determinism. The fairy tale told by the grandmother (another text-within-the-text) underscores the gloom of a dead world through the image of the orphan child who sets out on a search, only to find that the kindly looking moon is a piece of rotten wood and the sun a withered sunflower. But Woyzeck himself seems to affirm something different from this hopeless, preordained gloom: a vocation of victimhood that also implies the mystery of the human soul. Every human being is an abyss!

As for the meaning, or denial of meaning, implicit in the play, it must be said that the range of possible interpretations is wider than may at first appear. The fragmentary nature of the drama and the ensuing gaps encourage a variety of stresses. At one level, *Woyzeck* debunks false morality, taking to task what Büchner, in his correspondence, condemned as the big lie of "culture" and "idealism." The Barker at the fairground exhibits a trained horse, but is in reality out to mock man's "bestial rationality," by insisting on human submission to the calls of nature—a truth Woyzeck himself illustrates by urinating against a wall. What kind of culture is it, Büchner seems to ask, that does not first take into account unadulterated "nature"? Büchner, in this depreciating mood, anticipates the bitter honesty of Brecht's *Three Penny Opera:* "Erst kommt das Fressen, dann kommt die Moral." The Barker's horse sense lesson is deterministic in its own way: "Man, be natural; you were created dust, sand, and muck." [28]

At another level, however, the stress seems to be on the sociopolitical and economic implications. Woyzeck himself refers to "us poor people" ("Wir arme Leut") and to a life of hardship: "Nothing but work under the sun—sweat even in our sleep." Even death is determined by economic factors, as is made clear in the brief but telling episode with the Jew who sells Woyzeck the knife. The Jew sells it to him "cheaply," insisting that he will have an "economical death." Cheaply but not for nothing, he adds. The pawnbroker's expression "nit umsonst" is of course ambivalent, meaning "not for nothing" but also, in a more ironic way, "not in vain." Verbal manipulations mirror literal manipulations: Woyzeck is used as a guinea pig by the Doctor for his scientific experiments. Put on a steady diet of peas, he is subjected to the further indignity of hearing the Doctor assert that man is free, that the human will can control the muscle that controls the bladder.[29]

The tragic dimension of the play does not, however, come from its deterministic gloom, bitter fairy tale references, or political themes of oppression and exploitation. Rather, it is the *passion* of the protagonist— both in the etymological sense of suffering and the more ordinary sense of violent emotion—that retrieves tragedy in the antiheroic context. The most telling moment is doubtless the instant of revelation of raw sexuality as Woyzeck, standing outside the open window of the inn, watches Marie and the Drum Major dance by in a symbolic embrace to the accompaniment of Marie's repeated goading: "On and on. On and on." ("Immer zu— immer zu.") What follows is Woyzeck's outburst universalizing the metaphor of lechery:

> On and on! On and on! Keep turning, tumbling. Why doesn't God
> blow out the sun, so that everyone and everything can tumble and
> fornicate, man and woman, man and beast. Do it in broad daylight,
> do it on people's hands like flies. Woman! The woman is hot,
> hot.—On and on, on and on.

The significance of Woyzeck's outburst cannot be limited to violent jealousy leading to murder. Its real interest is that it unmistakably echoes the much broader range of King Lear's pungent diatribe when, in his spiritual agony on the heath, he discovers that he is "not ague-proof," and imagines sarcastically that he is once again sitting in judgment over one of his subjects accused of the crime of adultery:

> I pardon that man's life. What was thy cause? Adultery? Thou shalt
> not die. Die for adultery? No. The wren goes to't, and the small
> gilded fly does lecher in my sight. Let copulation thrive. . . . To't lux-
> ury, pell-mell!

The textual link is confirmed by the striking similarity of apocalyptic images which are so typical of Woyzeck's "demented" vision. Lear's speech about universal lechery leads up to the following fiery words: "There's hell, there's darkness, there is the sulphurous pit: burning, scalding, stench, consumption." [30]

Woyzeck's own language is characterized by a revelatory violence that harkens back to the Bible. He quotes, probably repeating words quoted by a preacher: "Isn't it written, and lo, the smoke of the country went up as the smoke of a furnace?" Talk of fire and brimstone and of terrible voices speaking to him lead to the Doctor's smug diagnosis of "aberratio mentalis partialis." But the highly metaphorized language is not a single character's symptom. The whole of Büchner's play is suffused with violent and colorful images, the more remarkable as they are set in the drabbest of contexts. Oneiric antitheses of light and darkness, heat and cold, set up fundamental oppositions, and tend to universalize human experience. The brightly lit fairground stands in dramatic contrast to Marie's dark room. Marie is "beautiful as sin," the earth "hot as hell," while hell itself is referred to as ice cold ("die Erd ist hölleheiss, mir eiskalt, eiskalt, die Hölle ist kalt . . .")—a venerable image of infernal extremes of ice and fire. [31]

These stark oppositions also maintain a steady link between sexual and religious imagery. The power of rhetoric is here of an unrhetorical nature; it does not depend on the verbal flourishes of any single protagonist and is neither grandiloquent nor "heroic." Rather it comes into being through embeddings of, or oblique references to, already existing texts, whether in the form of folk tales, songs, or ditties, which all seem to point to an indeterminate collective meaning that transcends any given individual. Shakespeare, it has been seen, provides a steady reference. So do the Scriptures. Marie, in a repentant vein, turns the pages of the Bible, and falls on the passage telling how the scribes and the Pharisees brought Jesus a woman taken in adultery. Reading about how Jesus said "Neither do I condemn thee. Go and sin no more," Marie begs for the ability to pray. The passage ends with a desperate evocation of her namesake, Mary Magdalene, washing Christ's feet with her tears and drying them with her flowing hair. [32]

The tragic and Biblical subtexts are themselves remarkably interconnected. Lear's vehement outbursts on the heath, as he divests himself of all false lendings, invoke hell, darkness, and the sulphurous pit. The result is a fascinating network of images, the significance of which lies beyond the ken of the unheroic hero. Yet in the process, the tragic spirit and the tragic status are somehow retrieved, in part through the age-old nobility of passion, victimhood, innocence, and alienation. In large part also because the antiheroic mode, stressing the banality of life and death, reaches out to universal man. But it is a reach that exceeds the antihero's grasp. [33]

◆ 3 ◆

GOGOL'S
"THE OVERCOAT"

THE MEANINGS OF A DOWNFALL

Akaky Akakyevich is the central character of Gogol's story "The Overcoat." Although Dostoevsky gave common currency to the term "antihero" in *Notes from Underground*, it is Gogol's Akaky Akakyevich who is the genuine, unmitigated, and seemingly unredeemable antihero. For Dostoevsky's antiheroic paradoxalist, afflicted with hypertrophia of the consciousness, is well-read, cerebral, incurably bookish, and talkative. Akaky Akakyevich is hardly aware, and almost inarticulate. Gogol's artistic wager was to try to articulate this inarticulateness.

The story, in its plot line, is simple. A most unremarkable copying clerk in a St. Petersburg ministry—bald, pockmarked, shortsighted, and the scapegoat of his colleagues, who invent cruel ways of mocking him—discovers one day that his pathetically threadbare coat no longer protects him against the fierce winter wind. The tailor he consults categorically refuses to mend the coat, which is now beyond repair, and tempts Akaky Akakyevich into having a new overcoat made, one totally beyond his means, but which by dint of enormous sacrifices, he manages to acquire and wear with a newly discovered sense of pride. But his happiness lasts only one short day. Crossing a deserted quarter at night, he is attacked by two thieves, who knock him to the ground and steal his coat. Drenched, frozen, deeply upset, brutally reprimanded by a superior whose help he dares seek, Akaky develops a fever, becomes delirious, and dies.

One can hardly speak of an interesting plot line. Yet this simple story lends itself to orgies of interpretations. There may be as many interpretations as there are readers. "The Overcoat" can be read as a parable, a pathetic tale, an interpretive puzzle. But to begin with, there is the temptation to read it seriously as satire with a social and moral message. In "The Nose," Gogol had already made fun of the rank-consciousness and venality of civil servants. In "The Overcoat," he seems to deride systematically the parasitical, lazy, phony world of Russian officialdom, whose members are the impotent mediators of a hierarchic and ineffectual power structure in which every subordinate fears and apes his superior. Early Russian critics, convinced that literature must have a moral message, read such a denunciatory and corrective satirical intention into the story, even though it is clear that Gogol constantly shifts his tone, defends no apparent norm, and systematically ironizes any possible "serious" message.

There is of course the temptation to read "The Overcoat" as a tale of compassion, as a plea for brotherhood. The pathetically defenseless little clerk, taunted and persecuted by the group, remains blissfully oblivious to the cruel pranks of which he is the butt, intent on his humble copying activity. Only when the jokes become too outrageous, or interfere with his work, does he protest ever so mildly. But here the tone of the story seems to change. For Gogol introduces a young man, recently appointed to the same office, who is on the point of sharing in the general fun, and who is suddenly struck by the strange notes in Akaky's voice which touch his heart with pity and make him suddenly see everything in a very different light. A true revelation emanating from an "unnatural" ("neeste'stvennaia") power allows him to hear other words behind Akaky's banal entreaty to be left alone. What he hears are the deeply penetrating, unspoken words echoing with poignant significance: "I am thy brother."

And with this voice from behind the voice comes the shocked awareness of how much "inhumanity" there is in human beings, how much brutality lurks in what goes as civilized society and civilized behavior. The apparent lesson in humanity given by the scapegoat victim seems, in the immediate context, to have an almost religious character, especially if one relates it to the narrator's comments, after Akaky's death, on how a man of meekness who bore the sneers and insults of his fellow human beings disappeared from this world, but who, before his agony, had a vision of the bright visitant ("sve'tliey gost'"). The man of meekness, the man of sorrows, like the unspoken but clearly heard "I am thy brother," seems to have a Christian, if not Christological, resonance.

But we might forget Akaky's name, and that we are not allowed to do. For the patronymic appellation not only stresses the principle of repetition (Akaky's first name being exactly the same as his father's), but the funny sound repetition is even funnier because the syllable *kak*—"like" (*tak kak* = "just as")—embeds the principle of sameness in Akaky's name, determining, it would seem, his single-minded, lifelong activity of copying and implicit condemnation to sameness. Regarding the many years Akaky served in the same department, Gogol observes that he "remained in exactly the same place, in exactly the same position, in exactly the same job, doing exactly the same kind of work, to wit copying official documents." But there is better (or worse), especially to Russian ears, for *kakat'* (from the Greek *cacos* = "bad," "evil") is children's talk for "defecate," and *caca* in many languages refers to human excrement. Affliction with such a name clearly relates Akaky to the garbage being regularly dumped on him as he walks in the street, and to his being treated with no more respect by the caretakers than a common fly. The cruel verbal fun around the syllable *kak* extends beyond the character's name, and contaminates Gogol's text. Gogol indulges in seemingly endless variations on the words *tak, kak, kakoi, kakoi-to, kakikh-to, vot-kak, neekak, takoi, takaya, kaknibud'* ("just so," "that's how," "in no way," "somehow," and so on), which in the translation disappear altogether. The exploitations of sound effects or sound meanings clearly correspond to a poet's fascination with the prestigious cacophonic resources of ordinary speech.[1]

One last point about the choice of Akaky's name, specifically the Christian act of "christening": according to custom, the calendar was opened at random and several saints' names (Mokkie, Sossia), including the name of the martyr Khozdazat, were considered, only to be rejected by the mother because they sounded so strange. Akaky was chosen because that was the name of the father. But Acacius, a holy monk of Sinai, was also a saint and martyr, and thus we return—especially since the Greek prefix *a* (*A*cacius) signifies *not* bad, therefore good, meek, humble, obedient—to the religious motif. If Akaky continues to copy for his own pleasure at home, this is in large part because the bliss of copying has a specifically monastic resonance. Gogol does indeed refer to his copying as a "labor of love."

At this point, new possibilities open up. Could "The Overcoat" not be read as hagiography in a banal modern context, or at the very least as a parody of hagiography? A number of elements seem to lend support to such a reading of the story in or against the perspective of the traditional lives of the saints: the humble task of copying documents, reference to the theme of the martyr ("moo'chenik"), salvational terminology, sacrificial motifs of communion ("I am thy brother"), Akaky's visions and ecstasies, his own apparitions from beyond the grave. But the most telling analogy with hagiographic lore is the conversion effect on others, first on the young man who has a revelation of a voice that is not of this world ("svet"), and toward the end on the self-admiring, domineering, Very Important Person on whom Akaky's ghostlike apparition makes a never-to-be-forgotten impression.[2]

The overcoat itself can take on religious connotations because clothing, in the symbology of the Bible and orthodox liturgy, often represents righteousness and salvation. The only trouble with such an interpretation— and Gogol has written *Meditations on the Divine Liturgy*, which refers to the priest's robe of righteousness as a garment of salvation[3]—is that the coat can have an opposite symbolic significance, that of hiding the truth. Hence the traditional image of disrobing to reveal the naked self. And there are many other possible meanings quite remote from the religious sphere: the metonymic displacement of the libido (the Russian word for overcoat—*shinel*—is appropriately feminine), the effects of virilization (in his new coat, Akaky surprises himself in the act of running after a woman in the street!), loss of innocence, and loss of "original celibacy."[4] The coat itself thus turns out to be a form of temptation (material acquisition, vanity, pride), and the devilish tailor is the agent of this temptation, just as the writer or narrator (is there not something devilish about the narrative voice?) "tempts" the reader into a succession of mutually canceling interpretations.

This provocative writer-reader relationship, sustained throughout the narration, casts a special light on Akaky's fundamental activity of copying—the act of writing in its purest form. It does not take much imagination (our modern critics discover self-referentiality everywhere) to see in Akaky's copying an analogue of the writer's activity. And like the proverbially absorbed writer or scholar, he is obsessed by his writing to the point of finding himself in the middle of the street while thinking that he is in the middle of a sentence. This self-absorbed and self-referential nature of Gogol's act of writing might be seen to imply a negative attitude toward the referential world, toward all that which is not writing. Much like Flaubert, who dreamt of composing a "book about nothing," and whom contemporary critics like to view as an apostle of intransitive literature, Gogol yearned for monastic withdrawal. Flaubert was haunted by the figures of the monk and the saint. Similarly, Gogol explained in a letter: "It is not the poet's business to worm his way into the world's marketplace. Like a silent monk, he lives in the world without belonging to it."[5]

Pushed to a logical extreme, this sense of the radical deceptiveness of life calls into question worldly authority, and leads to a destabilizing stance that challenges the principle of authority, a subversive *gesta* of which the real hero is the artist himself. There is indeed something devilish about

Gogol's narrative voice. It has already been suggested that the devil makes an appearance in the figure of the tailor who tempts Akaky into buying the coat. This caricature of the sartorial artist who quite literally is the creator of the overcoat, this ex-serf sitting with his legs crossed under him like a Turkish pasha, has diabolical earmarks: he is a "one-eyed devil" living at the end of a black staircase; he has a deformed big toenail, hard and thick as a tortoise shell; he handles a thrice mentioned snuff box on which the face of a general has been effaced (the devil is faceless); he seems to be nudged by the devil and charges "the devil knows what prices."[6]

This verbal playfulness seems to extend to the narrator himself, who undercuts his own narration in truly diabolical fashion by means of grotesque hyperbolizing, mixtures of realistic and parodistic elements, sudden shifts from the rational to the irrational, and elliptical displacements from epic triviality to unrestrained fantasy. Indulging in a game of mirages and foglike uncertainties, the narrator subverts the logical progression of his story. Ultimately, even the ghost is debunked, and we are back in the blackness of quotidian reality. In the Russian text, these shifts in tone and textual instabilities are even more insidious, since everything seems to blur into the undifferentiated flow of seemingly endless paragraphs.

This merging of discontinuities undermines any sense of plot, undercuts the notion of subject, and suggests at every point that what is told is *another* story, thereby teasing the reader into endless interpretations that can be neither stabilized nor arrested. Some of this is the inevitable result of a mimesis of inarticulateness, a narrative style that is the imitative substitute for Akaky's manner of communicating mostly through prepositions, adverbs, and "such parts of speech as have no meaning whatsoever." But the strategy of destabilization and fragmented diction also has a deeper subversive purpose. The non sequiturs and hesitations reveal the arbitrariness of any fictional structure, and in the last analysis subvert any authorial authority. The concluding page of the "The Nose" represents the narrator's critique of the story as incomprehensible and useless. The mediating self-negator is the fictionalized narrator identified in "The Overcoat" as the "raskazyvaiushchyi"—the narrating one. And this narrator, occasionally pretending to be ignorant or semi-ignorant (like Cervantes' narrative voice as of the very first sentence of *Don Quixote*), does not know in what town, on what day, on what street the action takes place—in fact, complains of loss of memory. All this, however, only accentuates the possible importance of the unknowable and the unsayable, while protecting the protagonist's sacred privacy. In "The Overcoat," the narrator clumsily speculates on what Akaky might or might not have said to himself as he stares at an erotic window display in the elegant quarter of St. Petersburg, and he concludes: "But perhaps he never even said anything at all to himself. For it is impossible to delve into a person's mind" (in Russian, literally: to creep into a person's soul).

"The Overcoat" is thus marked by conflicting and enigmatic signals, pointing to oxymoronic textures of meanings. Inversions hint at conversions. What is seemingly up is in fact seen to be down, while the reverse is equally true. The insignificant creature turns out to be capable of heroic sacrifices, while the powerfully constituted VIP with the appearance of a "bogatir" (hero) is cut down to human size by fright. On the other hand, when Akaky's fall is likened to a disaster such as destroys the czars and other great ones of this earth, one may well feel that Gogol is ironic about all heroic poses, heroic values, and heroic figures. When Akaky wears the new coat, his pulse beats faster, his bearing seems to indicate a newly discovered sense of purpose ("tzel'"), his eyes have an audacious gleam, he appears somehow to have almost become virile. Yet the overcoat is also the emblem of false values, of trivial passion, of a silly reason for a human downfall. One might wish therefore to read a deeper significance into these mutually canceling interpretations. In English, the word *passion* is fraught with a multiple significance: in the ordinary sense, it denotes intense and even overwhelming emotion, especially of love; yet etymologically, it signifies suffering. Love and suffering are of course linked in a grotesque manner in "The Overcoat." Whether such love and such suffering are commensurate with any objective reality remains unresolved in this story, which seems to say that any love is great no matter what its object, that love is all-powerful; and conversely, that any passion can drag one down, that the more intense it seems, the emptier it is. Gogol's style is in itself an admirable instrument of ambivalence: enlarging trivia, and thereby trivializing what we may for a moment be tempted to take as significant.[7]

What complicates Gogol's text for the reader is that it is not a case of simple ambivalence. It will not do to praise Gogol as a compassionate realist with an ethical message or to see him as a playful antirealist indulging in overwrought imagery and in the reflections of distorting mirrors. The hard fact is that Gogol is a protean writer whose inclination to offer a simultaneity of possible meanings allows for neither respite nor the comfort of a univocal message. If the narrator is center stage, it is because ultimately he becomes a performer, a buffoonish actor mimicking incoherence itself. Intelligent readers of Gogol—Boris Eichenbaum, Vladimir Nabokov, Victor Erlich, Charles Bernheimer, Donald Fanger[8]—have in varying degrees, and with different emphases, understood that rather than indulging in a feast of ideas to be taken seriously, Gogol delighted in verbal acts as a game—a game that implied the autonomy of narrative style, a declaration of artistic independence, and a thorough deflation of *l'esprit de sérieux*.

Perhaps there is an underlying autobiographic urge in "The Overcoat," and the verbal clowning and narrative pirouettes are telling a story in which the irrational takes on an exorcising and liberating virtue—much as the idiosyncrasies of Dostoevsky's *Notes from Underground* present a vehement protest against spiritually deadening rationality. What is certain is that Gogol needs to wear a mask. Haunted by the monsters born of his imagination, afraid to be unmasked, Gogol literally disappears in his writing by becoming a multiplicity of voices.[9]

But there is a danger in depicting Gogol as an escape artist struggling against his own demons at the same time as he struggles against the repressive reality he wishes to deny. Similarly, there is the risk of considerable distortion in the determination of formalist and poststructuralist critics to draw Gogol to the camp of radical modernity by seeing him exclusively concerned with speech acts and sheer rhetoricity. A multiplicity of meanings does not mean the absence of meaning. The real problem, much as in the case of Flaubert, who complained of the plethora of subjects and inflationary overfill of meanings, is that overabundance and multiplicity become principles of indeterminacy. Excess is related to emptiness. Gogol, too, seems torn between the futility of experience and the futility of writing about it, between the conviction that writing is the only salvation, yet that it is powerless to say the unsayable—aware at all points of the gulf between signifier and signified.

Nabokov may have come closest to the heart of Gogol's dark playfulness when he wrote: "The gaps and black holes in the texture of Gogol's style imply flaws in the texture of life itself."[10] To this one might add, however, that the hollowness of the gaps, the terrifying absence, is also an absence/presence: a void that asks to be filled by the interpretative act. The dialectics of negativity, so dependent on the antiheroic mode embodied by Akaky, displace the production of meaning from the almost nonexistent character and undecidable text to the reader, on whom special demands are being made.

4

DOSTOEVSKY'S
UNDERGROUND MAN

PORTRAIT OF THE PARADOXALIST

"I am a sick man. . . . I am a spiteful man. I am an unpleasant man." The obsessive and aggressive monologue of the underground man begins with these three brief sentences, whose tripartite nature stresses at the same time solipsistic self-enclosure and the link between a specific self and a generalized image. "I am a sick man. . . . I am a spiteful man. I am an unpleasant man"—three parallel yet modulated affirmations whose inner structure clearly plays on the separation as well as the tie between the personal pronoun *I* and the substantive *man*.

These three self-denigrating and intensely subjective opening sentences of Dostoevsky's *Notes from Underground* seem to promise a self-portrait. Hostile to himself, driven by what he calls a "hysterical craving for contradictions" (II, 1)[1], the underground man does, however, present himself both as a unique self and a representative type. He thereby undermines all binary oppositions, and complicates from the outset the very notion of a portrait. Herein lies this novel's first paradox. It is expressed in the first person, yet it speaks to us of the *other*. This initial paradox will be confirmed by the dialectical moves of the narration, as well as by the only external commentary, attributed to the fictional editor of these so-called "Notes." This brief terminal commentary defines the author of the notes as a "paradoxalist."

The self-portrait of this lover of paradoxes remains essentially derogatory. The underground man launches his monologue under the sign of a sickness, the chief symptom of which seems to be the morbid pleasure of experiencing and inflicting pain, and he sounds a double note of indulgence in physical suffering and hostility to doctors. Dostoevsky's protagonist looks at himself, judges himself, holds himself in contempt. If his moans are malicious, it is because he wishes to deny all dignity to his own suffering, but also to provoke a malaise, and to teach that to know oneself means to lose all self-respect.

This disparaging self-portrait is a physical portrait up to a point. The underground man sees himself as weak and puny; he compares himself to the sinewy officer, and finds his own awkward silhouette utterly ridiculous. He sees himself as a spiteful, petty official, gnashing his teeth and foaming at the mouth. He quite literally sees himself, for the underground man likes to watch himself in a mirror, painting his portrait so to speak *sur le vif,* from life. He sticks out his tongue at the mirror. In the room of Liza the prostitute, he suddenly sees reflected in a mirror his own pale, loathsome, nasty face, with disheveled hair, and he derives a keen satisfaction from appearing so revolting to the woman he will seek to humiliate in every possible way.

Needless to say, the physical portrait tends to become a moral and psychological portrait as well; the bodily images, in particular the so-called infirmities, are in reality metaphors, much like the gnashing of teeth and the foaming at the mouth. Dostoevsky's character compares himself to a hunchback, a dwarf, a cripple—but this is to suggest his moral defects, his vanity, his psychological deformity, his inertia, his bad faith as an inveterate poseur.

The image of a deliberate pose and the idea of portraiture are clearly on his mind. He not only refers ironically to the pose of an ideal model, trying to give his face an expression as noble ("blagorodnoe"—II, 1) as possible, but he specifically invokes the academic painter N. Gay, imagining sarcastically the hypothetical portrait of the respectable and self-important individual—the very type Sartre was to call a bastard, a *salaud*—and to whom Dostoevsky attributes physical and moral traits that seem to come straight out of the infamous gallery of portraits in *Nausea.* The underground man writes: "I will demand respect. . . . I live peacefully, I will die solemnly. Why, after all, it is splendid, perfectly splendid. And then, what a belly I would grow, what a triple chin I would establish, what a flamboyant nose I would produce so that anyone, at the sight of me, would say: 'Now here is someone, here is something real and positive'" (I, 26).

This hypothetical caricature-portrait only underscores the equivocal nature of the self-descriptive discourse in the first person singular. Dostoevsky derides any pretense at truth, since his protagonist, who refers in French to the famous opening sentence of Rousseau's *Les confessions* ("Je veux montrer à mes semblables un homme dans toute la vérité de la nature"), illustrates, through his own example, the impossibility of not lying when speaking about oneself. We face the old paradox of Epimenides. What credence are we to give to his statement that all the inhabitants of Crete are liars if the person who makes the statement is himself a Cretan? More than truth or veracity is at stake. Identity itself is in question. The underground man complains that he does not possess any definite quality, that he is, all told, a man without qualities. The original Russian is more precise, the word "svo'estvo" (I, 6), signifying a specific identity, made up of attributes belonging uniquely to a single individual. He refers to the golden dreams of such an identity, meaning thereby that such a fixed and solid identity is an illusion. This being so, the singular portrait becomes an impossibility. Specific identity eludes us. At best, we may speak of a multiple or collective portrait, in the same sense that the underground man's discourse is not really a monologue, nor even a dialogue, but a polylogue through which he divides and then multiplies himself.

The notion of a collective portrait is suggested by the image of the cripple which appears both at the beginning and at the end, thus framing the paradoxalist's notes. If from the outset physical deformity is a metaphor that stands for the character's pathological susceptibility, in the end this image is generalized and extends to everyone. "We all limp more or less," he writes. But this tendency to generalize appears much earlier. It is embedded in the author's note that precedes the text of the novel, in which the author affirms in his own name that persons such as the writer of these "notes" must exist in contemporary society, that he is in fact a characteristic type, representative of his generation, and that this type was bound to appear in his time and place. This deterministic note will of course itself be made ironic by the subterranean discourse, but it does establish a generalizing tone. Moreover, the idea of a collective portrait will be made explicit. Addressing his imaginary audience, the protagonist gives as an example a "friend," adding immediately: "But after all he is your friend, too—and indeed whose friend is he not!" (I, 7). Then going one step further, he qualifies this friend as a "collective personality." Toward the end he becomes even more precise, using the expression "all of us," which he knows will profoundly irritate his putative interlocutors.

About the underground figure himself, the novel provides two complementary definitions, one offered by himself, the other given as an objective editorial commentary. In the last paragraph, the protagonist, already defined as a *paradoxalist* by the editorial voice, defines himself as an antihero ("antigero'ey"). The two terms (antihero and paradoxalist) are so to speak coupled. The notion of antiheroism implies the subversion or absence/ presence of the questioned model, while paradox suggests a deeper meaning hidden behind a logical incongruity or provocative negation. Both notions inform an ironic thrust whose aim is to carry the underground message to its radical extreme. The word *paradox* signifies countertruth. The fictionalized adversarial listener comes close to the secret intentionality of the message in the garb of paradox, when he remarks: "You doubtlessly mean to say something, but out of fear hide your real meaning." (The Russian for real meaning is here "posle'dnoe slovo": "your last word"— I, 11.) But, how to decipher the concealed "last word"? The paradoxes of the antihero are no doubt conceived so as to place indirections, oblique approaches, and outright lies in the service of some truth.

The term "antihero" is certainly not ennobling, yet it can be understood to promise a measure of truth, since Dostoevsky explicitly opposes it to the idea of fiction. "A novel requires a hero," writes the underground man, "and here all the traits of the anti-hero are *expressly* gathered" (II, 10). We are given a negative, even devastating self-portrait: the underground man blackens himself as though on purpose. He hates himself even in his childhood and school memories. He describes himself in his tattered robe, browbeaten by his servant Apollon, and evokes with self-debasing satisfaction his humiliations, his fits of hysterics, his convulsions. He sees himself as insignificant, as loathsome in the eyes of others, and imagines—as the Russian saying goes—that they pay no more attention to him than to a common fly.

Yet the word hero itself, in the Dostoevskian context, is loaded with negative connotations. Beyond the posturings of the poseur, it points to the mental cruelty of the human type, who, when humiliated, seeks to humiliate in turn. In the presence of the prostitute Liza, the underground man thus assumes the role of a "hero." The word hero appears several times, always in a derogatory sense, and always with reference to the desire to dominate and subjugate. The protagonist dreams of seeing others grovel at his feet. What is at stake is the question of *power*: "I cannot live without exercising my power and my tyranny over someone," he explains (II, 9). Beyond power and tyranny it is human nature itself, including the capacity to love, that is in question. "Even in my underground dreams, I did not imagine love in any form except as a struggle. I always began it with hatred and ended it with moral subjugation" (II, 10).

The word hero carries other negative connotations for the paradoxalist. It points to intransigence, inflexibility, and the unreasonable desire for the absolute. The underground man observes that he can be neither a hero nor an insect, giving us to understand that his conception of the hero excludes the human dimension—any state, that is, of imperfection. "To be a hero or to grovel in the mud, there was nothing between," he writes (II, 2). To be an ordinary human being, we must understand, is simply not enough. The paradoxalist thus skips without any transition from an inflated sense of victory to the most spiritless abjection.

This oscillation between the ideal and the image of mud, this subversion of the heroic model conceived in terms of an inhuman desire for domination, goes hand in hand with the subversion of the narrative model. For in Dostoevsky's *Notes from Underground*, the place of action is not the concrete and objective outside world. The opening signals do not in any way answer the triple question associated traditionally with the beginning of any narrative construct: who? when? where? Here the voice is anonymous, and, from the start, the place of action is consciousness itself. The protagonist is not in an underground; the underground is in him. As he himself puts it, he carries the underground in his soul. What we are given is the mental staging of an internalized drama.[2] Such a reversal, together with the ceaseless wavering between yearnings for the ideal and for degradation, places priority on the vertical, metaphorical axis, at the expense of sequential narration. This dominant vertical axis is intimately related to the possible meanings of the image of the underground, "podpo'lie."

The semantic range of the term "podpo'lie" is particularly broad because of the dialectical nature of its positive and negative connotations. In negative terms, the image of the underground, announced both by the title of the book and by the title of part I, may suggest a retractile instinct, the desire to hide, a sordid shelter, a verminous existence, asocial behavior, the repression of the unconscious, the pathological need to elude normal human intercourse through shame and hostility. At the extreme limit, the image connotes death and burial. But the underground can also refer to courageous resistance, whether political or spiritual. And the voice that is heard coming from below could communicate a subversive, dissident, seditious message in revolt against an established authority or ideology.

But there is more: the image of death also functions as an image of life. And this not only because what lies below the ground could bring to mind the image of the nourishing root (a radical emblem of origin and foundation), but because the underground, the place of burial (one need only think of the catacombs of the early Christians), is also conceived as the privileged locus of prayer, of a spiritual message, and of resurrection. An ambivalent symbol of repression and revelation, the underground is thus at the same time a metaphor of sterile isolation and of a reascent toward light, suggesting the vocation to proclaim a momentous truth from the abyss.

This subterranean voice, endowed with a prophetic potential, belongs in the first instance to the confessional genre. We return to the self-portrait. The underground man claims to be honest and sincere with himself, to write for himself alone. But almost in the same breath, he observes that the poet Heine—referring to Rousseau's *Confessions*—asserted that it is impossible to tell the truth about oneself. Another model, however, looms behind Rousseau, who lies out of vanity. This model is Saint Augustine, who writes under the severe surveillance of God. The contrast is telling. Unlike Saint Augustine's utterances, which also come from below, under the eyes of an unimpeachable witness, the underground man's monologue remains specular, self-reflexive, devoid of any guarantee. The contrasting parallel between the Dostoevskian protagonist and the figure of Saint Augustine is by all counts ironic, highlighting a basic absence or *lack*. But this conflicting parallel allows us to glimpse the latent intentionality of the underground man's paradoxical discourse. Saint Augustine also wonders about the addressee of his message. ". . . to whom am I telling this? Not to Thee, Oh my God, but in Thy presence I am telling it to my own humankind." Indeed, Saint Augustine need not tell God, who sees and knows all; in full sight of God, cheating is out of the question. Augustine adds the following, which confirms the ironic resonance of the Dostoevskian voice: "And to what purpose do I tell this? Simply that I and any other who may read may realize out of what depths we must cry to thee" ("de quam profundo clamandum sit ad te").[3]

This voice emerging from the depths thus implies at the same time the idea of telling lies or telling the truth—and this precisely to the extent that the absolute witness is (or seems to be) absent or present. This paradox extends to the dialogical monologue of the underground man, who imagines or invents the *other*, yet argues essentially with himself. He addresses a public he calls "gentlemen" ("gospoda"), while fully aware that they are only a fiction. If he invents them, it is to divide and disperse himself. Even the objections he attributes to his listeners are of his own invention, and their laughter, which interrupts the flow of his words, is in fact his own laughter. He splits his personality, becoming the other. (Raskolnikov, in *Crime and Punishment*, will carry this split or rift in the etymology of his own name.) The underground man explains that he needs the other, his judgment, his glance.

Faced with a narration that reveals simultaneously solipsistic self-enclosure and a need for otherness, one is tempted to draw on existential analysis. Tzvetan Todorov proposes a typical existentialist formula: "The underground man does not exist outside his relation with the other, without the glance of the other."[4] It would be hard to overemphasize the importance of the glance. If the underground man invents the glance of the other, it is noteworthy that he himself, most often, tries to lower or even hide his eyes. He informs us that he has never been able to look people straight in the eye. He not only looks at himself with discontent and even hatred, despising in particular his face, but he fears the glance of the other as he fears the other's mocking laughter. He sees himself as seen, and if need be invents this glance that looks at him with revulsion. For he fears not being seen even more than being seen and judged.

This need and fear of the observing eye settles at the heart of this work a tragic ambivalence ("L'enfer c'est les autres," will be Sartre's formula) that corresponds to the psychological rift within the character. And this inner rift in turn refers to the profound but unstable rapport between the specific self and the representative human being announced in the author's note on the first page. There lies the true difficulty of a work that opposes and blends *one* and *all* ("odi'n" and "vse" [II, 1])—a work in which the penitent is also the judge, and the denouncer embodies the parody of what is being denounced. Camus, in writing *La chute,* was to remember this lesson.

The cleavage is not only structural, but conceptual as well. The events described in part II precede by some twenty years the kind of self-portrait proposed in part I, and this temporal inversion stresses the distance between two cultural moments, two generations, two ideological codes— namely, the romantic idealism of the forties and the prevailing positivism and determinism of the sixties.[5] A rift and an inversion that have much to do, as Joseph Frank has shown so well, with the central issue of suffering viewed as a purifying value, but also as a pretext for moral and spiritual sadism.

This duplicity also manifests itself on the philosophical level, since the idiosyncratic antihero, who wills himself outside and in opposition to the norm, is presented on the very first page as determined by the moral and intellectual climate of his time. It would seem that the puny, nasty, spiteful official stands at the same time for the principle of pure caprice, hence free will, and for determinism—embodying in his person one of the oldest philosophical dilemmas: the relation between freedom and necessity.

⚜

Here we move to the larger issues. By means of a self-portrait which is in reality a parodistic collective portrait, we are led to a serious critique of problems situated at the core of the Western consciousness: free will, consciousness itself, books and bookish culture, rationalism and the idea of progress, nostalgia for spiritual values. The underground man associates lucidity with suffering. Disease, in all the accepted meanings of this term, sharpens consciousness; but consciousness itself, or rather the hypertrophy of consciousness, is seen as a disease. According to the protagonist, an over-developed, overrefined consciousness is the characteristic affliction of modern man. He is aware that his intelligence is pathologically developed, that he is hyperconscious of his own thoughts and words. He knows that the effect is inertia, even paralysis. "Thus conscience," in Hamlet's words, "doth make cowards of us all." According to the underground man, only asses and mules are brave (II, 1). Once again, the individual symptom extends to the collectivity. The same page that treats hyperconsciousness as a disease refers to the city of St. Petersburg as an accursed place: an abstract, premeditated, deliberate, and rationally planned inhuman habitat.

In a different context, Italo Svevo was to develop this paradoxical relationship between disease and consciousness, insisting on the value of disease, real or imaginary, to the extent that it multiplied the resources of consciousness and reflexivity. But it is no doubt Baudelaire, a contemporary of Dostoevsky, who provides the most viable parallel with the underground man: same paralyzing irony, same sense of *ennui*, same internal exile, same divisive self-torture ("I am the wound and the knife"; "I am the slap and the cheek"), same condemnation to sardonic laughter in front of the sinister mirror.

And of course the image of the mirror leads us back to the reflexive nature of thought. In question here is the very notion of culture, staring at itself in the looking glass of a heritage that perpetuates itself through the imitation of models. The underground man places in doubt a culture that projects a bookish conception of the world. To be sure, he denounces the bad use of books; but in so doing, he points to culture itself as a problem. Modern man is seen as "morbidly cultivated" (II, 1). Reading is presented as a vice, and the text is studded with literary references (in addition to Heine and Rousseau: Pushkin, Lermontov, Nekrassov, and others), which function as a critique of the romantic lie and of self-indulgent literariness.

There is worse: books and their authors are seen as mediations capable of choking spontaneity and authenticity, conducive to bad faith and factitiousness. The underground man's behavior with the "other" is defined by him as scandalously bookish. The effect is dehumanizing, as his cruelty to Liza clearly shows. For it is when his behavior toward her is most atrocious, that it is defined as bookish "kni'jnaia" (II, 10). But we must make no mistake; we are not presented with an isolated, exceptional case. The underground man embodies the problematic point of encounter between culture and nature, and he concludes at the end of his book that without books we would be lost, that we are all "stillborn," our so-called culture being in fact a negation of the vital principle.

The idea of negation and negativity is applied to the entire century, which is defined as negative or negativistic ("otritsatel'ni"—I, 6). The principle of negation has of course traditionally characterized the denial of God. Dostoevsky must have remembered the famous line that Goethe puts into the mouth of Mephistopheles: "I am the spirit that always says no" ("Ich bin der Geist der stets verneint"). Yet the underground man's century, the century of the industrial revolution, is also the century of a most *positive* commitment to reason and progress. A purely material progress, the underground man would add, and even that is not so sure . . . For it is not at all self-evident that the evolved human creature of modern times is in any way less barbaric than the so-called barbarians of the past. Progress is far from visible, considering the march of history, with its increasingly perfected instruments of destruction, and the rivers of blood that continue to flow. As to progress through culture, the underground man observes that the most exquisite slaughterers have almost always been the most civilized gentlemen (I, 7).

Dostoevsky's critique reaches beyond questioning the rational evolution of history. It is rationalism itself that is targeted. This attack takes two forms, a mocking scorn for the formula "two times two makes four," and a radical hostility to the very idea of the Crystal Palace. The mathematical formula "two times two makes four" offends the underground man to a point of obsession. He compares it to a stone wall, to an unbreachable obstacle, literally a dead end. An emblem of the blind cult of the positive fact, the hated mathematical formula becomes the ultimate manifestation of the spirit that negates whatever is not subject to a scientific law. At some point, "two times two makes four" is called the beginning of death (I, 9). A spiritual death, to be sure. In the tradition of the *libertins*, the formula was recognized as a signal of atheism. Molière's Dom Juan, accused by his servant Sganarelle of being an unbeliever ("mécréant"), is asked by him whether there is anything, for instance the afterlife, in which he does believe. Dom Juan's terse answer comes promptly: "Je crois que deux et deux sont quatre" ("I believe that two times two makes four").

The underground man would say that better a crime than such a negative credo. What offends him above all is a so-called value system based on utilitarianism, which for him means the absence of values and the denial of free will. Hence his rejection of any deterministic system that would force a human being to obey the predictable laws of a calculating table, to be no more than a cogwheel, to have no more freedom than a piano key or an organ stop. We would say today that the underground protagonist rebels against the nightmare of a computerized human robot. He is appalled by the thought of a world that lacks the choice of suffering and the exercise of the human will. By saying no to the materialistic utopia advocated by the Chernyshevskys of this world, by refuting their blind optimism, Dostoevsky also challenges the idea, or rather philosophy—a perverse one according to him—of happiness and progress.

It is here that the metaphor of the Crystal Palace takes on its full meaning. If the formula "two times two makes four" turns into an obsession, the same is true for the Crystal Palace, seen as a utopian edifice, an evil Tower of Babel—but also as a protomodern architectural construct. Before serving as an underground metaphor, the Crystal Palace did indeed exist architecturally. Designed by Sir Joseph Paxton for the Great Exhibition of 1851, it was still an attraction during Dostoevsky's visit to London in 1862. Great Exhibitions—a significant feature of the nineteenth century— were meant to glorify the new industrial society. The Crystal Palace illustrates such a glorification in the very materials used, since it was constructed largely of iron and glass, much like the sheds of the great railway stations, those other cathedrals of modernity. Dostoevsky's metaphor evokes a futuristic construct, a new and perverse cathedral to celebrate the false and pernicious religion of progress and materialism. Faced with such a perversion, humanity can only shudder with horror, even if it does not understand the nature of this shudder. On the same page where the underground prophet evokes the Tower of Babel, he also maintains that man the builder has an instinctive fear of completing the edifice he is building (I, 9).

This almost holy fear, as at the thought of a sacrilege, suggests the paradox of a religious theme in a context from which God is absent. The central paradox of this elusive work might be its tendency and ultimate ability to convert negative into positive. To say no to a negation implies an affirmative message, much as in the logic of grammar a double negation cancels itself. To support the hypothesis of conversion one need only take a close look at the enigmatic section 10 of part I, in which the intimation of another reality, the notion of unsated yearnings, and of a lofty ideal are perceptibly articulated.

Even more surprising in this brief section are the striking Biblical images and injunctions. "May my hand be withered if I bring a single brick to such a building." A few lines later, there is talk of letting his tongue be cut off; and at the beginning of the following section, he refers to his longing for something he cannot find, to his great *thirst* as though he were in a desert. *Ja'jdat'* ("to thirst"), in the figurative sense of desiring, is a very strong verb indeed. The importance of this section of part I, with its implicit religious message, is confirmed by Dostoevsky's letter of March 26, 1864, to his brother Mikhail. He deplored the shape in which this section appeared in the periodical *Epokha*, and accused those "swinish censors" of having suppressed entire sentences, thereby deleting the passages where he deduced "the necessity of faith and Christ," but leaving intact those in which he seemed to rail at everything and *pretended* to blaspheme.[6]

In support of this hidden religious theme, there is also internal evidence, notably the special value bestowed on suffering. If the narrative voice stresses the almost voluptuous delights of suffering, it is not so much to spite his listeners with his morbid penchant, but because suffering is literally and metaphorically understood as *passion* in the etymological and Christian sense of the word (in Russian, *stra'st'*). And here is the point: according to the underground man, suffering is not even thinkable in the Crystal Palace. At the end of the book, in opposition to what is called "cheap happiness," suffering is explicitly referred to as exalting.

It is not surprising that the strategy of mobility and ironic inversion eliminates the possibility of a stable portrait. The very idea of catching or fixing the salient, durable traits of a subject—which a portrait is supposed to do—is incompatible with a work animated by the dynamics of contradiction. While stretching subjectivity to the extreme, *Notes from Underground* erases the line of demarcation between subject and object. Binary opposition is canceled as of the opening sentence. Situating the adversarial other in himself, the underground man becomes more than the other: he becomes *the others*. Essentially ironic in its instability, the obsessive monologue participates through its very mobility in a process that knows no end. That would seem to be the meaning of the concluding editorial comment concerning the absence of conclusion. "In truth," writes this fictional editor, "the 'notes' of this paradoxalist do not end here." We learn that he could not resist continuing them, indefinitely it may be assumed.

It is an ironic work also because the "paradoxalist" personifies that which he is not. In his intellectual biography, Joseph Frank observes that Dostoevsky carries the logic of the underground discourse to its furthest point, where the critique is fused with the object of the critique, where parody and satire become indistinguishable, and the parodic personage makes it difficult to see the target of the satire.[7] "Seeing through" is indeed the problem here. Accused and accuser all in one, the underground man is not only unstable, but opaque. This opaqueness of the underground discourse is doubtless the secret of its efficacy. It would seem that here universality is a function of an apparent absence of coherence, much in the way that a sense of victory, beyond the conversion of negative to positive, seems to stem from the triumph of irrationality. The underground man appears to say that what is most precious—our dignity, the freedom to choose (even that which can be harmful to us), our individual will—can be achieved only through the exercise of a perhaps noxious fantasy, in radical opposition to a "reasonable" view of ourselves and of the world. That is also, it would seem, the message of *Notes from the House of the Dead*, Dostoevsky's account of his Siberian prison experience, in which the inmates of the penal colony, all participating in a collective nightmare, affirm the dignity of their *selves* by means of the most eccentric behavior and attitudes. And yet their fierce individualism is also fused into a collective experience: even the most picturesque sketches drawn from these penitential memories never amount to portraits, but rather to representations of a collective consciousness and a symbolic projection of human freedom.

What may we learn or conclude from such a negative attitude toward the independent and stable portrait? The paradox of the disintegrated or disintegrating portrait or self-portrait seems to correspond to the refusal to bring out or invent an internal coherence, to the impossibility of knowing oneself, of possessing oneself, in spite of the obsession with the mirror. But does the underground man really seek to actualize and know himself? Can he in fact know or recognize himself, when he knows and recognizes himself in *others*? A portrait implies a certain specificity, much in the manner that a traditional novel, or a *roman d'analyse*, posits the importance and even the priority of a central, privileged subject—specifically of a "hero." According to Sartre, the modern writer must cease indulging in a literature of analysis. The reason given by Sartre relates to political ideology: the spirit of analysis has done enough harm; its only function would now be to perturb the revolutionary consciousness and to isolate human beings.[8] Dostoevsky, a century earlier, is revolutionary in another sense. The frantic monologue of his paradoxalist antihero is a multiple discourse that eludes and defies a static psychologism in order to favor a movement that admits of no respite, that transgresses and transcends the figurative notion of a frame.

FLAUBERT'S
"A SIMPLE HEART"

PATHOS AND IRONY

"A Simple Heart," so different in tone from Flaubert's novels projecting
the boundless dreams of Emma Bovary or Frédéric Moreau, seems to pay
tribute instead to the virtues of discipline, hard work, and self-denial embodied in the simple-minded peasant servant Félicité. But the simplicity
of the protagonist in no way affects the narrative strategies, which remain
complicated and ambivalent throughout.

Two exemplary passages illustrate this ambivalence. The first depicts
Félicité's beloved parrot, Loulou, enthroned, dead and stuffed, in the old
maidservant's little room, that inner sanctum which isolates her as much
as her deafness and the tiny circle of her ideas. This touching and pathetic
private space is described in the following manner:

> This place, to which few people were admitted, contained such a
> quantity of religious bric-à-brac and miscellaneous oddments that it
> looked like a cross between a chapel and a bazaar.

> Cet endroit, où elle admettait peu de monde, avait l'air tout à la fois
> d'une chapelle et d'un bazar, tant il contenait d'objets religieux et
> de choses hétéroclites. (186)[1]

"Chapel" and "bazaar" are here the two complementary and contradictory terms. The word "bazaar," which refers to a marketplace, connotes
metaphorically an atmosphere characterized by multiplicity, confusion,

disorder, heterogeneity—all of them notions tending to desecrate Félicité's room and which are confirmed by the expression "choses hétéroclites." The commercial metaphor quite obviously comes into conflict with the idea of "chapel," which tends rather to stress the spiritual and even religious nature of Félicité's private space.

Flaubert demands of his reader not a choice, but a simultaneous reading in which the suggested meanings, far from canceling one another, straddle and intermingle. Félicité's room is the measure of her limited and confused mind. Yet irony itself, in a typical Flaubertian manner, remains ambivalent to the extent that it targets and affects that which is its opposite. For the image of the chapel is, as it were, contaminated by that of the bazaar. The religious bric-à-brac (the pictures of the Virgin, the holy-water stoup made out of a coconut, and other *bondieuseries*) are inseparable from the water jug, the chipped plate, the medals, the little plush hat, the artificial flowers, and other old rubbish that adorn Félicité's room. The shell box that occupies the place of honor on the chest of drawers draped by a cloth "just like an altar" would seem to indicate that in this junkyard perspective Félicité's chapel is a bazaar after all.

The other typical passage illustrating Flaubert's techniques of ambivalence concerns not a description of a place, but an action, even an exploit. Coming home through the fields, Félicité protects Mme Aubain and her two children against a raging bull by flinging some clods of earth into the eyes of the galloping and bellowing beast, at the risk of being eviscerated. The elements of tauromachia, though of a parodistic nature, introduce a mythical and heroic note. The event was talked about in Pont-l'Evêque for many years, and takes on a legendary status. But if Flaubert uses the word "heroic," it is to stress the innocence of a character totally incapable of conceiving herself as such, totally incapable even of understanding the implications and resonance of such a word. To stand up to a bellowing bull is nothing out of the ordinary for someone like Félicité, who was raised on a farm and is familiar with animals. Her act or action in no way implies a deliberate behavior. Flaubert goes on to explain: "Félicité never prided herself in the least on what she had done, as it never occurred to her that she had done anything heroic."

Can one indeed be heroic without self-awareness? The ambivalence of this passage puts into question the very concept of hero or heroine. Much like the description of the chapel-bazaar, the episode of the bull at the same time affirms and subverts the tragic and spiritual dimension of the character and, by extension, that of the tale—without its being possible at any point to decide whether subversion or affirmation carries the day. What can be asserted is that Félicité's courage at every point—even in her way of picking up the knitting needles lying on the worktable after hearing of her nephew's death—is a function of her simplicity of mind and of her integration in an antiheroic, or nonheroic, literary system. With her high-pitched voice, her automatic gestures, her ageless face, she is the archetypal victim, the butt of the cruelty of circumstances and of those who hold her in contempt and exploit her. Incapable of conceptualizing anything, blending all the images of the illustrated geography book as well as those of sacred history, Félicité's unintelligence condemns her to an almost strictly literal vision of things—a literalness that paradoxically also gives her access to an almost poetic sense of wonderment. Betrayed, scoffed, beaten, violated by life as well as by those who crush her with their egoism and contempt, she appears like a distant cousin of Büchner's and Gogol's scapegoats—the soldier Woyzeck and the copying clerk Akaky Akakyevich—with the additional vulnerability of being a woman.

Hegel suggested that the death of tragedy and of the tragic hero coincided with the emergence of the Slave as a protagonist, the Slave being by nature incapable of understanding (and therefore of loving) his fate. But we are hardly in need of historical or literary theories to sense that no one could be more remote from the heroic model than Félicité, the *servante au grand coeur* who is already foreshadowed, on the podium of the agricultural fair in *Madame Bovary,* by the awkward and intimidated silhouette of Catherine Leroux, a living illustration of a half-century-long peasant servitude. Félicité's story has no story. Flaubert himself sums it up in one of his letters: "The story of a simple heart is nothing but the account of an obscure life" ("L'histoire d'un coeur simple est tout bonnement le récit d'une vie obscure").[2] Simplicity is in this context the equivalent all at once of insignificance, poverty of mind, humility, disposition to love and to serve, innocence in every sense of the term, and of a devotion that no disappointment or critical judgment can erode.

Ambivalence is inscribed into the title of the story. To the extent that this title is a synecdoche or, broadly speaking, a metonymy, it simply replaces the name of the character, a part of the body—the heart—standing for the whole of the person. But the distortion of a seemingly familiar expression—the adjective *simple* being normally coupled not with *coeur* but with *esprit (esprit simple)*—is a first ironic signal. Behind the innocence, purity, and natural goodness that the title seems to announce, one senses less positive attributes implicit in the unusual combination of adjective and substantive: lack of sophistication, simple-mindedness, not to mention mental debility.

But everything changes from the moment one suspects that the title hides a metaphor. In that case, the tale would tend toward a signifying unity, and *coeur simple* announces a theme which, at the extreme limit, might be that of sainthood. The story would still be about a humble servant, but also about an ideal which the character herself is in no way capable of comprehending. It remains to be seen by what means and in what terms metonymy is transformed into metaphor, or clashes with it. For metonymy and metaphor coexist in a state of tension in any narrative text. What distinguishes Flaubert's tale is that the tension between metonymy and metaphor becomes conflictual, and that this conflict itself becomes a theme.

Everything depends on the point of view. At the level of the character and of the sequential development of the story, the metonymic system seems to prevail, together with the reign of contiguity and parataxis. From the outset, Félicité appears in the context of a huge chunk of time. "For half a century the women of Pont-l'Evêque envied Mme Aubain her maidservant Félicité." This half century of the opening sentence contains an invasive substitution, almost a vanishing act: the person of Félicité is presented as nothing but the pretext for a collective envy of the bourgeois of Pont-l'Evêque. The principle of a substitution is amplified in the second sentence, which gives the reasons for the women's envy, namely the long list of Félicité's domestic activities: she does all the cooking, the housework, the sewing; she washes and irons, fattens poultry, churns butter—all in return for the absurdly small sum of one hundred francs a year. In other words, a list of chores here replaces the attributes of a human being. More specifically, Flaubert succeeds, by exploiting the principle of substitution at the level of narrative rhetoric, in depriving Félicité of her being, thus reducing her to pure function.

At the level of the character, that is from the point of view of Félicité, which Flaubert consistently differentiates from that of the narrator, the perspective remains almost exclusively metonymical. Whether it be dogma, a geographic map, or a book of engravings, she confuses signified and signifier, proving herself incapable of distinguishing, even in the most rudimentary manner, between symbol and sheer literality. Everything for her is real and immanent. Félicité glides from surprise to surprise, from bewilderment to bewilderment—a gliding that Flaubert takes on ironically, and translates into a narrative structure that proposes temporality, not through events and causal relations, but in terms of flow, monotony, and repetition.

We read at the beginning of a paragraph in part III: "Then the years slipped by, each one like the last . . ." But the sentence could have appeared at almost any point in a text which, through an inventory of routine, conjures up an essentially chronic temporality deprived of any dramatic saliency. No event has any hold on a time which stubbornly remains the time of daily reoccurrence and the return of seasons. The story is articulated by expressions such as "every Thursday," "every Monday morning," "about midday," "soon after," "from time to time." Not only is each week punctuated by the uncausal banality of the quotidian, but the sequence of years is nothing but a succession of repetitions: Easter, the Assumption, All Saints' Day—an undifferentiated time marked by domestic events, a story outside of History, it would seem. Flaubert seems to take pleasure in stressing the anachronistic nature of a time as flat as the fields and the sand beaches of Normandy. If mention is made of a 14th of July or of the 1830 Revolution, it is only to bring out the pervasive historical anaesthesia or absence of historical awareness. July 14th is mentioned ironically as an important date only because it is on this day that Félicité's nephew Victor signed up for an ocean voyage, and she felt unhappy at the thought of his long absence. As for the brief allusion to the fall of the Bourbon monarchy in 1830, it is there only to mark the arrival of a new sub-prefect, in fact the very one who is responsible for the presence in Pont-l'Evêque of the parrot Loulou.

The slow pace and sheer weight of time make of this tale a poem of mourning. "A Simple Heart" begins with anachronistic and posthumous signals, under the sign of decay. Mme Aubain is first presented in her quality of widow inhabiting a house that smells a little musty, the floor of the parlor being on a lower level than the garden. The tomblike atmosphere is further stressed by references to a defunct world, vestiges of "better days" and "bygone luxury," and the description of the permanently shut drawing room with its furniture covered by a dust sheet as though under a shroud. The old farmhouse, with its worm-eaten ceiling beams, also has an air of decrepitude. Funereal images prepare from the outset the inventory of death that punctuates the story of Félicité: the death of Victor and Virginie; the death of friends; the death of Père Colmiche, of M. Bourais, of Mme Aubain; the death of the parrot, and finally the death of Félicité herself—a reminder to Mère Simon, who attends her during her agony, that she herself will one day have to go the same way ("un jour il lui faudrait passer par là").

Not surprisingly, this mortuary poem is also a poem of memory and nostalgia. Félicité poignantly recalls the old days, much as Flaubert himself, at the time he wrote "A Simple Heart," indulged in sad recollections of the past, revisiting Pont-l'Evêque and Honfleur. Flaubert seems indeed to have heeded his friend George Sand's advice to cease writing ironic texts, and to gather instead and make literary use of the intimate emotions of his own past, to steep himself in precious memories stored up in his heart.[3] It must be with these gentle admonitions in mind that Flaubert described the tone of his story in a letter to Mme Roger des Genettes: "It

is not at all ironic . . . but on the contrary very serious and very sad. I want
to move sensitive souls to pity and tears."[4] In another letter, his indebted-
ness to George Sand is even more explicit: "I began *A Simple Heart* for
her exclusively, and only to give her pleasure." But here intrudes the irony
of fate. George Sand was never to read the story that she had inspired.
"She died," writes Flaubert, "as I was in the middle of my work. Such is
the way with all our dreams."[5]

But is it true that the tale is "not at all ironic"? Félicité's name itself,
the structure of the tale (which has Félicité's death coincide with summer
imagery of sunshine and children's laughter), the textual closure which
subverts the vision of opening heavens by juxtaposing the verbs *croire* ("to
believe") and *voir* ("to see")"Elle crut voir, dans les cieux entrouverts, un
perroquet gigantesque . . ."—all tend to undermine an edifying or consolatory reading. "And as she breathed her last, she thought she could see,
in the opening heavens, a gigantic parrot hovering above her head." The
provocative final sentence acts as a reminder that irony is always an incite-
ment to interpretation, a challenge to the reader. Even the most flagrant
irony may hide multiple meanings. That is the case of Flaubert's famous
parrot. Loulou's comic value cannot be denied: his rainbow colors, his endlessly repeated repertoire of three sentences, his uncontrollable shrieks of
laughter, his way of pulling his feathers out and of scattering his droppings
everywhere. After his death, artfully stuffed by the taxidermist, biting a
gilded nut, enthroned in Félicité's chapel-bazaar, Loulou will increasingly
appear as an iconic and symbolic presence, while lending himself even
more obviously to Flaubert's ironic intentions.

For Loulou, at a psychological level, functions as a substitute for unavailable human affection. But this pathetic ironizing of the unprivileged
sentimental life of the protagonist betrays a grain of perversity on the part
of the author. It will be recalled that in her outpourings of emotion, Félicité sees the parrot as "almost a son or a lover"; she bends over him with
maternal gestures ("à la manière des nourrices"); and their intimacy almost becomes a parody of sexual relations (Loulou climbs up her fingers,
pecks at her lips—184). Lover and mother: the incestuous model is of
course perfectly incongruous in the context.

But Loulou also functions as an ironic presence at the sociosatirical
level, illustrating the repetitive mechanisms of language and of the social
discourse, the mimetic tendencies of the group, collective psittacosis or
parrot disease. In one way or another, the parrot brings out the worst in
everyone: an addiction to clichés (all parrots, according to friends, should
be called Jacquot), stupidity (Fabu teaches him swearwords), cruelty (Paul
blows the smoke of his cigar at him).

Irony of course also operates at the conceptual level, notably with regard to religious and theological themes. The three sentences relentlessly repeated by Loulou recall the catechism Félicité ends up by learning as she hears the children's repeated recitations, while the number three may well allude to the Trinity, and the absolutely trivial first two sentences give way to the third element of the bird's repertoire: "Hail Mary!" The religious satire tends to become more acerbic when the stuffed animal is turned into a fetish/icon which Félicité confuses with the Holy Ghost, and which the priest, at the end of the story, accepts for the altar at the procession of Corpus Christi. Flaubert even makes fun of Félicité's mystical ecstasy by indicating that the "luminous ray" which seems to shoot forth directly from the stuffed parrot's glass eye is nothing but a simple reflection of a sunbeam. Thus Loulou is all at once a mystic fetish for the character, and for the author a tool of irony.

Narrative rhetoric, rather than the order of events or the structure of the plot, is here given priority, involving and putting into doubt the attitude of the author, which remains enigmatic precisely because of the shiftiness of irony. For laughter itself is enigmatized. When Bourais, the smug solicitor, roars with laughter, inordinately amused by Félicité's inability to comprehend a geographical map, the reader is surely not encouraged to sympathize with this cruel and vulgar laughter. What confirms this discrediting of laughter personified by Bourais (he turns out moreover to be an embezzler) is that Loulou makes fun, it would seem, of his arrogant hilarity. As soon as the parrot sees the figure of Bourais, he shrieks with laughter ("Dès qu'il l'apercevait il commençait à rire, à rire de toutes ses forces"—182). Polyvalent comic signals in "A Simple Heart" contribute to a strategy of destabilization which informs all of Flaubert's work. Years earlier, as he toyed with the idea of the "Dictionnaire des idées reçues," he entertained the dream of writing books conceived in such a way that the reader would not know whether or not he was being made fun of ("que le lecteur ne sache pas si on se fout de lui, oui ou non"[6]). The attitude toward religion remains particularly undecidable. Does "A Simple Heart" deride religious observances, Catholic dogma, faith grounded in ignorance, idolatry, and superstition; or does it communicate a latent nostalgia for an impossible innocence, for a lost and irretrievable simplicity? Clearly, the story cannot be read in a single perspective or at one single level. Side by side with an ironic reading, the text proposes other readings which cast a very different light on Félicité's antiheroic destiny.

A "tender" reading is thus not excluded; in fact, such a reading cannot be avoided. From beginning to end the text is steeped in an atmosphere of sadness, nostalgia, mourning, and is also suffused with a soft luminosity and a pious recollection of the past. Charged with intimate and even inti-mist poetry, the tale offers elegiac tonalities which are related no doubt to Flaubert's inner need, at the time he composed "A Simple Heart," to re-visit his own past. He refers in letters to his having willfully immersed himself in a "bain de souvenirs"; to having undertaken that pilgrimage to Pont-l'Evêque and Honfleur, which filled him with poetic sadness; to be-ing haunted by the tender ghosts of Trouville. Félicité will end up by em-bodying the very notion of tenderness. Reading himself, Flaubert explains to Mme Roger des Genettes that Félicité is tenderness itself, colloquially describing her as "tendre comme du pain frais." [7]

Hers is, from the outset, a total and selfless availability of affection, an ability to give of herself which almost makes of her a caricature of mater-nal devotion, pride, and self-effacement. When Virginie takes her first communion, Félicité watches her: ". . . in one of those imaginative flights born of real affection, it seemed to her that she herself was in the child's place" (". . . avec l'imagination que donnent les vraies tendresses, il lui sembla qu'elle était elle-même cette enfant"—169). This tendency to self-denial goes with a capacity for compassion and pain that at times has an almost animal-like quality. Occasionally pain opens the way to commu-nion in suffering, such as when Félicité accompanies Mme Aubain to Vir-ginie's room, and the two women, deeply moved, find themselves in a state of veneration in the presence of the dead child's relics—her dolls, her hoops, her more intimate possessions (her handkerchiefs, frocks, petti-coats) still revealing the shape and movements of her body. The scene con-cludes with an embrace, a kiss which, for a moment, make the servant and her mistress equal ("un baiser qui les égalisait"—180). It is of course an illusory equality, which does not prevent Félicité, when Mme Aubain dies, from weeping for her "as servants rarely weep for their masters" (188). In the midst of the emptiness that increasingly surrounds Félicité (absence of those she loves, deafness and solitude, disappearance of familiar objects, the house that goes on sale), Félicité continues to have the secret of trans-forming emptiness into plenitude. Yet once again, the author's irony puts all in question. Immediately after the emotional and equalizing scene of communion with Mme Aubain, a simple sentence is enough to make the reader smile about Félicité's "dog-like devotion" and "religious venera-tion." That strange sentence is in fact given the privileged status of a half-line paragraph: "La bonté de son coeur se développa" ("The goodness of her heart grew stronger").

It is possible of course—and this would constitute a third level of inter-pretation—that we are dealing with a hagiographic signal. Félicité re-mains, so to speak, incorruptible; nothing embitters her. She does have moments of sadness recalling the old days, and even a moment of real weakness after the brutal whiplash on the road to Honfleur, when the miseries and disappointments of her life all come back to her, well up in her throat, and almost choke her. But innocence and serenity characterize her, and lead her toward the sensuous fervor ("sensualité mystique"—192) of the concluding paragraph. Félicité dies with a smile on her lips. This sensuous fervor is evidently not without its own ironic potential for readers recalling Emma Bovary's voluptuous "élancements mystiques" on her deathbed.

The religious themes, to be sure, are extensive in "A Simple Heart." If Félicité never complains, it is because her resignation is a function of her holy innocence. Her "simplicity" gives her access to the supernatural. One of Flaubert's sentences is explicit: ". . . pour de pareilles âmes le surnaturel est tout simple" (". . . to minds like hers the supernatural is a simple matter")—177. Her room—this chapel or bazaar in which her deafness further cloisters her—is much like a convent cell. Albert Thibaudet was surely right when he spoke of the "religious and Christian rhythm" of the story,[8] though once again intertextual irony is at work. The alert reader of Flaubert will surely recall the "monastic rigidity" and deafness of the old farmhand Catherine Leroux, who in *Madame Bovary* functions as a counterpoint to Emma's amorous desire.

Whether ironic or not, hagiographic elements are without question present throughout the story. The style occasionally takes on a legendary quality ("Ce jour-là il lui advint un grand bonheur"—181). Félicité takes care of the victims of cholera; she protects persecuted people, cures the sick, cleans the filthy hovel of Père Colmiche, who is afflicted with a horrendous tumor, and changes his dressings. Nothing disgusts her; no chore seems to her too humble, too lowly. These hagiographic elements are confirmed by structural contiguities, namely the very ordering of the three stories that make up *Trois contes*. These three tales are quite evidently conceived under the sign of the central metaphor of the saint. "A Simple Heart" may be viewed as an introduction to, as well as a commentary on, the two other tales, which, chronologically regressive, are centered explicitly on the figure of a saint: the medieval figure of Saint Julian the Hospitaler, and the Biblical figure of Saint John the Baptist in "Hérodias."

If the hagiographic motifs are at the same time serious, parodistic, and demystifying, it is because the tale, within its compact structure, opens onto questions that reach far beyond the immediate context, some of which have a very personal resonance: the author's nostalgia for the values his irony seems to deny; a sense of mourning for a dead faith (according to Sartre, Flaubert's father killed it from the outset); the need to write a

"consolatory" text, as George Sand advised him to do.[9] In evoking an irretrievable innocence, Flaubert might well have felt himself irreparably excluded and bereaved. But broader cultural questions are also involved. Is a
religious faith extending to sainthood still possible, or even conceivable,
in the materialistic nineteenth Century? Was such a faith ever possible,
and is the belief in sainthood ever anything but "simplicity"? Yet how is
one to live in a world that no longer even has hope for faith?

Multiplicity of meaning, not at all simplicity, is at the heart of "Un
coeur simple," whose success depends on a complex mastery of narrative
techniques. This is no doubt what Ezra Pound had in mind when he stated
somewhat hyperbolically in one of his letters that Flaubert's tale "contains
all that anyone knows about writing."[10] Pound did not explain what exactly he meant, but one can easily list Flaubert's technical skills: control
of prosody and rhetoric; displacements of point of view that do not com-
promise the integrity of the narrative voice; internal economy; ironic articulations; shifts and interplay of tropes (specifically of metonymy and metaphor) which make it possible (and necessary) to read the text at the same
time as a negation and an affirmation of values. A technical prowess which
in no way impedes the elaboration of a highly poetic texture: poetry of
setting, of silence, and of a recaptured past.

But the real challenge Flaubert chose to meet is more radical still. He
set out to have the reader enter into the unintelligent and unintelligible
intimacy of a human being deprived of the ability to articulate impressions
and emotions which, if articulated, would lose their immediacy. Flaubert's
long-standing desire is well known: to write a book about *nothing*, a book
that would "hold up by itself" through its internal strength. Recalling
the mathematical laws that preside over the most sublime architectural
conceptions, he formulated, in a letter to George Sand, the dream of finding the unique and necessary relation between the precision of language
and the precision of form, aiming to achieve a total harmony which ultimately would minimize the importance of both the subject and the character.[11]

To be sure, "A Simple Heart" is not a book about nothing, and it would
be easy to relate the tale to the key themes of *bovarysme:* the need to transfer dreams, the tendency to objectify desire by assimilating it to an external reality (whether Emma's lovers or Félicité's parrot), the repetitive nature of the imagery, the recurrent notion of a "mystical sensuality." As
for writing a book about *nobody,* Flaubert seems less concerned with the
insignificance of the character than with the radical gap between the functioning of the personage and the functioning of the text. Which is to say
that the text's unity and significance do not come from the fictional char-

acter, but from the tensions artfully set up between the text and the world it describes.

But what does such a dissolving or even disappearance of the protagonist (or "hero") mean? It so happens that at the exact time that Flaubert began "A Simple Heart," he declared to George Sand that in his writings he wished to avoid the "Accidental" and the dramatic: "Pas de monstres, et pas de héros!"[12] ("No monsters, and no heroes!"). This terse statement casts light on the antiheroic intentionality of Flaubert's literary project. At the rhetorical level, what matters to him is to maintain simultaneously a link and a gap between the tropes. At the level of the character Félicité, everything seems to relate to metonymy: heterogeneity, the gliding by of time and images, contiguity, parataxis, resemblance, confusion in all the senses of this term. But the text also offers a metaphorical latency that derives from the act of reading rather than from the action represented, and that tends toward an underlying analogical unity. The work thus maintains throughout a tension between the chapel and the bazaar.

This tension is all the more unresolvable in that neither the image of the chapel nor that of the bazaar remains stable and likely to be assimilated to the principle of homogeneity. This conceptual wavering ultimately characterizes the writer's own activity. In his study at Croisset, which he viewed as a monastic cell, Flaubert also liked to surround himself with miscellaneous oddments and bric-à-brac; he too installed a stuffed parrot. The chapel-bazaar was here displaced into a *chambre-écritoire* or "gueuloir," a displacement corresponding to a more significant displacement confirmed by all of Flaubert's work. The "de-heroization" of the hero, a marked tendency especially since the "passive heroes" of *L'education sentimentale,* is related to the pessimistic and idealistic notion that art, at the same time a form of withdrawal and abnegation, demands a heroic sacrifice. What is involved is nothing less than a very modern notion, the notion of the heroism of art. A closer and closer bond is taking shape in Flaubert's mind between the idea of sainthood and the vocation of the artist—a bond that also implies the relation between the writer and the impenetrable monumentality of Bêtise, the sacralization of art based on the complete understanding of life's inadequacy, and the disconsolate awareness that neither art nor the artist will ever be up to the dream of the absolute. Hence a literary *bovarysme* that goes far beyond the story of Emma Bovary. For much like Kafka, who was to be one of his closest readers, Flaubert knew all too well the insatiable desire to attain an ideal that remained out of reach, as well as the need to punish himself for his dreams by subjecting to an implacable irony his sense of a deep want.

ITALO SVEVO, OR THE
PARADOXES OF THE ANTIHERO

Literary glory came to Italo Svevo in 1925, late in his life, and only because James Joyce had alerted his Parisian literary friends about *Confessions of Zeno* when it failed to gain recognition in Italy. The solid Triestino businessman, by then in his sixties, could not believe that his old dream of literary fame had come true. In a letter to Valery Larbaud, dated September 15, 1928, he described himself as a "sixty-four-year-old kid" ("bambino di 64 anni"—I, 764).[1] The oxymoron applies throughout his life. For he was early on haunted by old age, yet remained disarmingly childlike. World-weary but unresigned, vulnerable, available, capable of wonder, neither the writer nor the paterfamilias could ever take himself seriously or define himself.

Italo Svevo was a "stranger" in more ways than one. Born in Trieste, he was an Austrian subject; educated in a German school, he strove to become an Italian writer, though his native idiom was the Triestino dialect, and he thus found himself condemned to write in a language that was not his own; steeped from early childhood in an ethos of commercial pragmatism, he discovered in himself a compelling artistic vocation; being a Jew, he resided in a world that tolerated but remained essentially hostile to him. Svevo/Schmitz not only lived in a Mediterranean city at the margins of the Austro-Hungarian empire, but his sense of personal marginality casts light on a peculiar configuration of themes and problems in his life and work: the ironic treatment of bourgeois values, to which he remained profoundly attached; the concomitant interest in and suspicion about the psychoanalytical theories that reached him directly from Vienna; the false stability of the social and moral order on the eve of World War I, as well as the discontinuities provoked by this cataclysm; the ambivalent status of a world astride the Austro-Hungarian and Mediterranean mentalities; the complex relationship between the confessional mode, ironic subversion, and the interplay of bad faith and authenticity. His self-awareness as an assimilated Jew gave him poise, but without dissipating— quite the contrary—a cultural, if not social malaise that partly explains his need and taste for indirections, oblique approaches, ambivalent strategies, systems of transfers and disguises, and, above all, for self-protective and self-revealing paradoxes.

For the cultural historian, Svevo may well embody the paradoxes and inner contradictions of Trieste. For the literary historian, the problem is somewhat different. For it is one thing to reflect the mentality of a group, to be affected by its paradoxes; it is quite another to exacerbate these paradoxes and to structure them thematically. Svevo's writings habitually exploit the resources of *Witz*. His is the voice that states that the bandage is the noblest part of the body; that he sees everything and understands nothing; that he is an expert in failure; that the bird in the cage is reluctant to fly away for fear of being locked out; that he has no pact to sign with Mephisto, being equally afraid to grow old and to live his life all over again; that real tragedy is the absence of the tragic; that only the future can unveil the past; that literature is necessary in order to struggle against opacity and insincerity, but that transparency would be lethal to literature; that writing is at the same time a sickness and the only salvation; that lies end up by telling the truth; that any affirmation comes close to its own negation.

Paradox is at the heart of Svevo. The title of his most famous novel, *La coscienza di Zeno*, is like an emblem. For Zeno, whose family name is Cosini ("little thing," "insignificant object"), is phonetically close to the Italian *zero*, and etymologically closer still to *zeno*, the stranger or alien. This latter sense is confirmed by Zeno's comment concerning the last letter of the alphabet, his own initial, as he recalls the fascination he experienced for the common initial carried by his future father-in-law's four daughters: Ada, Augusta, Alberta, and Anna. "My name is Zeno and I felt as if I were about to choose a wife from a far country" (64). But above all, the name of Zeno brings to mind Parmenides' disciple who, according to Aristotle, founded dialectics, the art of refuting the opponent by taking as a point of departure principles accepted by him. This Zeno is famous for a series of paradoxes—the race between Achilles and the tortoise, the arrow that never reaches its target—all of which tend to demonstrate, on the basis of a hypothesis of discontinuities, the impossibility of ever reaching an aim.

Spatio-temporal paradoxes are thus bound up with the name in the title. But the title's substantive is richer still in implications: the word *coscienza*, in the English sense of *consciousness*, coming into play against the notion of *conscience* or moral sense. On the one hand, there is the awareness of one's psychic presence, which, according to Svevo, is the cogito of the reflective animal ("I suffer, therefore I am") and which inflicts a steady reminder of an incurable wound, the traumatic "grande ferita" alive in his consciousness (180; II, 752). And to be aware of the self also means, for Svevo, to be aware of repressed feelings and perhaps even to hope for self-possession. On the other hand, consciousness is precisely what makes self-possession elusive, if not impossible. For *coscienza*, to the extent that it means good or bad conscience, implies scruples, doubts, remorse, a sense of guilt, and willful blindness; it can lead to bad faith.

This hyperactivity of the self-reflective consciousness is also what leads to passivity, even paralysis. Hamlet's words come to mind: "Thus conscience doth make cowards of us all." Too much reflection inhibits us in the face of action. Zeno becomes a caricature of such inhibition: having learned that at least fifty-five muscles enter into action each time we take a step, he can no longer walk without limping. But in the Svevian context, the sense of paralysis is exacerbated by the desire to feel pure and innocent, the fear of remorse, the need to exculpate oneself and to have what all his fictional characters yearn for: "la coscienza tranquilla" (III, 40). Hence the constant gliding from one sense of the word *coscienza* to the other. Hence also Svevo's attraction to the confessional mode, which, from the very start, remains linked to a feeling of powerlessness, and to the practice of alibis, subterfuges, transfers, and half-truths.

For the Svevian consciousness, the desire for truth remains dialectically bound up with the fear of truth. In his *Profilo autobiografico*, Svevo maintains that it is human to want to delude ourselves ("ingannare se stesso") about the nature of our desire so as to reduce the pain of the inevitable disappointment ("disinganno"—III, 809). In this intertwining of truths and lies, the lie becomes an instrument of truthfulness. Zeno is a compulsive talker, a spinner of tales. Only Augusta, his maternally smiling wife, understands from the beginning that Zeno's habitual fictions or lies give away his deeper self precisely because they are invented by him. His lies, or rather his ways of lying, are his truths. The novel keeps shuttling between deceptive justifications and the realities which these deceptions unveil. A network of self-indulgent lies surrounds apparently trivial episodes: Zeno's escape from his screaming infant; his forgetting the prenuptial ceremonies involving Ada; his fake indignation concerning his brother-in-law's adultery. In each case, he reveals an essential aspect of his character to himself, but can achieve this insight only because of the protective network of lies.

At bottom Zeno is convinced that language is flawed, that it is simultaneously an illness, a necessity, an inadequate mediation, and a tragic event ("tragico avvenimento"—311; II, 877–78), for words cannot be taken back. Once a word has been pronounced and has struck, no repentance, no blurring can help. Chronically shifting and unreliable, language is, moreover, always alien and alienating. This no doubt is the significance of the gap Zeno experiences between his Triestino dialect and the Tuscan literary idiom that will never be his own. The gap is in fact symbolic of every effort at verbal expression—and, more specifically, of the separation between ordinary speech, literary discourse, and the ceaseless mobility of our consciousness. Zeno complains that his psychoanalyst, a hostile interpreter of his written confession, has no notion of what "writing in Italian means to us who talk dialect but cannot express ourselves in writing." And he adds, raising his lament to the level of a general truth: "A written confession is always mendacious. We lie with every word we speak in the Tuscan tongue" (384). Yet on the same page Zeno maintains that lying means inventing or, better still, creating.

The novel's central paradox is the problem of writing. Not only does the author of this written confession describe himself as ill, but he views life itself as a disease. To write takes on a curative value, a meaning that is structured into the doctor's preface. But precisely to the extent that the difficulty of living leads to salvational writing, the writer-patient ends up loving the illness that leads him to the writing-remedy. The remedy thus implies that the disease allows for a creative, as well as a negatory, potential. The last word scribbled down by the old man in "La novella del buon vecchio e della bella fanciulla" is the word "Nulla" ("nothing"—III, 62).

The preference for illness and literature (even if it leads to failure) over the cure is confirmed tersely in Svevo's letter to Valerio Jahier: "He is a great man, that Freud of ours; but more so for novelists than for patients" (I, 857). Elsewhere Svevo admits that he developed a distaste, not for Freud the man or thinker, but for the idea of psychoanalysis as therapy. Psychoanalysis as a heuristic inquiry was bound to intrigue him. Throughout his work, there are traces of an original trauma, as well as an interest in the expressive structures of dreams and strategies of transfers and repetition. What Svevo dislikes about psychoanalysis is not its theoretical thrust but its claims of clinical cures. Svevo is much too committed to protecting his illness ("proteggere la propria malattia"—III, 688).

The ironic link between disease and health, as well as the problematic relation between lies and truths, is at the heart of Svevo's work. In another

letter to Valerio Jahier, Svevo asks: "Why should we wish to be cured of
our illness? Must we really deprive humanity of what it has that is most
precious?" Recalling Schopenhauer, Svevo adds that those who are
healthy, or pretend they are, deserve our pained laughter (I, 859–60). A
comment such as this casts light on Zeno's punning declaration that his
diabetes is for him infinitely sweet ("una grande dolcezza") and that he
cherishes his illness (II, 936). The doctor's preface, which offers from the
outset a lesson in interpretative instability, functions in the same paradoxical context. By setting up an unresolved hostility between the psychoana-
lyst-reader and his writer-patient who has interrupted his treatment, the
preface discredits both the doctor and the notion of health itself. The book
thus begins under the sign of a refusal to be cured—a refusal which, at
the end of the novel, is proposed as the true cure. The hostility toward the
medical profession is summed up in the scatological name of the doctor
who attends Zeno's dying father: Coprosich, from the Greek *kopros*, or excrement. The significance of this hostility, however, goes beyond the shortsighted diagnosis of the psychoanalyst who stubbornly uncovers proof that
the son wished his father's death. The paradox of the patient cured of the
desire to be cured calls for a different explanation.

The words paradox and antihero are wedded. This association is of course
not new, having acquired its literary status in Dostoevsky's *Notes from Underground*, which begins with the same double signal: hostility to doctors
and pleasurable acceptance of disease. At the end of the book, the underground man, defined as a "paradoxalist," refers to himself as an "antihero"
("antigero'ey"). The antiheroic mode implies the negative presence of the
absent or subverted model, while paradox retrieves hidden meanings
through provocative negations or contradictions. Dostoevsky pushes contradiction to its extreme, much as he does with irrationality, placing his
aggressive negation of the notion of progress in the service of an implicit
affirmation of spiritual values. To achieve this, he also undermines, as we
have seen, the hidden authority embedded in the confessional mode. Unlike the voice of Saint Augustine, also speaking from out of the depths,
the compulsive monologue of Dostoevsky's antihero remains unreliable.
Deprived of an absolute witness, such a narrator can only evoke a mendacious autobiographical tradition. What is more, he does everything to deni-
grate and discredit the self. In Italo Svevo's case, the tone is less acerbic, less strident, less oracular, more gentle—and the stakes are not the
same. But the principle of self-denigration is also at work from beginning

to end. The old man in "La novella del buon vecchio e della bella fanci- ulla" is not the only protagonist of Svevo compelled to look in an accusa- tory mirror and to see himself insignificant and miserable ("misero e pic- colo"—III, 48).

The tendency to deprive his protagonists of any strength of character is a constant feature of Svevo's fiction. He himself refers to every single one of them as "abulico," or lacking in will power. This refusal to grant his personages any heroic status projects into his stories a debilitating self- irony ("ironia di se stesso"). The only heroism left is in daydreams, and these inevitably lead to a sense of defeat (II, 440; III, 802–9). Constantly present in its very absence, the heroic model is a reminder of a deep-seated ineptness. Svevo likes to evoke the Darwinian theory of natural selection, the harsh law of life in which the weak are vanquished and disappear. To his young wife, Livia, he writes that a man's value comes not from what he is, but "from what he succeeds in conquering." The image of Napoleon appears repeatedly, and in a variety of contexts. In another letter to Livia, he recalls that early in life he had dreams of a destiny similar to that of Napoleon (I, 117, 59). But Napoleon is an ironic signal, too: he is the impos- sible and even undesirable model. Svevo's younger brother Elio, who died at only twenty-three, touchingly confides in his diary his boundless admi- ration for the older sibling and budding writer, whose witness and chroni- cler he chose to be during their adolescence. "How well I have written his history!," he noted, adding humorously: "Napoleon never had an historian who admired him as much as I admired Ettore.[2] The Napoleonic reference was certainly significant in the context of a success-and-career-oriented mercantile society that could not take the artist seriously.

Elio Schmitz's diary, a witnessing mirror for the future novelist, sets up recurrent themes: dissatisfaction with the self, a vocation of discourage- ment and failure, a gentle melancholy rooted in the conviction that happi- ness (like health) is impossible, the acceptance of disease because it allows one to embrace passivity and to settle in what he was to call "senilità." Even the father, who was an oppressive spokesman for the all-powerful commercial ethos (but obsessed and even paralyzed by financial worries), is ironically described as inept—an "inetto," precisely the title Svevo was to choose for his first novel. To be sure, what is absent from Elio Schmitz's diary (for Italo Svevo it came only with time) is a very peculiar sense of the comic, the characteristic *Witz* of Mitteleuropa, colored by Jewish hu- mor. This humor, at the same time self-deprecatory and consoling, goes together with Svevo's predilection for the type of fable which, in its smil- ing gentleness, brings out even more cruelly a feeling of inadequacy, impo- tence, and deep-seated pessimism.

The expression of this feeling occasionally takes on a buffoonish cast. Svevo imagines having a son who also dreams of a Napoleonic destiny but who in fact comes closer to the ludicrous role of Travetti, a lowly character straight out of a comedy in Piedmontese dialect (I, 59). Svevo recognizes that he is clumsy, indecisive, absent-minded. Like Signor Aghios (in "Corto viaggio sentimentale"), who is unable to find his train at the railroad station, Svevo has a real talent for making mistakes or heading in the wrong direction. Ineptness is, in his case, part of a pessimistic system, tending to humanize and trivialize suffering. Margherita's remark in *Senilità* comes to mind as she refuses to take off the boot that hurts her: "There's always got to be some pain" ("Già qualche male ci dev'essere sempre"— II, 465). Giovanni in *La rigenerazione* is equally resigned: sooner or later something unpleasant is bound to happen (IV, 493).

The banality of such statements must not deceive. Svevo's pessimism is radical, and so to speak, absolute. It implies a ceaseless awareness of the tedium of life and of suffering and death, yet also the fear of the posthumous glance. "The ultimate memory of life remains lonely suffering." This diary entry sheds light on Svevo's yearning for oblivion. The addiction to memory only heightens the nostalgia for the waters of the river Lethe (III, 817–40).

The cruel law of survival through struggle and violence extends beyond generalities. In *La rigenerazione,* there is talk of the shipwrecked man on the raft who saves himself by cannibalizing his friend (IV, 454). The true horror of life is more basic still, almost unutterable. It is suggested in the Kafka-like nightmare at the end of the astonishing short story "Vino generoso," in which the protagonist sees himself condemned without trial by some irrational will called the Law; he is to be choked to death by a terrible engine in a ceremony named "holocaust"—an atrocious sentence he tries to elude by offering his daughter as a substitute. The deep horror of this nightmare is ironically stressed by his remark about his children, who are happy to be alive "because they know nothing yet" ("perchè loro non sanno niente ancora"—III, 74, 76–77).

But in this tragic perspective, knowing is not a matter of age. Similarly, the much-glossed word *senilità* is not to be confused with mental impairment. *Senilità* refers neither to the pathology of old age nor to precocious decrepitude, but to a very special kind of inertia—"the inertia of the dreamer" (I, 122)—which accompanies the tragic sense of life, the ceaseless meditation on human vulnerability: an insight that only sharpens suffering and produces a keen sense of having lost that which one never really possessed.

Aging and death, though a terrifying commonplace, remained for Svevo a constant surprise. How could as "serious" a matter as growing old happen in his silly life, he asked himself. In another humorous note, meditation on time is presented as "la mia specialità" (III, 835, 838). Once again, paradox structures Svevo's thought. Offended and unhinged by the aging process, Svevo nonetheless declares himself in a hurry to get old ("Attendo con impazienza d'invecchiare," he writes to his wife (I, 164), and in "L'avenire dei ricordi" (III, 299), recalling the child he was, he presents himself cheerfully as "il vecchio" (the old man). But this humor must not deceive. Death and aging are linked to a meditation on time, not merely because they signify an ultimate finality, but because they are a permanent presence in the act of living. The demise of each instant ("Tutto a me d'intorno muore giornalmente . . ."—III, 822) causes an unmedicable anguish. For Signor Aghios death is the very given of life (III, 195); and in *Senilità*, Svevo observes that the notion of death can become all absorbing (II, 588). In a letter to Livia, written shortly after their marriage—she might have preferred receiving more cheerful missives—he reminds her of his obsession: "You know how much the thought of death is always with me" (I, 210).

This steady awareness of evanescence makes inertia an object both of fear and of desire. It also explains the autobiographical impulse: the will to fixate in the instability of writing the permanent failure called life. In a note of January 10, 1906, that brings up the erosive nature of time, Svevo specifically associates the verb *fissare* ("to fixate") with the word for autobiography (III, 822). But this literary "fixation," holding out hope of self-possession, is itself subject to the reign of flux. Conversely, Svevo makes it clear that every effort to give form and stability to thought by means of the "graphic sign" is a sure way of imprisoning it and of inhibiting its development (III, 816). Paradox thus extends to writing itself. Literary ambition goes hand in hand with the conviction of not having lived up to his vocation, of not having found his own voice, of being a failure, a *fallito*, as a writer (III, 813; I, 76).[3] Having reached the age of forty, Svevo claims to have given up literature, which he defines as "ridiculous and harmful" (III, 818); yet in fact, writing—much like Zeno's famous last cigarette—is a bad habit, a disease for which there is no cure. "La cura non riuscí," Svevo comments ironically after a new relapse into the illness called literature (III, 689).

The true paradox lies deeper still and turns against itself. Svevo relishes the sweetness of defeat insofar as he has learned to transform defeat into victory. "No salvation outside of writing," he concludes in one of his diary entries ("Insomma fuori della penna non c'è salvezza"—III, 816). But defeat can be converted into victory only by making the courage of lucidity, based on the feeling of a radical lack, the theme of one's work. The moment of that literary *eureka* came to Svevo early in his life. On February 24, 1881, Elio writes in his diary that Ettore, then barely nineteen years old, has just declared that he found his true subject, "Modern Flaw" ("Difetto moderno"). The word *difetto* is all the more revealing in the context: the same word appears in the preceding sentence, there referring to a physical defect which seems to have exempted young Svevo from military service.[4] We return to the antiheroic theme.

卐

This theme is solidly rooted in Svevo's work, even in his first novel, originally entitled *Un inetto*—an inept man. His publisher constrained him to adopt the banal title *Una vita* (*A Life*), but it is obvious that the original title best fits the story of Alfonso Nitti, whose very name (nix, niente, nihil) carries a negative resonance. Nitti, who lives on daydreams and vague desires, ends up by committing suicide, aware of being unfit for life's struggles. Timid, clumsy, indecisive, inefficacious, vulnerable, easily discouraged and haunted by his lack of courage, this young bank employee, frustrated by his inferior social position, feels ill at ease in his own skin and is aware himself of his role as antihero. He seeks refuge in the vain illusion of being a writer, but quickly comes to realize that he better give up trying. The result is a yearning for nonaction and nonparticipation, a desire to be merely a spectator, or better still, to settle in the cozy somnolence of premature old age. Hence also a sense of the futility of life, an almost superstitious allegiance to his protected childhood, a not so secret wish to return to the mother, which recalls the syndrome of defeat at the end of Flaubert's *L'éducation sentimentale,* when Frédéric Moreau, taking stock of the ruins of all his dreams, yearns for a retreat to the maternal womb and wishes for nothing more than a somnolent life "in the shadow of the house where he was born."[5]

The originality of Svevo's first novel, *Una vita*, stems in large part from a deliberate and subversive rewriting—with a stress on what Svevo calls the "heroic comedy"—of literary models that are already antimodels. In *L'éducation sentimentale*, Flaubert had undertaken a novel about a "passive" hero. Svevo, whose protagonist's head is crowded with bookish memories, must have remembered, as he described Nitti's wanderings through the streets of Trieste, the gray and humid cityscape of Flaubert's novel, filled with drifters, gloom, and chance encounters. But there is also the model of Stendhal. Much like Julien Sorel, Alfonso Nitti penetrates into a social world in which he resents feeling inferior, goes about seducing the daughter of his employer, conceives of love as strategy, forces himself to commit acts of boldness that go against his nature, is torn between the desire to be the aggressive lover and the fear of humiliation, while remaining haunted by the dread of being taken for a vulgar social climber. Nitti does not, of course, have the charm, the fervor, the energy of Julien Sorel. Nor does he have the dash of Rastignac, the hero of Balzac's *Le Père Goriot*. The Balzacian model is indeed also subverted. Like Rastignac, Nitti is a young provincial out to conquer the big city; like him, he tries to learn the rules of the social game and feels ashamed of his clumsiness. The great hive ("alveare") of Trieste, with its hunger for money, is an echo of the humming beehive ("ruche bourdonnante") that Rastignac surveys from the Père Lachaise Cemetery at the end of Balzac's novel. But there is a difference. Rastignac challenges the big city with his famous words of defiance ("A nous deux maintenant!"), while Alfonso Nitti, glimpsing the city from a moving train, chooses to flee (II, 316).

The detailed description of Nitti's bureaucratic banking job further degrades the model of the traditional *Bildungsroman*. It is a labyrinthine world of paperwork, circumlocution, dark corridors, petty rivalries, and living caricatures; a cruel and hierarchical world, devoid of energy and human warmth. The same demeaning features afflict the lower-middle-class ambience of his lodging house, a milieu of sordid quarrels, underhanded dealings, and histrionic posturings capable at best of parodying "la commedia eroica" (II, 396).

The antiheroic mood of Svevo's second novel, *Senilità*, is more complex and more subtle. A work of truly classical rigor, combining structural balance and psychological discontinuities, this novel—much admired by Joyce—is a masterpiece on the theme of self-deception, bringing obsessive motifs and the most commonplace reality into ironic coexistence. Emilio Brentani, a tired young aesthete living with his anemic sister, has fallen in love with a *fille du peuple*, whose animal-like beauty and sexuality have an immediate provocative effect on him. He suspects of course that she has been promiscuous with almost all of Trieste. Nevertheless, though constantly surprised and wounded by her perverse ingenuity, he accepts to live with lies and compromises, in part because abjection protects him from genuine involvement. His jealousy becomes pathological. He feels paralyzed by the fear of suffering, and at the same time envies the open virility of his rivals. For Emilio is a weakling who lives expecting the worst, and who seeks refuge in irony while dreaming of a decisive, even violent act. But violence is at most self-directed. Suffering from a powerless rage, all he can do is bite his own hand. Daydreams of violence and crime end up tiring him. Emilio seeks refuge in sleep or in fantasies of algolagnia that allow him to cuddle his own pain. A crushing bad faith suffuses not only his relations with Angiolina, to whom he freely offers moral lessons as a self-styled "maestro di virtù" (II, 440), but his feelings of remorse toward his sister, which he transforms into self-pity. An idle aesthete until the very end, he perceives Wagner's sound effects and synesthetic harmonies as an invitation issued by the heroes and the gods to retreat in their company to a world of transfiguration and transcendence (II, 521–22).

This imaginary victory is to some extent taken over by the text itself, namely in the epilogue of the last three paragraphs, which James Joyce especially loved and had learned by heart. For Brentani's memory becomes the scene of a strange transmutation that blends Angiolina's carnal beauty with the dead sister's moral qualities. The metamorphosed Angiolina, endowed with radiant spirituality, ultimately appears as the symbolic figure of "la donna triste e pensierosa." Still the woman lover, this Angiolina, whom memory has reshaped, "thinks and cries" as though the secret of the world and of her own existence had been revealed to her. The ironic distance between the lyric symbol and the mediocre setting is not, however, incongruous. It is underscored by the ambivalences of the Triestine landscape, which serves throughout the novel as a background to the bitter love story. This landscape, whose light is filtered, dark, lunar, at times carrying reverberations of a dying fire, provides a cruel and poetic commentary on the hero's unheroic passion.

茁

Twenty-five years of silence intervened between *Senilità* and Svevo's major novel, *La coscienza di Zeno* (1923)—twenty-five years punctuated by the businessman's routine, the prolonged calamity of World War I, the discovery of psychoanalysis, and chronic resentment about his lack of success as a writer. This time, however, success did come, and the victory was heady. But a more significant success is inscribed in the very texture of the novel: the Svevian antihero wears the enigmatic smile of the victor who remains faithful to his weaknesses and to his defeats.

From beginning to end, *La coscienza di Zeno* is structured ironically in terms of its temporal schemes. Though it gives the story of a life (childhood, the father's death, marriage, marital infidelities, professional activities), time is not linear but internalized. The novel imposes the obsessive time of repetition and recurrence. Referring to a certain period of his life, Zeno himself speaks of the same scene "that was repeated *ad infinitum*" (141; II, 718). If his childhood seems so important, it is because it accompanies him throughout his life, and he remains a perennial child. The real story is thus played out against chronology: the principle of psychological simultaneity counters and negates the linear time of everyday life and conventional narration. Svevo sees life itself as a textual space that denies the sequential nature of events by stressing repetitive patterns. Zeno's dream of himself as an infant having an erotic dream is a good example. In this dream, he sees the baby dreaming of a perfectly beautiful woman (his mother?) whose patent-leather shoes, visible beneath the hem of her skirt, fascinate him, and whom he yearns to possess by eating little bits of her "at the top and the bottom" ("al vertice e alla base"—388–389; II, 930–31). Rereading his own confessional manuscript (more attentively, it would seem, than his psychoanalyst), Zeno is struck by the similarity between this dream and another dream described two chapters earlier, in which he kisses and devours the neck of his mistress with mad lust, inflicting terrible wounds that do not bleed (181; II, 753). A complex system of transfers (mother-wife-mistress) is at work throughout the book.

Another episode, placed at the very beginning, prepares the synchronic reading. In Zeno's initial attempt to recapture the past, what rises before him is the image of a locomotive puffing up a steep incline. He at first thinks that the image has no connection with his past. But later, in the chapter on his father's death, it is precisely the image of the panting locomotive which is linked, not to the memory of childhood, as Zeno at first believed, but to his father's laborious breathing on his deathbed, and therefore to an unremitting sense of guilt.

The different memory schemes set up ironic tensions made up of misunderstandings, hesitations, approximations, and discontinuities. Remembered time coexists with the time of remembering, the time of writing, the time of reading. For Zeno is a far better reader of his own lived and written text than is his discredited analyst.

To these temporal tensions Svevo adds the ironic complication of point of view, as the discredited doctor of the preface discredits in advance the author of the manuscript, whom he accuses of fabricating a heap of lies. The narrator is in fact not to be trusted; he is the notoriously "unreliable narrator" so characteristic of the confessional mode or first-person narration. We do not know, after all, whether Dostoevsky's underground man does not defame himself on purpose. Did he really behave like a lout with Lisa? Does Lisa even exist? Similarly, did Camus's judge-penitent in *La chute* really see a woman fall into the Seine without doing anything to come to her rescue? The entire episode is perhaps an invention that serves the aggressive intentions of what Camus himself qualifies as a "discours orienté." We face again the paradox of Epimenides. What are we to make of the statement that all Cretans are liars if the speaker is himself a Cretan.

No verification is available. Much like the analyst, we can only go by what Zeno says—or, rather, by how he says it. And even if Zeno wished to tell the truth, is he really able to do so? Beyond his linguistic difficulty (the symbolic gap between the literary idiom and the Triestino dialect) lies a basic problem: "I remember everything, but I understand nothing," Zeno observes (29; II, 621). With even greater irony, he calls himself "a magnificent observer" but a "perfect ignoramus" ("grande ignorante"—298; II, 855). What is certain is that Zeno sends constant signals concerning his unreliability—his bad faith, his silences, his half-truths. He denigrates himself, insists on his guilt and incompetence, brings up, with self-directed irony, typical traits of the antihero: lack of courage, the habit of procrastinating and of seeking refuge in sleep, fear of emotional involvement, hypochondriacal behavior. He makes fun of the difficulty he has always had of stopping once he is in motion, and of getting started when he is at rest.

Such humor is in itself a problem. Zeno loves to provoke laughter at his own expense, precisely insofar as he fears to be the butt of laughter. All of Svevo's writings attest to this ambivalence of laughter. Watching himself laugh in a mirror, Svevo notes in "Soggiorno londinese" (III, 685) that laughter never reveals, but hides what one thinks. The mask of laughter most often betrays the repressed desire of a counterstroke or of vengeance. It is because he fears the laughter of others that Signor Aghios becomes the other who laughs.

Self-abasement is dialectically bound up with the awareness of the admired model. The antihero can exist only if the heroic model remains present in absentia, by preterition. Such a presence-absence is implicit throughout *La coscienza di Zeno*. For Zeno, giving up smoking is a step toward becoming perfectly virile, becoming "l'uomo ideale e forte"; marriage is the choice of a companion and second mother, who can inspire him to lead a manly life of struggle and victory (II, 661); sexual rivalry parallels the exploits of "medieval heroes" who fought for ladies they had never seen (291; II, 48). But the contrasting reminders of the "model," the ones who succeed where Zeno does not, are even more explicit. In addition to Napoleon, Caesar, Don Juan, heroes of history and literature, there are the heroes of mythology (Achilles and his famous spear, Hercules and his labors), but above all—and most ironically—the figure of Oedipus, who marks the fundamental interpretive rift at the core of the novel. For his psychoanalyst, Oedipus signifies the well-known complex diagnosed by Freud; but for Zeno, Oedipus is Sophocles' hero. Zeno's refusal of the diagnosis and of the therapy thus indicates more than resistance, defiance, or blindness: it is a way of retrieving the sense of the tragic. Zeno expresses his delight at the diagnosis, but simultaneously deconstructs the Freudian interpretation in order to reinstate the dignity of suffering. Zeno claims to be delighted because the Oedipus complex elevates him to the "highest nobility" ("più alta nobiltà"—383; II, 926). What he attains by establishing his mythological pedigree is precisely the pride of his disease and of his introspection. For the Oedipus of Sophocles' tragedy is not so much the unhappy creature who killed his father and married his mother as the willful consciousness that had the courage to pursue truth and to discover (and uncover) himself.

The novel stresses interpretive hiatus and instability: the interpretation of disease is but the obverse of the disease of interpretation. Throughout the novel, signs and connotations carry multiple meanings. The last cigarette suggests the condemned man's last wish, but also the hoped-for cure from a bad habit, an impossible resolution, a procrastination that only increases desire and pleasure, a decision reached in bad faith, and above all, a temporal and psychological relation between the *last* and the *first* cigarette—the first one representing a desire to imitate the world of adults, an initiation into virility, and even a rivalry with the father, who, as it happens, is the unknowing victim of his son's thefts. In the narrative context, this rite of passage (the cigarette will continue to act as an erotic stimulant) occurs with the tacit complicity of the mother, whose indulgent smile adumbrates the smile of the future spouse. But if the metaphor of the last cigarette presides over all betrayed resolutions (perpetuating and sharpening the guilt of pleasure and the pleasure of guilt), it also functions in the creative drama of the recaptured past: smoking the most recent cigarette helps to recreate, and even to invent, the time of the first cigarette.

One calls someone who smokes one cigarette after another a "chain smoker." The image is doubly apt, since it evokes an enchainment to a habit as well as a chain of temporal continuity. Similarly, the chapters of Svevo's novel, prepared and linked by the image of the chain of smoke, impose the concatenation of a story—not so much in the sense of a plot (or "knot" that is to be unraveled by a dénouement), as of a chain of words, a spoken chain. Zeno is fully aware that words are events. "It is strange how a word can bridge time," he observes. "It is itself an event that is linked to other events" (325).

The chain metaphor extends to the structure of the novel. The chapters follow one another, linked by the image of the cigarette and the perpetually postponed resolution to stop smoking. The initial episode of the first cigarette gives way to a series of chapters whose titles suggest a chronological progression, but which in fact are all determined by thematic repetition: "The Death of My Father," in which the guilt of having probably wished this death is combined with the awareness of never being able to prove one's innocence; "The Story of My Marriage," which tells of the search for a new father and the traumatic discovery of rivalry in love; "Wife and Mistress," where adultery uncovers an entire system of transfers and substitutions; "A Business Partnership," which is in reality the story of a repressed love and of a corroding jealousy of his brother-in-law, Guido, who ends up committing suicide. Zeno's fundamental "mistake" (he follows the wrong cortege and thus misses Guido's funeral) betrays his sense of guilt for his hidden crime and for a victory based on his rival's death. The final chapter, entitled "Psychoanalysis," which is in fact a farewell to analysis under the double sign of war and commercial success, affirms the material victory of the weakling. But one may glimpse another victory in the shadow of the apocalypse of the last page, the apocalypse without revelation brought about by the superbomb. It is a victory that recalls Pascal's "thinking reed," or that of a smiling Sisyphus facing the absurdity called life. Zeno has learned that disease exists as life itself exists, that life is in fact disease, and that the only way of eliminating disease would be to end all life. This no doubt is the meaning of the surprising last page of the novel where Zeno imagines that a super-powerful explosive—an invention of the near future—will be detonated and that "the earth will return to its nebulous state, ... free at last from parasites and disease," but also from all other forms of life, including humans.

We return to the inverted health-sickness motif. Ever since the opening pages, the antihero had the intuition that sickness alone allowed for meaning and dignity. From the outset, Zeno understood that analysis was not useful to disease, but that disease was useful to analysis. He remarks that "health cannot analyze itself" (152), and he knows that for him there is an intimate bond between pain, thought, and writing. Pain, he explains, is what led him to write fables dictated by exasperation. The paradox of salutary sickness has its confirmation in the pernicious health embodied by Augusta and by all those for whom the notion of health goes with law, order, moral smugness, *esprit de sérieux*, and trust in authority. For Sartre, they are the reprehensible many who deny their nausea, need to believe in heroes, live out a life of lies, and refuse to face the fact that they are sick—that is fragile, mortal, human. The Svevian antihero converts this false health into disease ("la converto in malattia"—II, 725), aware that in his consciousness of his weakness lies his true strength.

Hence Zeno's essential superiority over Guido and all those others who believe they have an innate right to success and who lament, as soon as events betray their trust, that life is "hard and unjust." Zeno, who considers himself an expert in failure, knows that life is neither just nor unjust, neither beautiful nor ugly, but, as he puts it, "original" ("la vita non è né brutta né bella ma è originale")—and that this "incomparable originality" of life situates it outside of any possible preconceived meaning. Such a view also implies the courageous acceptance of the unalterable absurdity of a world in which man, having appeared by accident, remains a stranger, an intruder ("... l'uomo vi è stato messo dentro per errore e ... non vi appartiene"—312–13; II, 866–67). Svevo comes very close here to an existential sense of the tragic, rooted in the courage of despair.

The closing of *La coscienza di Zeno* remains enigmatic. The catastrophe of the superbomb exploding at the center of the earth, a terrorist act by means of which the bespectacled human animal will destroy itself, represents a horrible hypothesis but also an ultimate irony, as this self-destruction will eliminate at the same instant every microbe, every parasite, every disease. Zeno/Svevo prefers instead to accept the discomfort of living, refusing the privileged point of view of the future perfect, which is an accomplice of death; unwilling also to gamble on literary posterity, Svevo proposes in his own understated way a hymn, if not to life, then to the difficulty of living. The originality or absurdity of existence becomes an antidote against a poisonous sense of victimhood. The great wound of consciousness and conscience is, he knows, incurable. But this great wound, this almost heroic *grande ferita*, also signals a victory that wears an ironic smile. For the smile of such a victory is inseparable from the consciousness of defeat.

7

IDIOT SCHWEIK, OR
IN PRAISE OF CUNNING

Jaroslav Hašek's good soldier Schweik says "yes" with a happy grin, but continues stubbornly to think "no." Stretching army obedience to the point of mockery, this jocose wartime orderly, in a world gone mad, stands typically at attention and "humbly reports" to his superiors. Schweik plays out the role of imbecile with an artfulness that parodies and denounces the imbecility all around him. Some of the less obtuse officers suspect that he is making fun of them, and order him to wipe the silly expression off his face. But on second glance, they conclude that the exaggerated tenderness of his gaze is a sign of mental debility rather than insolence. In fact, some years before the outbreak of World War I, the medical experts of the Austrian army had officially certified Schweik as "feeble-minded" and recommended that he be discharged. But that was before the Austrian army needed cannon fodder.

Czech readers of Hašek's satirical novel, which appeared shortly after the war, soon became familiar with Josef Lada's illustrations.[1] Lada caught the tone and spirit of the work accurately, and his caricatures helped define the ultimate shape of Schweik's silhouette: his stocky body, his ample buttocks, his distended trousers, his thick pointed nose, his kepi perched over his plump, unshaven cheeks. This lighthearted figure of the common man of Prague seems to be empty of meaning. Whether on parade or solidly seated in front of his beer, Schweik looks like a bemused witness of cruel stupidity, while his body language remains enigmatic.

The disarmingly jovial soldier Schweik, a dogcatcher by trade and a brave drinking companion, is hardly a war hero. The collective madness of a world war makes of him a resigned but secretly resisting victim of Austrian militarism carried to the point of absurdity. In his ironic preface, Hašek stresses Schweik's status as antihero: he is a "modest, anonymous hero" who has nothing in common with the Napoleons and Alexanders of this world. And yet the "glory" of this insignificant man will not fade, the author promises; it might in time eclipse that of the grand actors on the stage of history.

Unheroic to his very core, Schweik is by craft and instinct a survival artist. His flaws are his strength. Simultaneously clumsy and resourceful, he turns mishaps into adventures. He ultimately even succeeds in being captured by his own army. Yet there is nothing of the *schlemiel* in him. A somber humor colors and determines his actions. A rheumatic recruit, waving his crutches with pseudo-patriotic enthusiasm, Schweik has his cleaning woman push him to the induction center in a wheelchair. When accused of being a malingerer, he is forced to undergo a regime of enemas, quinine, and bromide, which is also meant to cool a jingoistic war ardor bordering on parody. For this crutch-waving "simpleton," who sings war songs and shouts war slogans in the streets of Prague, is sly in his persiflage. His pretended innocence deflects political provocations, just as his digressive anecdotes—be they on distemper in puppies—serve to divert and disarm police surveillance.

It is not by chance that Schweik's function throughout the entire war is that of officer's orderly—a type Hašek characterizes as inclined less to heroic deeds than to saving his skin, poisoning the existence of his superiors by acting out the age-old role of "cunning slave" (162). His military epic is thoroughly unheroic. It is an endless sequence of humiliating constraints, punishments, drudgeries, and pointless missions. Schweik's tribulations illustrate the petty servitudes of military life, which often make it preferable to be locked up in the garrison goal than to perform one's duties as soldier.

In Hašek's novel, antiheroism is not a simple matter of character typology. The aim is not merely to put into question individual heroism by stressing the virtues of passive resistance. At stake is a radical denunciation of the values which, over the centuries, have made it possible to glorify war. This denunciation cannot be put more bluntly than by the so-called "volunteer" whom Schweik meets in the jail cell of the Marianské garrison: "Heroes don't exist, only cattle for the slaughter and the butchers in the general staffs" (300).

The debunking of the word "hero" may bring to mind Voltaire who, in chapter 2 of *Candide,* refers to the battlefield as "heroic butchery" and defines the Bulgar "heroes" as disembowelers and rapists. But Voltaire's "heroes" are at least actively violent. With Hašek, the hero is the helpless victim. Being crippled or massacred is what defines the hero. To put it axiomatically in Hašek's perspective: the hero is he who dies in absurd and horrendous circumstances called the glorious defense of the Fatherland.

The demystification of *la gloria militar* has its comical side, such as the story of Lieutenant Kretschmann, back from Serbia with a leg wound, having been gored by a cow. Hašek indulges in anecdotes of a scatological nature: the countless stomach pumpings inflicted on soldiers suspected of malingering; the martyrdom of Cadet Biegler, who lusts for a Gold Medal and who, instead of seeing glorious action, suffers the indignities of chronic diarrhea that forces him to spend the war in toilets where the sound of the pulled chains and the flushings of water is the closest he comes to the din of battles, cavalry assaults, and the thunder of guns. But scatology does not exclude grimness. An abandoned metal chamber pot becomes the emblem of the battlefield after the carnage. All the while, the general is obsessed by the regulation of field latrines and "shitting" schedules (535), as though the victory of the Austro-Hungarian monarchy depended on sound defecating discipline. The point is that war is a macabre, excremental farce.

The devaluation of military prowess is also dependent on preposterous references, similes, and metaphors that establish incongruous parallels with great figures of history, mythology, and literature in the best mock-heroic tradition. The exploits of Napoleon and Alexander, Hercules' labors, the adventures of Odysseus, are obvious topics in this mock-heroic perspective. The most insignificant individuals and the most ludicrous situations call for perverse comparisons. The good soldier Schweik, returning from one of his misadventures, is compared to the Greek god of theft (404); the corporal with the expressionless watery eyes brings to mind Dante in hell (333); the army chaplain emerging from his drunken stupor is likened to Gargantua awakening in his priapic glory (340). When Schweik loses his way in search of his unit, Hašek invokes Xenophon's *Anabasis*. A long chapter is entitled "Schweik's Budejovice *Anabasis*"—a doubly ironic classical allusion, since the word anabasis connotes at the same time marching and retreating. There is talk also of Caesar's legions marching toward the north without the help of maps.

In the same spirit of derision, Hašek invokes the *Odyssey*, the "glorious times" of Roman domination, Nero's ferociousness, the cruelty of the emperors signaling the death of the wounded gladiator. These are only a few of the many irrelevant similes or references, all of which, however, carry a polemical significance. The fall of Carthage, Nineveh in ruins, the arthritic soldier on crutches who is off to war like Mucius Scaevola despite his burnt arm, Schweik absorbing devastating doses of quinine powder with even greater composure than Socrates swallowing his hemlock, are images that tell a story.

The story they tell is one of horror and hatred of war. Subject and tone are not new: Hašek knows his models. When he has Schweik sing "awe-inspiring war-songs" (56) in which the blood flows freely and arms and legs go flying in the air, when he refers to the "delights of war" ("vojen-ských radostí"—592, 598; III, 147, 152), the reader recognizes the type of lexicological inversion that characterizes the antimilitaristic pages of Voltaire's *Candide*. Hašek systematically uses the words "glorious" and "gloriously" in a derogatory fashion. "The Glorious Licking" is the title of part III of the novel. What is new, however, in this epic of defeat and ineptness, is that Schweik's stance and survival strategy, despite certain affinities, do not make him a picaro, or a Sancho Panza, or a Candide.

The good soldier Schweik knows how to avoid traps, how to extricate himself from messy situations; he is what the French call a *débrouillard*. But his skill is not limited to beating the system. Schweik is essentially a subversive, engaged in a resistance struggle—even though this resistance takes on an apparently passive form. His weapons combine fake deference, sabotaging obedience, and a rhetorical arsenal of non sequiturs, digres-sions, and obliquities. He is the tongue-in-cheek artist of a fierce logic, carrying logic itself to its self-discrediting extreme. He explains that sol-diers love to be shot at: it exhausts the enemy's ammunition. He relishes playing the role of imbecilic worshiper of authority. Law and order must be maintained at all costs! "Every cripple must be at his post" (56). His verbosity is his screen. Evasive verbal tactics turn out to be a strategy of insolence. He emulates and imitates to the point of caricature, breaking down from within the rhetoric and ideology of officialdom. The indirec-tions of his speech patterns (he has an outlandish anecdote for every occa-sion) project a dark, accusatory humor. In depth, Schweik cherishes forbid-den things and forbidden notions—"zakázaný věci" (575).

His cheerfulness is both simulated and spontaneous, allowing him to protect an independence that does not show its true face. Inner freedom, hidden and stubborn, is what counts. The yarns he spins, the anecdotes and false analogies he lavishly offers, exhaust and disconcert his superiors by the sheer abundance of words, while illustrating, through the sense-lessness of his discourse, the senselessness of the military establishment and of the war machine. He makes use of mimetic amplifications and sty-listic parody to denounce the vacuity and aberration of official slogans. "God save our Emperor, Franz Joseph! We shall win this war!"—"I ... don't want to hear of peace until we are in Moscow or Petrograd." "I'll ... serve his Imperial Majesty to my last drop of blood." (143, 739, 12.)

The overstatement of stereotypes might be attributed to an instinct for comedy. Hašek surely wants to provoke laughter, and his own laughter is often coarse and scabrous. But when the pub owner claims to have removed Emperor Franz Joseph's portrait because of the flyspecks that defiled it and is arrested for saying that flies "shitted" ("sraly") on his Imperial Majesty, it is clear that gross comic effects are turned into political satire. Satirical devices pervade the novel: damning juxtapositions and parallels (the murderous military expedition into Galicia is compared to intellectual tourism, and the name of Humboldt is evoked); trivialization of the horrendous and amplification of triviality; lexical incongruities recalling the playful effects of Gogol's style.

Hašek exploits these devices with a view to discrediting the most venerated institutions and beliefs: the hallowed clichés of patriotism; the hysterics of genocidal militarism disguised as duty and honor; religion made to sanctify atrocities. Hašek is not merely irreverent, as when he has army chaplain Katz state that he chooses to "represent someone who doesn't exist" (139). Moral indignation is the keynote, as he evokes frontline liturgies, the chaplain's sanguinary declarations before the slaughter conceived in the name of God, glorification of war under the sign of the cross, the archbishop blessing the bayonets so they may pierce more deeply into the bellies of the enemies. This kind of rhetoric inspires the official "historian" of the battalion, who, in bardlike fashion, sings the praises of the "heroes" and also waxes ecstatic at the thought of a sharpened bayonet penetrating bellies, cutting "as through butter" ("vjéde jako do másla"—581; III, 136).

The story of the good soldier Schweik—together with the novels of Henri Barbusse, Roland Dorgelès, and Erich-Maria Remarque—doubtless ranks among the great antiwar texts. But only Louis-Ferdinand Céline, in *Journey to the End of the Night,* has shown the hellish idiocy and naked horror of war without even a trace of indirect glorification, without the least hint of redeeming the heaps of bleeding flesh through the discovery of virile fraternity. Hašek's method is unremitting and devastating in another sense, in large part because he does not show life in the trenches, and never describes the fighting, thus never providing an opportunity for the display of courage. The approach remains indirect, yet he evokes with ruthless precision the transport of human chattels toward the slaughter of the front, dismembered limbs hanging from charred trees, torn bodies writhing half alive and tangled in barbed wire, smells of excrement and putrification filling the air after the carnage.

By exhibiting absurd patriotic zeal, by extolling war with macabre unconcern and praising it as great fun ("že je vojna špás"—I, 80), Schweik indicates that his simple-mindedness must not be taken literally. Sly and patient, concealing his guile behind a screen of words, this unassuming spokesman for the underprivileged of this world intuits that absurdity must be embodied to be denounced, that one can best hold it up to laughter and scorn by mimicking it outrageously.[2] Hence, the importance of the jocular mode: playfulness is not only essential for survival and sanity; it is a mighty weapon of subversion.

At the time totalitarian regimes were at their zenith, Czeslaw Milosz identified the crafty tactics—defensive as well as offensive—that made it possible to resist tyrannical ideologies. In *The Captive Mind*, he referred to the practice of *ketman* in the Islamic civilization of the Near East and Central Asia (a practice that had been described by the French diplomat and writer Arthur de Gobineau).[3] According to Milosz, the dissident intellectuals of modern Europe have learned to adopt just such a method, based on hiding one's real convictions by "playing out" the very role one despises and hates, by pretending to believe that which one secretly abhors and combats. The practice of *ketman* bestows value on the militant lie, sharpens wits, allows one to remain faithful to one's most cherished beliefs in a world where the infidel is in power.

The point of encounter between simulated submissiveness and inner freedom is also the place where antiheroism can affirm itself as a form of courage. *Ketman* produces its own brand of heroes, who, at the core of their beings, see themselves as protagonists of a resistance, whose masked dissidence is meant to sap the foundations of power. It is, however, a dangerous intellectual game, for the mask may adhere.

The originality of Hašek's novel has much to do with a mutinous "ludism" that represents neither an intellectual's exploit nor a pretext for elitist pride. There is no hint of protecting a private sanctuary. Instinctive rather than cerebral, *ketman* as practiced by Schweik functions at a popular level. Schweik represents an essentially "Czech" resistance to Austria and its militaristic spirit. This ethnic populism is, moreover, dealt with thematically. The German and Austrian officers, highly suspicious of the Czech units (50 percent of Czech soldiers are said to be "politically suspect") consider the use of the Czech language as the equivalent of a subversive act. Hašek comments in his own name that the ordinary Czech carries disrespect for the Emperor "in his blood" (215–16).

The Czech salutation "Nazdar!" is a patriotic reply to the German "Heil!" (315). Schweik, who shares his compatriots' innate disrespect for the Emperor and for patriotic hyperbole, is filled with contempt for "idiotic old Austria" (234). On the one hand, there is the myth of the unity of the Empire, of the great family of nations, of the unshakable solidarity of the diverse peoples under the Austro-Hungarian Monarchy; on the other, a rebellious spirit that toys with dreams of treason and desertion. A fellow soldier, who was a schoolteacher in civilian life, teaches his comrades what to say when they reach the Russian side, how to say in Russian: "Hello Russian brothers, we're your Czech brothers, we aren't Austrians" (392).

The balkanization at the heart of the Empire, ethnic hatreds, vicious brawls between Hungarian and Czech soldiers, brutal treatments inflicted on the Jewish population—these seem to be endemic features of Schweik's world. (One might even speak of an extension of the Jewish theme: the gambling and hard-drinking army chaplain is named Katz; the field altars as well as other devotional objects, rosaries, and holy images, are supplied by the Jewish firm Moritz Mahler in Vienna.) But this is not the main point. What counts is the author's capacity for wrath, the personal voice that comes through and which, under pretext of diverting the reader with Schweik's droll feats and misdeeds, stigmatizes institutions, as well as human nature corrupted by power and authority. It is not by chance that Schweik indulges in the commerce of stolen dogs. Meditating on the destiny of the stolen pinscher, Max, whom he has procured for his lieutenant, Schweik concludes philosophically: "After all, by and large every soldier is stolen from his home too" (199).

Truth is not cozy. Addressing his reader directly, Hašek inveighs against all the hypocritical "swine" ("sviňáci") who are offended by crude, truth-telling language, while themselves experts in turpitude. Things as they really are may not be pleasing, but to disguise and embellish reality is profoundly immoral. Life is not a finishing school for proper young ladies (214). Behind the realistic speech patterns and the popular common sense, it is not difficult to note revolutionary political attitudes. At times, such views are explicitly stated. In the chapter on Schweik's "anabasis," Hašek observes that the yellow and black horizon (the colors of the Austrian flag) begins to be overcast with "the clouds of revolution" (280). There are premonitions of collective mutiny. Already entire battalions have gone over to the Russians, and a call for group desertion lurks almost like a message in the background of Hašek's text. The heavy pre-storm weather seems to announce insurrection. The "voluntary" soldier, who does not mince words when he speaks of how everything stinks of rottenness in the army, prophesies the political awakening of the people and the revolt of the masses.

In this dark atmosphere, premonitory of greater upheavals, the perspective remains restricted to the horizon of the "little man." Far from naive, however, this perspective is essentially ironic, in the sense that *eirôneia*, a feigned inadequacy or ignorance, is the art of dissimulating and minimizing in order to reveal.[4] Schweik's secret is that his strength derives from his apparent weakness. Occasionally, his toughness shines through, as when he ejects an intruder with a bouncer's skill, or forcefully brings his drunken superior back to his lodging. But even though he is endlessly resilient, and can prove himself decisive when circumstances call for it, his are typically secret strengths and hidden victories. Schweik carries a disguise and is never observed from within. His pudgy face remains serene. His store of anecdotes protects his equanimity. He is not only popular in the sense of being well liked, but other characters in the novel see him as already legendary. "So you're that famous Schweik," says the commandant of the military convoy (335).

Ultimately, Schweik represents more than the Czech man of the street. He becomes the symbol of the common people under any repressive and totalitarian regime. An unheroic passive resister, he possesses the essential virtues, including courage. Mischievous, but deeply honest and loyal, disinclined to be anyone's dupe, but capable of assuming his responsibilities, Schweik knows that he is neither alone nor unique. His comrades—even the army cooks—are fond of him. But this "popular" figure (popular in all the senses of the word) is also a disturber and perturber, unsettling minds and shaking convictions. In this capacity, Schweik's role as defier of values and conventions joins up, unexpectedly, with that of the intellectuals, though in a more occult, less vulnerable, and perhaps more efficacious manner. In a world of censorship, all writing is suspect, and independent reading (and thinking!) are viewed as forms of rebellion. The corporal's aggressive contempt for the soldier who had been a newspaper editor betrays a deeper hostility. He reacts in characteristic bloodthirsty fashion upon learning that a "political" newspaper editor has been executed in Moravia. "It serves editors like that right. They only stir the people up" (338). Executions by hanging or firing squads have indeed become the fashion.

Intellectual heroes do not really appear in Hašek's novel—at least not directly or explicitly. By temperament and wisdom, Hašek preferred to translate his political and intellectual themes into the register of antiheroism, using as his exemplary figure a conscript who has been certified as an "idiot." But if indeed Hašek's book is in praise of cunning, then this praise must not be limited to Schweik. It might be difficult to separate or distinguish the good soldier from his author.

MAX FRISCH

THE COURAGE OF FAILURE

Max Frisch's second diary or sketchbook, *Tagebuch 1966–1971*, concludes with the image of a stubby column standing incongruously all by itself in the loggia of his Swiss country house, where he sips his coffee in the evening. Its origin is unknown, its presence inexplicable. It is an unpretentious column, made not of marble but harsh granite, with nothing festive or noble about it. It is so short that one can touch its capital, and quite ugly—potbellied and slightly misshapen. This comical column, Frisch reports, is both touching and familiar; one does not hesitate to empty one's pipe against it. Yet its plebeian presence is not only reassuring, but vaguely meaningful, even poetic. It has weathered centuries, not proudly but with a quiet courage. It stands as a symbol of strength and survival, its sturdy profile drawn against the twilight and the first evening star. The last paragraph of the sketchbook plays equivocally with images of pathetic reality, fortitude, and even hints of transcendence.

Frisch's two published sketchbooks (the other, earlier one is *Tagebuch, 1946–1949*), both steeped in the historical and political realities of the day, repeatedly indulge in ambivalences of this sort. As he visits devastated German cities immediately after the war, Frisch's reactions are typically hostile to notions of the "heroic." Yet there is also nostalgia for the heroic mode. In what may be read as an emblematic scene, he describes acrobats performing on trapezes and tightropes high above the ruins of Frankfurt. Their daredevil exploits culminate in a truly frightening "deathwalk" on a rope attached to the steeple of the cathedral, as the powerful searchlights weirdly illumine the ruins of the city. What strikes Frisch is not so much the suspense and drama of a performance that appeals to his theatrical instinct, as the free courtship with death—one he describes (having recently visited Nazi death camps) as a "good death," that is an individual death, a freely chosen "personal death," very different from the extermination that awaited the victims of the Lager. In most telling words, Frisch speaks of the acrobats' "playful" death ("spielerische Tod"), and defines it as a "human death." Implicit is the age-old idea of dignity through free will. Some pages earlier one finds indeed the terse assertion: "Human dignity, I feel, lies in freedom of choice" (*Tg.* I, 227, 146).[1]

Freedom associated with a chosen death—an essentially heroic notion—is brought out more sharply in the many pages of the second sketchbook (*Tagebuch 1966–1971*) devoted to the notion of suicide. Rebelling against decrepitude and the ravages of age, Frisch imagines a hemlock society significantly named Voluntary Death Association (Vereinigung Freitod) (*Tg.* II, 96 ff.). But heroic longings and motifs have been present from the start; they inform his dramaturgical instincts. Frisch, the man of theatre, understood even better than the Bishop in his *Don Juan or the Love of Geometry* that we all need figures who dare do on stage what we can only dream of doing in life. We want to witness the exercise of a human will; we expect heroes in literature to make decisions that play into the hand of fate, though we suspect that a presiding fate is an illusion and that life is frustratingly devoid of an ordering principle. Frisch, who is intent on participating in a modern dramaturgy of frustration, recognizes the heavy weight of the classical heritage: the dramaturgy of fate and peripeteia. Unlike his *homo faber*, who claims not to care about the heroic myths of antiquity, Frisch is keenly aware of the heroes in the epic and tragic tradition who exercise their will and indulge in their appetite for catastrophe.

Tragic and mythical figures are metaphorical presences in his work: Oedipus, Agamemnon, Odysseus, Persephone, the Erinyes. The tension between truth and heroic illusion is brought out, according to Frisch, in the conflict between Don Quixote, the glorious victim, and the world that mocks him. To state that Cervantes ends up by saying yes to the-world-as-it-is does not deny that we all love the knight's error. But the implication is that the hero finds himself allied to untruth, that the heroic illusion needs to be denounced, and more so than ever in our own times. The hero's perspective is of necessity posthumous. Aiming at transcendence or eternity, he is not engaged in the present, no matter how dramatic his action. In some interesting pages about Brecht, Frisch explicitly contrasts the commitment to the heroic hereafter ("Jenseits") with a relation to the here and now ("Diesseits")—*Tg.* I, 254.

The antiheroic stance, much as in the case of Georg Büchner, has obvious ethical and political implications that are brought out sharply in *The Chinese Wall* (*Die Chinesische Mauer*, 1947), a play that inveighs against the dangerous yearning for heroes in our era of mass destruction. Despite his lifelong critique of the "Swiss" values of caution, self-interest, and practicality, Frisch tends to use the word *Held* ("hero") as a negative term. *The Chinese Wall* makes the point that "heroes" have done enough harm over the centuries by transforming history into a vast graveyard, that the time has come to rid the world of the conquerors responsible for mass slaughter, that the day of heroes and tyrants is over. The Emperor's daughter derides her father's values and silly talk of victory. What matters to her is not hero worship, but human survival. She knows that there is greater courage in allegiance to life, that what is most difficult is to be a genuine human being. But for every outspoken Emperor's daughter, there are the Cleopatras of this world who "believe in the victor," and are ever ready to love men who "make history" (G. 92).

It is not surprising that at the same time as he was deflating the image of the Napoleons of history Frisch also wrote an ironic play about another type of conqueror, the legendary Don Juan, incongruously emphasizing not his quest for women, but his yearning for intellectual and spiritual adventures. The very title of the play—*Don Juan or the Love of Geometry* (*Don Juan oder Die Liebe zur Geometrie*, 1952)—subverts the model and the legend. Don Juan's father complains that his son is not interested in women, that he spends his time in the bordello playing chess, that he is not committed to the virile arts. Though Don Juan fought at Cordoba against the Arabs, he is filled with contempt for martial exploits. As far as he is concerned, "heroes" are at best good for looting and for burning libraries. His love of geometry and chess brings him closer to being an intellectual hero. For the intellectual, Frisch explains in his postscript, the world exists to be put into question. Frisch's Don Juan does indeed love ideas far more than women; he lusts for an ideal, and even flirts with the notion of a monastic existence. What matters to him is the search for an inner life, the courage to discover or create his own authenticity. The paradox is that he entertains a narcissistic relation with his self, yet cannot take himself seriously, aware as he is of playing a role. The metatheatricality of the work stresses the tensions Frisch sets up between Being and Play ("Sein" and "Spiel"—G. 99). In such a ludic context, the heroic concept is evidently unstable. The risk-taking involved comes closer to pure spectacle than to a self-aggrandizing confrontation with fate. We return to the metaphor of the acrobat.

With time, the unheroic stance became more pronounced. It is at the core of Frisch's late novel *Man Appears in the Holocene* (*Der Mensch erscheint im Holozän*, 1969), which conveys a character's progressive senility in third-person narration, but as though experienced from within. Herr Geiser, a seventy-four-year-old widower living in retirement in a Ticino village, watches his physical and mental decrepitude, while all around him storms and landslides provide a background that is a simulacrum of the deluge. The metaphorical setting is that of a geological time of creation, erosion, mutation, and successive extinction of species. In a Beckett-like atmosphere of non sequiturs and futile bits of encyclopedic information that recall some of the most devastating pages of Flaubert's *Bouvard et Pécuchet*, the old man's disintegrating mind takes stock of itself as he gradually loses his sense of time and reality. Consciousness is here linked, even more cruelly than in Svevo's work, to undoing and defeat. "Heroic" allusions seem particularly ironic in the decidedly unheroic Ticino village. The legend of Hercules leading an entire people across the Alps, mythical dragons, apocalyptic images, dreams of adventurous escape and freedom, only underscore the ineffectuality of resisting the outrages of time and change.

Despite its poetic descriptions of landscape, snow, and fog, the Holocene novel is perhaps the least appealing of Frisch's works, though it is intensely revealing of his basic fears and obsessions. In a nonfictional and more personal manner, the two sketchbooks are of course more explicit. Frisch's political awareness, his capacity for indignation, the vigor of his enthusiasm for human rights, his sensitivity to the rift between culture and morality, do not dispel underlying personal doubts and uncertainties. Repeatedly, he alludes to the isolation of the artist, to his own ambivalent attitudes toward morality and violence. Self-questioning, in the form of self-addressed unanswered questionnaires, betrays his uneasiness and frustration. Suspicious of his own intellectual relation to reality, he yearns for an unmediated relation to life. He envies what he takes to be the joyful, unself-conscious, fearless physical presence of the Italian workmen he watches on his way to the beach (*Sk.* I, 80). He, too, would love to love life. Characteristically, it is in the proximity of the Etruscan tombs that his fictional Gantenbein experiences the greatest pleasure in living.

Such a joy is highly dependent on weakness and fear. Art for Frisch is not only a struggle against fear, but a hymn to it. "One sings out of fear," he stated in a 1958 speech dealing with the writer's vocation. In a diary entry of 1949, when he was in his late thirties, he made the emphatic point that none of us has as yet experienced death, only the fear of death — "Todesangst" (*Tg.* I, 369). That omnipresent fear goes together with the intense, bittersweet awareness of all forms of evanescence.

In this respect, his autobiographical book *Montauk* is most revealing. On the surface, it depicts the aging writer's weekend love affair with a young woman journalist. Oscillating between the novelistic third-person narrative and the first-person autobiographical or diary mode, *Montauk* recounts an escape into the immediacy of the present. At a deeper level, it is the account of how late in the game it is. Beneath the surface glow of tenderness and autumnal attachment to life, there is an underlying sense of weakness and failure, an essential difficulty in accepting or tolerating himself, a perception of his own superfluity. Time has come, Frisch feels, not only to talk of, but to face death. Fear of death and recognition of defeat inform this moving book, which can indeed be read as Frisch's third published diary.

Yet this preoccupation with death and defeat also takes on a positive value. In a key entry of his *Tagebuch 1946–1949*, Frisch refers to the eternal boredom of the Greek gods, who are unthreatened by any sense of finality. Awareness of our mortality is thus seen as a precious gift, a "köstliches Geschenk" (*Tg.* I, 306). Frisch goes one step further. Understanding from the start that fear and courage go hand in hand, he writes of "courageous fear" ("tapfere Angst"—*Tg.* I, 10), and in one of the most striking pages of the first *Sketchbook*, defines life itself in terms of fear. "There is no life without fear" is not merely a statement of fact, but a precondition. It is *angst* which, in an almost Pascalian sense, makes consciousness such a uniquely human attribute, and the source of our dignity.

It is not surprising that Frisch's pessimism remains ambivalent. He would have preferred, he says, not to have been born. But on the other hand, there is the joyful acceptance of the very life he did not desire, even the repeated temptation to sing a song of praise. The last words of the novel *Gantenbein* are: "Leben gefällt mir" ("Life appeals to me"). And in the explicitly personal *Montauk*, we read in capital letters: "TO BE IN THE WORLD: TO BE IN THE LIGHT" (G. 103). Ultimately Frisch never reneged on the early impulse to sing not so much the exceptional and heroic, as the ordinary human experience: "unsere Welt zu dichten" (*Tg.* I, 198).

The courage to see one's own weakness and translate it into strength is repeatedly viewed as a high attribute. This may explain why both *Sketchbooks* contain a number of short fictional pieces projecting figurations of the antihero. A fairly elaborate project for a film to be entitled *Harlequin* allegorizes the corrupting effect of power and the dehumanizing nature of hatred and fear in a burlesque fairground setting. A parody of Dostoevsky, under the ironic heading of "Glück" ("Good Fortune"), proposes the re-emergence of the underground man in twentieth-century Switzerland, heavily stressing the character's self-lacerating indulgence in his own re-pulsiveness, absurdity, and abjection ("Niedrigkeit"—*Tg.* II, 357 ff.).

In a more caricatural vein, Frisch conceived the character of Kabusch—an avatar of the eternally ineffectual and victimized *schlemiel.* This Kabusch, appearing in various social and professional guises in a Swiss setting, always misses out, always is the butt of jokes, always gets things wrong. Superfluous, yet somehow needed by the group, such a Kabusch, according to Frisch, would have to be invented if he did not exist. When one Kabusch disappears, another has to be found (*Tg.* II, 277ff.).

At times, these antiheroic silhouettes include objectively successful types such as the slightly balding surgeon/lover in "Sketch of a Mishap," who, on a pleasure trip with his mistress, is propelled toward the silly car accident in which he kills his companion. Similarly, a section called "Statics" delineates the self-doubting, self-denouncing, and self-denying figure of a pathetic professor of mechanics in a school of architecture, a figure weighed down by incurable clumsiness and riddled by indeterminate guilt.

These fictional projections are not merely digressions or inserts. They are related to personal concerns, to a not so vague feeling of inadequacy and even guilt concerning his craft and vocation as writer. For what is the writer's mandate? Frisch seems to ask. As time goes on, he appears to be increasingly aware that language implies a deadly separation from shifty reality, that it represents a mediating system which condemns us to stereotypes and prejudice. The paradox of language is that it not only fails to tell the "truth" (immediacy being always betrayed), but that, aware of its own emptiness ("Leere"), it is committed to expressing the inexpressible.[2] Revealingly, the very page that develops this paradox of language as separation and falsehood also refers to the Tower of Babel (*Tg.* I, 194–95). The result is a tragic challenge. "One cries out because of the terror of aloneness in a jungle of unsayable things," Frisch confided in a speech given in Zurich in 1958.[3]

The awareness of language as separation and negativity goes with another discomfort Frisch develops in his sketchbooks and fictional writings: the concern over the nefarious effect of image-making. The oft-repeated word *Bildnis* (image, effigy, likeness) significantly appears on the same page that associates the Tower of Babel with the mendacity and alienating power of language. Image-making is seen as essentially hostile to the mystery of life and love, which must remain ungraspable ("unfassbar"—*Tg.* I, 27), thus leading Frisch to invoke the Mosaic prohibition that would seem to question artistic representation itself.

The anxiety about language and image-making is ultimately related to the mystery of the self and the problem of identity. It casts light on the dialectics of silence and language so important in all of Frisch's work, in particular in his novel *Stiller.* The desire to communicate with the inexpressible is at the root of one of the most paradoxical statements in that novel: "We possess language in order to become mute. He who is silent is not mute. He who is silent hasn't even an inkling who he is not" (291). This self-seeking, self-creating rather than self-describing potential of language, is to be understood in the light of the novel's two epigraphs from Kierkegaard, which deal with the difficulty of choosing oneself. Such a choice is difficult because it clashes with the ultimate impossibility of becoming another.

The paradoxical double project seems to imply mutually exclusive thrusts: to get to the "self"; and in a more playful mode, to construct or even invent this more imaginative self as if it were another. This self-creating quest would explain why the figure of Montaigne looms larger over Frisch's work than even Kierkegaard's. In his second *Sketchbook*, Frisch quotes a passage from Montaigne's essay "On Experience" that describes aging as a process of transformation and elusiveness. "Thus do I melt and slip away from myself" (*Tg.* II, 75). The largely autobiographical *Montauk* is even more manifestly placed under the sign of Montaigne. The prefatory remarks addressed to the reader end with an invocation that includes the date Montaigne gives in his own foreword to the *Essais:* "Mit Gott denn, zu Montaigne, am ersten März 1580." Intimacy of subject and object in *Montauk* is illustrated by the constant alternation of first- and third-person narrative—the Ich-form and the Er-form about which he speculated in the *Sketchbook* (*Tg.* II, 308–9). Seeing the self as a role to be played, or tried out, is not only part of a self-deciphering enterprise ("to write is to read one's own self"—*Tg.* I, 19) and of a constructive playfulness that underlies the fiction-making process; it suggests the philosophical dimension of the identity quest. Drawn to the notion of *homo ludens*, Frisch expressed the belief that "play" ("Spiel"), in a speculative as well as dramaturgical sense, represents a higher form of existence[4]—a belief he placed in an existential perspective in the postface of his Don Juan play, where he drew the distinction between Play and Being ("Spiel" and "Sein").

A link somehow connects Montaigne, Kierkegaard, and Huizinga, the author of a well-known book that has given currency to the notion of *homo ludens*. This seemingly incongruous mental network lends particular significance to *Gantenbein*, one of Frisch's most experimental texts, in which he successfully rivals some of the boldest practitioners of the *nouveau roman*. The novel, whose full title is the hypothetical "Let My Name Be Gantenbein" (*Mein Name sei Gantenbein*), has at its center a character who, in a supreme form of role-playing, pretends to be blind. The metaphor of blindness operates on a variety of levels. Love makes one blind, as the saying goes; and Gantenbein, up to a point, protects the happiness of his marriage, for nothing really remains hidden from him, and he hardly needs to be jealous. He has in fact true vision, enjoying as he does an unadulterated view of all the acts and arts of deception. But behind the metaphor also lurks a bitter political significance. The world needs people who are silent about what they see or know.

Jealousy is of course not so easily avoided or repressed. Frisch himself seems haunted by the memory and pain of it. Referring to Othello, he comments at some length in his *Sketchbook* on the fear of feeling one's inferiority, on the horror of imagining that which may never have happened (*Sk.* I, 270–72). At the same time, the experience of jealousy provides a link with the fiction-making process, exacerbating inventiveness. "I lust for betrayal" ("Ich lechze nach Verrat"—G. 244), says Gantenbein. Role-playing, in this perspective, becomes distinctly nonheroic; the focus is on nonoccurrence, on that which literally did not take place. *Gantenbein* is punctuated throughout by the formula "I imagine ..." ("Ich stelle mir vor ..."), a formula suggesting an imaginary spectacle.

The concept of a nonoccurrence, or nonstory, comes close to Flaubert's stated wish to write a book "about nothing" ("un livre sur rien"), a book that would achieve significance through structure and style alone. There is mention in *Gantenbein* of a type of film "that has no story at all," in which the only event is the "movement" of the camera itself (173). Paradoxically, the absence of a specific story implies the multiplication of stories. The premium is on invention—"Erfindung." "What you are telling us is a lot of inventions," complains one of the characters, and Gantenbein agrees. Adventures of stories replace stories of adventures. The anonymous corpse floating away "without a story" at the end of the novel signifies a farewell to traditional narrative in favor of a narrative process of enigmatization requiring role-playing as well as the encouraging gullibility of a listener such as the cocotte in *Gantenbein* or the prison warder in *Stiller.* What is at stake is the need for stories.

Prison and language are at the heart of Frisch's key novel, *Stiller.* The story begins in a Swiss jail where the sculptor Anatol Stiller is busy writing an account of the circumstances that brought him to such an unheroic setting. Language is, however, at the same time logocentric and incapable of leading to anything but silence and negativity. Stiller finds that there are no words for the reality of his self-alienation. The novel predictably dismayed many of his Swiss readers.

The clean, well-lit Swiss prison cell, where Stiller stubbornly denies that he is Stiller, is like a symbol of the prisoner's country. The totally functional, "humane" Swiss prison, a model of hygiene and respectability, provides no apparent ground for indignation—not even the traditional cobwebs or mildew on the walls. This is no Bastille to be stormed! The denunciation is all the more damaging because this smug guiltlessness and "Swiss innocence" are seen to be the opposite of genuine freedom and spiritual boldness. The cell is a reminder not only of the oppressive and hemmed-in nature of modern society, but of a collective dedication to false freedom, which is not the monopoly of Switzerland. If all of Switzerland feels like a prison to Stiller, it is because it illustrates the broader unconcern with the problematics of freedom, a spiritless satisfaction and lethargy of the soul.

A sociopolitical reading of the novel is both unavoidable and misleading. The critique of society quickly veers toward a quest for private salvation. The redemptive thrust is prepared by the Kierkegaard epigraphs, the early fear of repetition ("Wiederholung"), the ascetic impulse to equate necessity with free choice, the difficulty of choosing oneself, the monastic dream merging with the prison motif. Self-centeredness and logocentricity are obvious impediments to the salvational process. That is perhaps why the structural and rhetorical devices of the novel so consistently serve disjunctive and decentering strategies, tending not so much to dissolve the assumed ties between the word and the world as to challenge a logocentricity symbolized by the prisoner status. Dreams of flight correspond to yearnings to become the *other*. Condemnation to the inner jail leads to a desire for metamorphosis. This hope for a liberating transformation may at first appear to be an attempt to break out of sterilizing solipsism. The refusal to be trapped in a given identity may even be construed as a heroic drive, a form of existential courage. But this would-be heroism soon degenerates into the heroics of false freedom. Ultimately Stiller comes to understand that the hope to escape is his true prison.

The prisoner in his cell writes and talks compulsively about himself; yet this self is radically called into question. Though indulging in self-seeking games, Stiller refuses to acknowledge his identity. Sought by the Swiss police after abandoning his wife and disappearing, this degraded Odysseus has now been arrested, upon his return to his hometown, in possession of a suspect American passport carrying the symbolically blank name of White. Odysseus also, at one point, claimed to have no name.

The figure of Odysseus pervades Frisch's novel, as does the Odysseus-motif of the homecoming. Stiller-White, abandoning and then returning to his Julika-Penelope, brings to mind the model of one who was also a cunning storyteller, a master of disguises. Only the fact that there is a *model* of this stature spoils it all. In fact, the presence of models is perceived throughout as an oppressive reality, a threat to genuine responses. Fixation on the "model" condemns one to inauthenticity.

The tyranny of models is a function of the larger tyranny of imitation. "We live in an age of reproduction," observes Stiller. "We are tele-viewers, tele-hearers, tele-knowers"—all by proxy (151–52). Even our so-called inner life, it would appear, is secondhand. The writer, in his cellular privacy, is perhaps the one who knows this most acutely. How indeed, he wonders, is he to prove that he does not know jealousy through Proust, Spain through Hemingway, the labyrinthine quest through Kafka? A double question lurks behind this perplexity. Is unmediated experience possible? Is it desirable? Involved is the very nature of artistic representation—mimesis—and its potential betrayal of life. For artistic form fixates and imprisons the flow of life, denying mobility and becoming.

Stiller's prison cell is not the only image of incarceration in the novel. Almost every setting assumes carceral characteristics—whether it is all of Switzerland or the crowded hold of a ship, the New York Bowery, a confining hotel room, or the *Magic Mountain*-like sanitorium where Julika, Stiller's tubercular wife, lies wrapped up in blankets on her veranda-jail. The prison motif invests the novel, extending—beyond the locales—to psychological states: the discomfort of being in one's own skin, the yearning to break out of one's ethnic or racial group, the desire to elude condemnation to the prison of self. Love and marriage are perceived as particularly grim forms of imprisonment, servitudes that condemn the partners, unable to save or even reach each other, to live behind their private walls or, like two people enchained, each choking the other with murderous possessiveness. The artistic impulse, which might be deemed liberating or sublimating, only intensifies the denial. Writing binds. Significantly, Stiller is not merely a spinner of tales, but a professional sculptor—a *Bildhauer*, a hewer of images—transmuting living reality into the rigidity of stone.

Image-making, Stiller's profession, is thus presented as the prison of art, a principle of repression and death. The Penelope figure, in one of the symbol-laden anecdotes, is transformed by the narrator into the mythological figure of Niobe, the woman metamorphosed by Apollo and Artemis into a stone image. The image-making process, including the mental images we impose on those we claim to love, is seen as a sin against life, a form of psychological and spiritual incarceration.

The religious connotations are inescapable. A young Catholic seminarian, a fellow tubercular patient in the sanatorium, explains to Julika that it is a sign of non-love and spiritual death to form an image of the other. The ultimate reference is to the Second Commandment. "Thou shalt not make unto thee any graven image. . . ." Revealingly, when the guilt-ridden Stiller translates his awareness of being the murderer of his wife into a nightmare, he imagines a crucifixion scene in which, under the surveillance of German soldiers, he fixes a photograph of Julika to a tree with drawing pins.

Prison motifs correspond to life-killing forms—specifically to image-making, whether interpersonal or aesthetic. But confining walls, literal and symbolic, also galvanize imagination and serve vision. "I sit in my cell, look at the wall, and see Mexico." From within his prison house, Stiller in fact sees further and deeper, into the very bowels of the earth, as well as into the recesses of his psyche. In an extraordinary episode omitted in the American paperback edition, Stiller recounts to the gullible turnkey his discovery and perilous descent into what turns out to be the Carlsbad Caverns in New Mexico. The omission is inexcusable, since Frisch himself refers to this cave as an underground "arsenal of metaphors" (G. 125). The cave in which the two explorer-friends are trapped becomes the mythical setting for a tragic escape feat. It is compared to Orpheus's Hades, to Ariadne's labyrinth, to a fairy tale nightmare. During this journey to the end of night, familiar reality appears inverted; the first large cavern recalls the nave of Notre Dame. But it also provides an analogue to the sculptor-protagonist's existence and problems, with its inhuman forms of stone and the entrapment of the two friends—the symbolic couple—culminating in the murder of the one by the other.

Imprisonment thus stands in a paradoxical relation to mythical and heroic models. Nostalgia for the heroic is found to be a form of escape, and the heroic quest an illusion, just as flight or hope for escape only reveals a sense of false freedom. What Stiller comes to understand, against the imaginary heroic backdrop he conjures up in his metaphoric prison cell is his own essentially unheroic nature. Better still, he comes to see the nonheroic human truth as a fundamental value. This discovery takes courage, honesty, and time. Stiller's painful memory of what he calls his "Spanish defeat" makes him relive indefinitely the intense humiliation of that moment during the Spanish Civil War when he failed to live up to his own heroic expectations. His failure to fire a gun at a critical moment becomes for him the haunting symbol of his inadequacy and non-virility. It takes a woman to question his heroic assumptions. Sibylle, hearing him blame himself dejectedly for being a failure ("Versager"), cannot understand why he should choose to feel ashamed of being as he is. After all, who asked that he be a fighter or a warrior, that he be what he is not? She puts it in more general terms: "You men, why do you always try to be so grand?" (224). The implied feminine criticism of so-called virile attributes once again underlines the danger of models. It also suggests the value of nonheroic virtues.

These values in turn militate against heroic concepts and poses. In depth, they seem to harmonize with latent religious motifs: apprenticeship of humility, surrender to a higher authority, willingness to emerge from the prison of self as an insignificant and powerless person, renunciation of the proud claim to be one's own savior. Pride, heroically or theologically conceived, seems indeed to be the target. At one point, Stiller and his rival/ friend the public prosecutor Rolf, in discussing the excessive demands we make on ourselves, refer to the well-known line in Goethe's *Faust:* "Him I love who craves the impossible" ("Den lieb ich, der Unmögliches begehrt!"). They agree that this "ominous" line could only have been uttered by a demonic figure (282; G. 243).

Stiller's private quest transcends his critique of modern society. Through the problematics of freedom, the unheroic hero reaches a new level of consciousness, if not a revelation. Stiller explicitly rebukes his fellow citizens for not sensing that freedom is a *problem*. Other writers, Stendhal for instance, have shown that between diverse orders of freedom there exist profound incompatibilities. Freedom understood in political terms easily clashes with a notion of inner freedom. But no one more suggestively than Frisch has related the freedom of the inner life to a kind of silence. This silence is inscribed in the name Stiller, in his muteness, his stammer, his eventual withdrawal from the world and the word. He is fully aware that the four walls of his artist's studio are a monastic enclosure protecting a "hermit's" existence. Pursuing a monastic freedom dream in prison, he gradually learns to value the prison of the inner life, and to want to reach the still center of the self. The willful acceptance of prison corresponds to the understanding that necessity can be freely chosen. Hence, the prayer for nonescape, the recognition that flight is not freedom.

Unheroic self-acceptance and acceptance of failure in *Stiller* represent a deeper sense of homecoming than seems at first implicit in the Odysseus motif. There are hints at self-love that acquire a spiritual, if not religious dimension. One of the characters points out that the injunction to love our neighbor as ourselves implies axiomatically that we must love ourselves as we were created. Such an acceptance of self means accepting and even loving the prison of selfhood. To accept oneself, we are told, requires the most vital of life forces—"die höchste Lebenskraft" (G. 243). What is more, only this self-acceptance can set one free. Many of the detailed accounts in the novel, including the apparently extraneous Genoa episode of the flesh-pink cloth Rolf carries like a symbol of permanent humiliation, have a religious potential.

Stiller himself is perfectly aware of a latent monastic wish. Who has not had the desire to become a monk?, he asks himself (150). Less explicit, though no less evident, is the hagiographic perspective on what could be defined as negative sainthood. From this perspective, it is only fitting that Stiller's ultimate withdrawal from the world should be accounted for by a witness-scribe, the public prosecutor Rolf, who imagines that his now silent friend, the author of the prison notes, is ready to provide a sequel to be entitled "Notes in Freedom." But Stiller remains silent.[5]

This sense of incompleteness is a reminder that *Stiller*, a typically decentered fictional construct, depends on agile and resourceful reading. Friedrich Dürrenmatt aptly observed that Frisch's novel could hardly be read or understood without the reader's playful participation.[6] The ironies of a book in which the protagonist's defense counsel is insensitive to him, while the public prosecutor turns out to be a comprehending friend, presupposes indeed a putative or hidden reader capable of glimpsing a different form of courage behind the worn-out, discredited modes of heroism and sanctity. In Camus's *The Plague*, published only a few years earlier, one of the protagonists had raised the question of whether it was possible to be a saint without God. The narrator's answer, as we shall see in the next chapter, was that he did not aim at being either hero or saint, that he felt greater kinship with the defeated than with saints and heroes, that what interested him was to be a human being—perhaps a more demanding task. Judged in such terms, Stiller himself might have agreed that his life had been a failure. But such a failure, the reader is given to understand, holds both a meaning and a promise. That a larger image of the human is on trial appears very clearly from the title of Frisch's next novel.

🙞

The title of that novel, *Homo faber*, points to failure of another kind. It stands in clear distinction to *homo sapiens*, the biological species of primates capable not only of reason, but of knowledge and wisdom. It also differs from the notion of *homo ludens*—playful, speculative, artistic man. At best, *homo faber* suggests a partial, specialized, technological human capacity. Once again, Frisch's narrative technique points to writing as a compulsion. After Stiller's seven "notebooks," we have in *Homo faber* two retrospective reports or bundles of notes also meant to be read by a reader in the text. In either case, the story is told by an unreliable first-person narrator; but in *Homo faber* the instabilities and ironies of retrospective narration bring out a sense of inevitability or fate. Classical allusions to Oedipus, the *Oresteia*, the Erinyes, Demeter and Persephone, further underscore the sense of tragic irony.

The obsessive travel motif here takes on regressive characteristics as Walter Faber, the pragmatic UNESCO engineer, finds himself unexpectedly impelled, first to the Guatemalan jungle and a confrontation with the primeval scene, then to Italy and Greece, and a return to classical antiquity and the world of myths. What seems like a series of chance events turns out to be a fated quest in search of origins, a return to the sources of nature and culture. On the way, Faber encounters various figurations of death and nothingness which help him discover or retrieve his true being and a meaningful sense of the mystery of life.

The narrative devices in *Homo faber* may at first appear less complex than in *Stiller*. But Frisch's handling of the first-person narration, with its built-in unreliability colored ironically by the presence of a hidden reader (Hanna, the wronged mother), further stresses the specifically tragic irony inherent in retrospective foreshadowings, and deftly pits the apparently accidental against a growing awareness of the workings of fate. Faber's rational or technological approach to life leads him to interpret exceptional events and coincidences in light of the law of probability, as chance or contingency, as occurrences to be reassuringly accounted for in statistical terms. He would never admit, at least not in the early stages, that a higher necessity might be at work, and that this bizarre string of coincidences represents instead the rigorous concatenations of a fate that leads him to incest with his daughter Sabeth, whose existence had never been revealed to him, and for whose tragic death he must eventually hold himself responsible.

The theme of incest, the age-old prohibition, unavoidably recalls the world of Greek tragedy. In particular, one is reminded of the story of Oedipus, whose myth brings home, among other things, the paradox of insight and blindness. Frisch obviously set out to tap the resources of Greek mythology. Hanna as a young girl dreamed of traveling through the world like Antigone, leading a blind old man. There are allusions to other figures: the Erinyes vengefully pursuing the guilty, Agamemnon murdered by his wife Clytemnestra, the keen memory of his having sacrificed their daughter Iphigenia. The metaphor of blindness occurs repeatedly in Faber's account. He feels "like a blind man"; he is perceived by Hanna as "stone blind." The mythical reference becomes almost explicit when Faber, horrified by what he now knows, yearning for self-obliteration, contemplates blinding himself. "I sat in the dining car thinking. Why not take these two forks, hold them upright in my hands and let my head fall, so as to get rid of my eyes?" (203).

As Walter Faber and Sabeth, having met on an ocean liner, set out on their "honeymoon," which carries them from Paris all the way to Greece, he at first does not know that she is the daughter of Hanna, the woman he almost married twenty years earlier, much less that he is her father. All along the journey through Provence, Tuscany, and the region of Rome, museums and archaeological sites are reminders of mythological antiquity. Though Faber claims to be insensitive ("blind," as he puts it) to art and ignorant about mythology, he is nonetheless impressed by Etruscan sar-cophagi, by a relief representing the birth of Venus with a lovely flute player at her side, above all by the stone head of a sleeping Erinys who, in a certain light, seems disturbingly awake and quite wild. But the most revealing classical reference, a clear proof that his self-proclaimed blind-ness is only partial, occurs after the "homecoming" to Greece, when the whole truth is about to be known. As Faber takes a bath in Hanna's apart-ment, he is assailed by the vague fear—no doubt a memory of Clytemnes-tra's vengeance—that Hanna may enter the bathroom and kill him from behind with an ax (141).

Hanna's own awareness of mythology is of course hardly surprising; she is a trained archaeologist, and works in an archaeological institute. The world of gods, myths, and fate is familiar to her as part of her job. She feels at home, as it were, with Oedipus, the sphinx, and the Erinyes. But the vengeful Erinyes play a more personal and threatening role in her life. For Hanna is not without her own heavy guilt. She has, after all, withheld the truth about Faber's fatherhood from him. Worse still is her particular form of hubris, for she has transgressed a natural law by her desire to have a child without a father, one that would belong exclusively to her. This possessiveness appears as a fundamental protest against all men, against the very presence of the male principle in the world. So as not to have any children with the man she did finally marry (Faber's old friend!), she had gone to the extreme of having herself sterilized.

Hanna's story illustrates, in her own terms, an essential gender conflict. Man sees himself, as she explains, as "master of the world"; woman is forced, though to no avail, to learn "the language of the master" (144). This feminine resentment goes beyond the problem of interpersonal rela-tions. Hanna feels that as long as God is masculine, woman is "the prole-tarian of Creation," that she is kept down, disinherited, exploited. The sources of her anger lie deep. There is the memory of the time when, as a child, she wrestled with her brother, was thrown on her back, and made a vow never to love a man. Her anger was in fact not with her brother, but with God, who made girls weaker than boys. She even founded a secret girl's club dedicated to abolishing Jehovah! (192–93).

Hanna's story has an implicit mythological referent. She herself cannot be unaware of the legend of the Greek earth goddess Demeter, worshiped as a mother goddess, and her daughter Persephone, also known as Kore, the maiden who was abducted and made queen of the Underworld by the god Hades, while Demeter, in maternal grief and wrath, made the earth barren.[7]

At the novel's literal level, Faber's compulsive rationality makes him a limited, flat, singularly unheroic character. His addiction to machines and gadgets (electric razors, typewriters, cars, turbines, robots, movie cameras) determines his outlook to the point where technological metaphors color his perceptions. As he helps Sabeth climb down a ladder in the ship's engine room, he compares the feel of her strong and slender hips to that of the steering wheel in his Studebaker. His is a case of impeded vision: the movie camera becomes a substitute for reality. But this willed blindness is also the symptom of a pride that takes on a distinct anthropocentric, misogynic, and "Western" hegemonic form. Faber is appalled by the French travel companion in the jungle who keeps talking about the decline of the white race. Faber himself is convinced not merely that a technological profession is a "masculine profession" and science a "masculine monopoly," but that man-the-engineer can and must be the "master of nature." His Swiss background makes him reject the German notion of a "master race"; yet he comes close to something objectionable in the way he praises the idea of population control, and even goes so far as to state that man must snatch procreation out of God's hand (78, 137, 108–9).

A whole world of values and meanings is closed to Faber. His lack of interest in dreams, folklore, literature, art history; his lack of imagination and his indifference to myths and demons (he only knows of Maxwell's demon, so named after the famous British physicist)—all this is symptomatic of a broader absence of curiosity whose worst feature is his indifference to the *other*, whether women or "natives." Contempt and fear characterize his attitude toward what he views as the primitive. His horror of elemental forces is telling. His encounter with the slime of the jungle is for him a traumatic experience. Revealingly, he compares the mire of fertile decay to pools of "menstrual blood," and later remembers the French saying that death and the earth are both feminine ("[L]a mort est femme . . . la terre est femme"—69–70), an association foreshadowing the Demeter motif.

Negative criticism of the technological ideology is appropriately formulated by a woman. Hanna tells Faber that he has lost a spontaneous, unme-

diated relationship to reality, that the technologist's "worldlessness" is the
negative skill of so ordering the world that one need not experience it.
She sums it up with the somewhat enigmatic statement that technologists
attempt to "live without death" (178–79). What the statement implies is
that Faber, living by the time of clocks and timetables, understands neither
the qualitative nature of temporality, nor the value of life made precious
by an awareness of vulnerability and death.

Hanna acutely senses what the reader comes to realize, namely that
Faber's account is given in bad faith. He repeatedly claims not to have
known, to have been surprised by events, when all along it is clear that he
suspected, yet falsified and justified the unjustifiable. The unreliable first-
person singular narrative is a particularly useful resource, for it allows
Frisch to project a consciousness at the same time self-deceptive and self-
revealing.

Faber's bad faith as the "technological" man, willfully indifferent to
mystery and mythology, is brought into sharp relief in the bathroom scene
in Hanna's apartment, when he so dramatically conjures up the memory
of Agamemnon's death. But to be self-deceptive also means to be partially
aware. Ironically, it is self-deception that makes the revelatory moment
possible. And revelation can lead to conversion, even if it comes almost
too late.

Such a conversion and ensuing new vision are prepared in *Homo faber*
by the early, unsettling experience of the forced landing and the confrontation with the jungle. Nature seems to take its revenge against arrogant
technology as Faber faces the elemental slime, the inhuman heat, the vul-
tures, the stench of fecundity and oxymoronic "blossoming decay" (51).
The apparently senseless proliferation of life and death offends him, as
though the jungle's ability to swallow up everything meant the defeat of
Western culture and the surrender to nothingness. All along the novel's
trajectory he encounters figurations of death: his own death-mask face in
the lavatory of the Houston airport, the death's-head laugh of the termi-
nally ill Professor O., the funereal mound near the via Appia, the tomb of
Caecilia Metella in the Roman Campagna, his vivid yearning for non-
being.

The real conversion occurs late in the novel, after Sabeth's accidental
death, when Faber, returning from a second visit to the jungle, stops over
a few days in Havana. This Cuban episode culminates in a revelation; it
also brings about a transformation and a resolve. The revelation has to
do with the sudden awareness of the luminous beauty of the indigenous
population: their flowing walk, their voluptuous skin, their provocative
hips, their animal-like sexuality. What Faber experiences is more than

erotic desire: it is rather a kind of metaphysical lust rooted in his sense of inadequacy. His sexual fiasco in Cuba only intensifies a new appetite for intimacy with the world. Faber discovers the epiphanic joy of being here and now, and for the first time catches himself in the act of singing the praises of life. (191, 210.)

The psychological metamorphosis and craving for deeper harmony with the physical world is typified by Faber's newly acquired metaphorical verve. With Sabeth, he used to play a verbal ping-pong game of inventing metaphors to describe the landscape; but he always lost the competition. Now he continues to play the game of metaphors by himself and has become good at it; and this metaphoric perception of reality, panharmonic in its nature, is closely bound up with Faber's new resolve to which he himself alludes in terse, poetic terms:

My resolve to live differently.
My joy. (182)

The lesson and the resolve bring the novel to its full-circle conclusion. As Faber flies back to Athens, this time not like the blind man he was when he flew out of New York in the snowstorm, he vows never to fly again. His wish now is to walk on the earth, to smell hay and the resin of the pine trees, to "grasp the earth" (206). The yearning is for the *hic et nunc* of a close embrace of life, the celebration of some vast nuptials that might help him conjure away the time by which he has lived. This epiphanic view of life brings Faber close to an almost religious vision: the experience of "eternity in the instant" (210).

We return to the mythical dimension of the book. It is a "return" indeed: the cyclical and recurrent time of myth, holding up hope for retrieval, renewal, and survival, stands in opposition to linear, progress-oriented time, which is *homo faber*'s time of obsoleteness and supersedure.[8] Faber's ultimate rejection of what he himself qualifies as the "American way of life" must be interpreted in this light. The denunciation of this "linear" way of life is to be read not as a political, but as a psychological and moral condemnation of modern Western society, and thus as a form of self-denunciation. The gawky "Coca-Cola people," the backslapping gadget lovers and vitamin eaters who stand with their whiskey glasses and broad grins at cocktail parties and view themselves as the protectors of the world become the emblem of our technological world with its obsessive notion of efficiency and fake youthfulness, its cosmetized corpses, its self-blinding optimism spread out "like a neon carpet in front of the night and death" (185–86).

Faber ultimately seems to agree with the young travel companion in the jungle who kept chattering about the decline of Western technological man. This notion of a fall from a sense of plenitude and nonfragmented reality probably accounts for the novel's pervasive recourse to mythology. Hanna, who lives in daily professional contact with the figures of myth, explains that her archaeological job means patching up fragments. "I stick the past together" (144). The image makes sense at the literal level. But it is also a symbol of a more fundamental attempt to rescue forms and values from time and ruination—a typically modern struggle for spiritual survival summed up in a memorable line of T. S. Eliot's "The Waste Land": "These fragments I have shored against my ruins."

The question of modernity is central to Frisch's work, though he voices it in a less strident and theoretically less provocative fashion than some of his contemporaries. Throughout his writings, he posits a void that asks to be filled, a negativity that signals the need for an absent plenitude. At the core, there is the awareness of fragmentation and discontinuity. In spite of the scope and flow of Frisch's prose, one may appropriately speak of an aesthetic of the fragment. In some remarkable pages of the first *Sketchbook*, Frisch in fact developed a brief theory of modernity based on the preference for the fragment and the sketch. He argued that a late civilization such as ours, suspicious of the sterility of closed forms, puts its trust instead in open-endedness, momentum, and the dissolution of inherited forms (*Sk.* I, 82).

The use of the diary form, with its mobile present indicative, is not limited to the sketchbooks. In his fiction as well, Frisch repeatedly exploits the stylistic and thematic resources of the diary and the notebook which allow him to stress the elusive, the transformational, the multifaceted. Hence, the special significance of the Hermes figure appearing in the form of lecture material at the center of *Gantenbein*. For Hermes, as the passage explains, is a figure of "multiple meanings"—a "vieldeutige Gestalt": god of thieves, rogues, and merchants, notorious for his craftiness and cunning, Hermes is the joyful bringer of good luck and opportunities, but also a misleader (literally seducer, "Irreführer"), a silent guide of dreams and messenger of the gods, as well as the invisible harbinger of death. Polyvalent rather than ambivalent, the figure of Hermes, as evoked in *Gantenbein*, corresponds at the mythological level to the notion of *homo ludens*, and participates in the playful subversion of myths.[9]

Such playfulness is hardly frivolous. The unheroic, strictly human dimension requires special courage. Already in *The Chinese Wall*, Frisch called for the end of "heroes," who are always on the side of violence and lies. The really courageous task was to resist the seductions of might and murderous victories in order to become what is most difficult: a human being. Once again, one is reminded of Dr. Rieux's refusal, in Camus's *The Plague*, to side with heroes and saints; of his low-key, yet proud desire to be both less and more: "être un homme." How different this rings from Malraux's haughty affirmation that man's true fatherland is where the darkest clouds gather. Frisch, like Camus, prefers to be more modest: "Our home is mankind"—"unsere Heimat ist der Mensch" (*Tg.* I, 150).

THE VOICE OF CAMUS

NEITHER SAINT NOR HERO

Priorities

In the plague-ridden city of Oran—a treeless, soulless city which symbolically turns its back on the beauty of the sea—a character by the name of
Tarrou voices the opinion that the only really important question in our
time is how to be a saint without God. Tarrou, who appears somewhat
overshadowed by Dr. Rieux, may in fact be a more important character
in *The Plague* than is usually granted. Unlike Rieux, who is committed
without illusions to a largely hopeless struggle against the plague, Tarrou
entertains yearnings for an impossible purity. To this nostalgia for the
absolute, Rieux responds with a more modest, but perhaps more ambitious demand. Heroism and sainthood, he says, do not appeal to him.
"What interests me is being a man." ("Ce qui m'intéresse c'est d'être un
homme.")[1]

Though disagreeing on this crucial issue, the two friends are allies in a
common battle. One might even say that Tarrou is Rieux's alter ego in the
sense that Tarrou makes heard a voice that will not be silenced. Coming
as it does just before a symbolic swim under the stars, their dialogue about
sainthood and humanity may well reflect Camus's internal debate around
the subject of moral commitment. Precisely at the time Camus was writing *The Plague*, he referred in his notebooks to negative sainthood, "a heroism without God." Yet shortly after, he observed that he was indifferent
to greatness, that he always found it "difficult enough to be a man"—
almost Rieux's words. Camus's ambivalence displays his lasting desire to

circumscribe modern forms of courage. "Modern heroism" is an expression featured prominently in *The Myth of Sisyphus*.[2]

A great deal could be said about the myth of Sisyphus in Camus's thinking. A legendary king of Corinth, Sisyphus is condemned in the underworld to pushing a huge stone up a hill; as soon as it reaches the top it rolls down and has to be pushed up again. For Camus, Sisyphus's ceaseless labor becomes the emblem of the human condition; yet he likes to imagine that Sisyphus finds pride and happiness in his crushing fate. Lucidly, he accepts the apparently absurd rules of a game to which he did not give his consent, and refuses to cheat. Acceptance and submission are, however, not the same. The lesson of Sisyphus is that the absurd can acquire meaning if one plays the game in a spirit of proud revolt. *L'homme révolté* (*The Rebel*) is more than the title of a polemical book; it is a pervasive notion in the work of Camus.

The theme of courageous lucidity permeates Camus's earliest writings. Already in *Noces*, the twenty-five-year-old author extolled tragic lucidity in the face of death. From the start, he saw the rejection of hope and consolation as the condition of human greatness. Contempt for lying and cheating as the mind struggles with a reality beyond understanding underlies the even earlier work *L'envers et l'endroit*. "I hate cheating. Utmost courage means keeping one's eyes wide open on the light of life as well as on death."[3]

Even courage, however, is decried, or at the very least put in an ambiguous perspective. It is simply not a priority. In his notebooks, Camus qualifies the Western cult of courage as "repugnant."[4] It is revealing that the narrator in *The Plague* paradoxically proposes as the real hero of his chronicle the touchingly ludicrous and insignificant figure of Grand. The name itself is ironic, carried as it is by a meek, slightly pathetic government employee "who had nothing of the hero about him."[5] His dream is to write a novel, but he cannot get beyond the first sentence. In his desire to compose a perfect opening sentence, he writes it over and over again with Sisyphus-like determination.

The real point of Grand's mock-elevation to the rank of hero—besides recognizing the goodness of his heart in joining the sanitary squads—is to demote heroism from its traditional preeminent position. The first place goes not to the heroic ideal, but to what Rieux calls, somewhat vaguely, "the noble claim of happiness" ("l'exigence généreuse du bonheur"). For even in times of crisis such as the plague—perhaps especially in times of crisis—there is nothing shameful according to Rieux in "preferring happiness." It is significant that this apologia of happiness is addressed to none other than Rambert, the man who fought as a volunteer in the Spanish Civil War, and came to the conclusion that bravery, by itself, is cold and murderous. "I don't believe in heroism": Rambert's terse statement comes not as a denial of the possibility of courage, but rather as a way of placing bravery below sunnier values.[6]

No Armistice

To say that Camus's love of the sun nurtures his sense of revolt is not stretching a point. The revolt is directed against an order of things which for want of a better word Dr. Rieux calls "creation," namely the conditions of existence that unavoidably include suffering and death. It is this revolt that inspires the doctor's struggle "against creation as he found it." But such a revolt remains ambivalent. Nature is to be fought. "What's natural is the microbe." All positive values—health, integrity, morality—are, as Tarrou explains, a product of the human will. Yet "nature," if it does not provide values, is a source of beauty in Camus's work. To turn one's back to the perfect shape of the bay and the beauty of the sea is a form of spiritual death. The inhabitants of Oran are thus unaware, at least at the beginning of the novel, of the unique landscape, the luminous hills, the peerless coastline.[7]

The symbolic charge of the novel is unmistakable from the earliest signals on. The title points to a contagious, epidemic disease. By its very nature, the plague is a collective affliction, involving collective responses, and calling for collective measures. The famous plagues of history (Rieux mentally surveys their recorded horrors) suggest not only natural, but man-made calamities such as wars. Biblical references, too, come to mind. Specific mention is made of the plague in Egypt, the scourge of God that humbled proud Pharaoh in the well-known episode of Exodus. And this in turn leads to religious and philosophical considerations which are at the heart of the debate that opposes the doctor and the priest.

If the title of the novel is richly symbolic, the Defoe epigraph centered on the prison image seems to announce an allegorical structure. Contemporary readers found it difficult to resist a topical reading. The plight of Oran could easily be read as a representation of France under the German occupation. Allegory and symbolism thus come into a complex, at times uneasy relationship—an uneasiness that appears to have troubled Camus when he observed in his notebooks that *The Plague* was really a "pamphlet."[8]

The key elements of the novel's brief opening sentence confirm this complex relationship between symbol and allegory. "The strange events described in this chronicle occurred in 194–in Oran." The temporal indication transparently identifies the period of the war and the Occupation. On the other hand, the city of Oran, which is not in metropolitan France, represents the ordinariness of any "modern" community. It is a negative place, symbolically without birds, without trees or gardens, without any intimations of nonmaterial values. As for the word "chronicle," with its suggestion of historical immediacy, it announces the tone of a modest, anonymous witness of collective events, as well as the moral importance of witnessing and memory.

Camus chose for his central character, chief witness, and principal chronicler the figure of a medical practitioner committed to his patients and to his daily rounds. The implicit lesson is not only that of dedication to a profession, to a *métier*, but to what Camus likes to call the "métier d'homme"—an expression difficult to translate, for *métier* means profession, craft, trade, work, occupation, but also skill and experience. To practice the "métier d'homme" is thus to be a fully involved human being. Such involvement is part of the apprenticeship of solidarity, of "belonging here," of accepting a collective destiny.

The keenest lesson, however, is that of exile, a notion central to Camus's thought. For exile, as is made clear in *The Plague*, is not so much an existential state as a potentially redemptory awareness of an inner void to be filled: a nostalgia, or homesickness for something lost long ago and largely forgotten, as well as an urge to move forward.

The result is a futile courage in the image of Sisyphus. Dr. Rieux knows, alas, that no victory can ever be lasting, that the struggle against the plague in all its forms, though necessary, means a never-ending defeat. But this is not a reason for letting down one's guard. The deadly bacillus may be here to stay, or reappear when one least expects it. Hence the need for permanent watchfulness. There can be no armistice in the insurrection against suffering. The midnight swim of the two friends symbolizes a happy distraction, a momentary release from the plague; but it is a happiness that forgets nothing. And after that privileged moment of respite, after that idyllic intimacy with the warm autumn sea and the dome of the sky, they both know that they must return to the struggle.

At the core of this will to struggle there is memory and the duty of witnessing. The words witness and witnessing appear four times in quick succession at the beginning of the final chapter, at the precise moment the plague seems to have disappeared or retreated, and the narrator-witness is appalled by the irresponsible happiness of an entire population quick to forget, and even to deny the recent horrors. This denial once again brings to mind recent historical and political calamities, including the gas chambers of the camps. Referring to the thick fumes that come from the furnaces in which the bodies of the plague victims were burned, Rieux points up the shame of silence and forgetting.

This tragic, understated sense of testimony is perhaps what separates most tellingly Camus's message from the rhetoric of heroic witnessing in the work of André Malraux. Yet there are points in common. Camus's reference to the plague victims waiting their turn in shackled impotence brings to mind the wounded political prisoners at the end of Malraux's *Man's Fate* waiting their turn to be tortured and executed. Malraux's French title, *La condition humaine*, hints at a common ancestry in one of Pascal's famous prison images describing the human condition.

> Imagine a number of men in chains, all under sentence of death, some of whom are each day butchered in the sight of the others; those remaining see their own condition in that of their fellows, and looking at each other with grief and despair await their turn. This is an image of the human condition.[9]

But the two writers' affinities around the Pascalian image of the human condition must be put in perspective. Camus may admire Malraux, but his work can also be seen as a reaction. From his earliest days, Camus was aware of Malraux's intellectual presence. Malraux's tone and ideas, even when inspired by themes of despair, "are always tonic," Camus observed in *The Myth of Sisyphus*. Yet ever since *Noces*, Camus rejected what he calls the "bitter philosophy," the heroic lesson of *grandeur*. Malraux—and this no doubt indisposed Camus—cultivated a literature of extreme situations, showed himself to be a master of dramatic contrasts and grandiose images, and spoke what he himself described as the "obscure and pressing language of modern prophets."[10]

The Scandal of Death

Much like Dr. Rieux in *The Plague*, Camus is suspicious of oracular grandiloquence, preferring at every level to deflate aggrandizing images and myths. He observes in his notebooks that the figure of Don Juan, for instance, is no longer conceivable in contemporary terms: "Neither sin nor heroism" seem possible.[11] As for the modern artist's freedom and creativity, they are linked to an antiheroic metaphor Camus strikingly unfolds in his essay "The Artist and His Time." The writer's vigor in our times depends, he explains, on being the direct opposite of Alexander, the conqueror who cut the Gordian knot with his sword. The artist is defined as a "contre-Alexandre" who, instead of severing it brutally, ties the Gordian knot of civilization once again.[12] Such a tying or binding goes with the artist's vocation of modesty and honesty, with his refusal to glorify himself. Camus's Nobel Prize acceptance speech similarly insists on the artist's responsibilities, as well as on the limits and limitations of the artist's role in society, on the need for scrupulous honesty.

Dedication to truth is underscored at the beginning of *The Plague* when Rieux refuses to grant an interview to a Parisian journalist because the latter cannot give him full assurance that nothing will be kept back. According to Rieux, testimony is valid only if it is given without reservation ("sans réserves").[13] Such concern for the naked truth leaves little room for heroic attitudes, and this is because tragedy is a daily, not an exceptional reality, demanding not gestures or feats suitable for grand occasions, but the relentless and undramatic courage of living. That such a notion of unheroic courage is not an abstraction, but a very early intuition, is made clear in Camus's posthumously published autobiographical manuscript *The First Man*, which evokes his childhood in Algiers.

Like other children, he had dreams of heroism and glory. At the public library, he devoured cloak-and-dagger novels in order to satisfy what he calls "the taste for heroism and panache." But these were books, and Camus's true apprenticeship of life was not bookish. His loathing of violence, for instance, seems to go back to a childhood fistfight, when he inflicted a black eye on a classmate and realized that "vanquishing a man is as bitter as being vanquished." He associated this somewhat commonplace experience of a school fight with the revelation that "war is no good."[14]

This early awareness of the ugliness of war takes on special poignancy as Camus's childhood and school years were lived out in the shadow of a recent world war. In the Algerian perspective, this war was quite literally a senseless calamity, sending large contingents to fight and die in defense of a country far in the north—a country which they were supposed to love as their "fatherland," but which in fact was for most of them just an abstract word, *patrie*. Camus's father was mortally wounded at the battle of the Marne, leaving his one-year-old son fatherless. Camus's entire boyhood was affected by images of war and death. He remembered with keen precision how he and his friends played on the grounds of the Home for Disabled Veterans, where the mother of one of his schoolmates was chief laundress. The presence of crippled veterans, men who had lost one or several limbs in the war, lent pathos to the children's games and to the rapture of the fragrant vegetation.

Even Camus's primary school teacher, who became a surrogate father for him, was a veteran who read moving passages from Roland Dorgelès's war novel *Wooden Crosses* aloud to his class. When Monsieur Germain realized that little Albert, seated in the front row, stared at him with his face bathed in tears, sobbing uncontrollably, this created between teacher and child a bond for life.

"Who taught you all this?," Dr. Rieux is asked in *The Plague*. The answer comes promptly: "la misère" ("suffering").[15] This answer has a personal ring. Poverty and intimations of death were at the core of Camus's apprenticeship of life. As an adolescent, he spat blood; he later had recurrent bouts of tuberculosis. In the preface to the early collection of essays *L'envers et l'endroit*, he explains that he was spared the double danger of resentment and self-satisfaction because his roots were in a world of poverty and stark sunlight. He had understood early on the bitterness not only of war, but of history, which disinherited and oppressed. Camus's moral sense responded at the same time to the calamitous nature of history and to the realization that a collective destiny casts doubt on the possibility of private salvation. But he also knew that "collective destiny," with its obvious threats to the individual, can be another form of tyranny exercised in the name of history. The central message of his 1957 Nobel Prize speech is that the writer must serve not those who make history, but those who are subject to it. A fundamental belief in human freedom runs counter to the "committed" grimness of some of his fellow intellectuals. It is fair to say that Camus never swerved from his early statement in *Noces*: "The world always ends up overcoming history."[16]

Yet Camus is hardly subject to naive optimism. His appetite for life remains grounded in what he perceives as the scandal of death. Loss and retrieval are at the core of his personal mythology; they illumine the notion of exile to which he returns so often. His tragic perception was formulated with some juvenile grandiloquence in *L'envers et l'endroit*: "There is no love of life without the despair of living." In his later notebooks, he goes on to explain that there can be no human truth outside the lucid acceptance of death, without, moreover, any hope of an afterlife. Lucidity replaces faith. Ever since the sensuously pagan *Noces*, Camus maintained that such inconsolable clear-sightedness was in itself an act of faith.[17]

Horror of death, in Camus's experience, engenders the passionate desire to live. This desire is exacerbated by the ironic awareness of nature's indifference to human suffering. But unlike Alfred de Vigny, who, in his famous poem "La maison du berger," denounced Nature's deafness to human cries, Camus holds the paradoxical view that despair accounts for joy. The dialectical nature of this link comes into sharp focus in any number of statements about the dependence of the notion of happiness on the awareness of misery. The truth of our condition is bitter. But an essential part of this truth is that every negation contains in germ a flowering of affirmations ("une floraison de 'oui'").[18]

Lucid acceptance of the inevitable becomes an act of faith precisely because there is no transcendence in Camus's scheme of things. The human body is inevitably subject to aging, disease, decay. Yet that body is our "only truth,"[19] compelling us to love the imperfect and the finite. On this subject, Camus can wax both lyrical and polemical, extolling as "sacred" the flesh that Christians have been taught to hold in contempt. Countering what he refers to as centuries of "Christian perversion," Camus preaches not redemption but convalescence. Pascal's message of human frailty may move him; but the fear and trembling that are meant to lead to God fail to convert him.[20]

Camus's earthbound outlook is summed up in Koliayev's terse reply to the devout Grand Duchess in *Les justes:* "All my appointments are on this earth." Elsewhere, the author speaks directly. "My whole kingdom is of this world." The same this-worldly attachment comes through in Meursault's answer, when shortly before his execution in *The Stranger,* he is asked by the prison chaplain how he imagines the afterlife: "A life in which I could remember this one."[21]

The basic stance is at once nonreligious and antireligious. From the posthumous autobiographical novel *The First Man,* one gathers that religion had no place in Camus's family, that there never was talk of God. Yet Camus displays not merely indifference, but downright hostility to what he views as the deceptions and illusions fostered by religion. Sisyphian courage is the rejection of the meaningless world of the gods.[22]

The deeper resonance, decidedly antimetaphysical, is however not devoid of a poetic and even spiritual register. Camus likes to imagine a divine order "without human immortality." He recalls that Odysseus rejects Calypso's offer of immortality, and sees this allegiance to the human abode as the central meaning of the *Odyssey.*[23] In Algeria, where he grew up, as in Delphi, which he visited, he experienced "l'angoisse du sacré," a sense of holy dread in the face of eternity.[24] But his most intense lyrical emotions continue to be related to the sense of hereness and to his preference for the finite. One sentence in *Noces* perhaps best captures a ring that is lyrical and spiritual by preterition: "The world is beautiful, and outside of it there can be no salvation."[25]

Exile: The Emptiness at the Center

Despite the deliberately understated, often colorless nature of his prose (in part because of it), Camus's fiction, as exemplified by *The Stranger* and *The Plague,* is laden with poetic instants that are evanescent and lingering, like whiffs that heighten the intentional flatness of the tone, and provide intimations of some other reality. The contrast between the studied

neutrality of the narrative style and such fleeting lyrical evocations is especially noteworthy in *The Stranger*. Meursault, the narrator, shows himself
repeatedly sensitive to the hills, the sea, the melancholy beauty of evening
hours. He responds to the colors of the earth, the changing light, the
gracefulness of a line of cypress trees, the summer smells, the familiar
sounds of the city.

This poetic disposition is hardly surprising in view of the many landscape evocations in Camus's early texts such as *L'envers et l'endroit, Noces*,
and even the philosophically ambitious *Le mythe de Sisyphe*. It is even
more evident in his personal writings—his notebooks, and *Le premier
homme*. Camus makes much of his longing for the sea, the light on olive
trees in Italy, the memory of shimmering bays, the early morning dew
on the ruins of Tipasa. His fundamentally sensuous perception extends to
children's games, the forms of the human body, the beauty of sports.

The Camusian mixture of unglamorous matter-of-factness, troubling
(yet reassuring) ordinariness, and sporadic lyrical expansiveness accounts
for much of the special achievement of *The Plague*. Exhausted by the daily
struggle against the epidemic, Dr. Rieux finds renewed confidence and
energy in the hum of the city carried by the gentle breeze, the hoarse
blasts coming at night from distant ships in the harbor, the unconcerned
movement of crowds in the street, the routine sounds of a nearby work-
shop.

The blend of humdrum existence, misery, and acute awareness of
beauty is even more striking in the transparently autobiographical pages
of *The First Man*. The evocations of Algiers and Algeria are keen and
suggestive: ephemeral twilights, the passing of seasons, the departure of
the swallows, ravines filled with scents, summer days when the sky gets
colorless with heat. The teeming districts of Algiers are vividly rendered
with their narrow arcaded streets, the peddlers and their stands, the food
stalls, the mingled religious and ethnic groups.

On the manuscript of *The First Man*, Camus noted that he wanted this
book to be "heavy with things and flesh." Human contact, friendship, solidarity—these are words and concepts that carry a concrete meaning for
him. One of the memorable passages in *The Plague* describes the noctur-
nal swim proposed by Tarrou to Rieux "for friendship's sake." The two
dive from a boulder into the moonlit waters that rise and sink near the
pier. As they swim side by side and in the same rhythm in the tepid sea,
they experience a sensuous communion, as well as a respite from the
plague. They both find it silly to live only in and for the plague, meaning
that it is senseless to live only in and for history. There are other values.
But those values exist because the plague and history cannot be denied.

The sense of happiness and freedom felt by the two friends during their swim is in fact dependent on the presence of the plague, and their need to fight it.

Yet the commitment to the struggle and the underlying sense of moral duty remain decidedly nonheroic. The tone of the early writings is sensuous, if not hedonistic. Camus made it clear to himself from the outset that he was not in quest of a harsh philosophy of "greatness." In *Noces,* his nuptial song of human at-homeness in a nature indifferent to human suffering, he declared his antiheroic as well as his antimetaphysical stance. Commenting on his own ambiguous attitude of love and rebellion, he concluded: "In this great temple deserted by the gods, all my idols have feet of clay." [26]

It is not surprising that desert images pervade his works. They press themselves forward in the collection of stories revealingly entitled *The Exile and the Kingdom.* The schoolteacher in "The Guest" experiences true exaltation as he faces the vast desert space he has come to love. The protagonist in "The Adulterous Woman" surrenders to the erotic allurements of the desert wind, the swaying palm trees of the oasis, the boundless horizon, and experiences the desert night as an overwhelming sensuous fulfillment. Her nomadic yearnings act like a reminder that something fundamental has been missing or has been forgotten.

This is the symbolic meaning of exile as developed in *The Plague.* For exile is not merely a literal separation from one's home and beloved, nor an understandable feeling of imprisonment in the beleaguered city. It is the increasingly keen awareness of a lack, an absence, an emptiness at the center of one's life. In *The Myth of Sisyphus,* Camus stated aphoristically that the intellectual outlook of an individual was basically his or her nostalgia, that true exile would be the loss of memory of one's home—a loss depriving one at the same time of any hope of a promised land.[27]

The notion of such a purifying nostalgia (in the original sense of *nostos* = return home) accounts for the metaphorical value of Greece in the writings of Camus. The apparently irrelevant digression about Greece in *The Fall,* with its evocation of the sharp outlines of the archipelago, the glittering waters, the endless islands appearing on the horizon, is intended to suggest a joyful world of purity and innocence that contrasts with the drabness of the Dutch setting. The narrator observes that Greece drifts somewhere within him, "on the edge of [his] memory."[28] This internalized metaphor clearly corresponds to Camus's own symbolic inner landscape. His notebooks contain any number of references to his Greek nostalgia. Because the Greek idea of the tragic appears to him essentially rooted in the evidence of beauty, he maintains that the world in which he feels

most at home is that of Greek myths. At one point, the thought of redemptive exile is specifically associated with sailing over Greek waters and experiencing the sight of islands covered with flowers and columns as a "second birth."[29]

Satanic Virtue

Such a commitment to innocence may surprise readers who have learned
to associate the name of Camus with the Parisian intellectual establishment of the postwar years, and in particular with the tenets of literary
Existentialism. These tenets are best exemplified by Jean-Paul Sartre's
views about the function of the writer. Camus no doubt subscribed to some
of them: that the writer must embrace his own period, that he writes in
the present and for the present, that his mission is to reveal the world and
its injustices, that every word and every silence have repercussions. Where
the two did not see eye to eye, and ultimately clashed, was with regard to
the Sartrean assertion that no one is innocent, and that the primary obligation of the writer is to give society a bad conscience.[30]

If not anti-intellectual in substance, Camus grew increasingly suspicious of intellectuals as a group, associating them with the Parisian scene
he knew well, but where he always felt like an outsider. Parisian polemics,
of which he became a victim after the publication of *The Rebel*, he found
distasteful. He called Paris a "jungle," maintaining that he preferred engagé individuals to the notion of "engagé literature" which, under the
militant banner of Existentialism, held a reductive view of human beings
as exclusively subject to history.[31]

Outright negative comments about intellectuals occur with frequency
in Camus's writings in the 1950s. In a speech delivered in Italy, he asserted
that many European intellectuals were "disgusted with themselves."[32] His
chief targets, however, were the intellectuals of Paris, principally Sartre
and his epigones, whom he accused of bad faith, hypocrisy, intransigence,
and lack of compassion behind the pretense of fighting social injustice. In
a terse entry in one of his notebooks, Camus takes Sartre to task directly
as personally and intellectually "disloyal." The very title of Camus's play
Les justes suggests his dislike for the politically self-righteous who are always ready to condemn. Another notebook entry, under the heading "Existentialism," is more pointed still: "When they accuse themselves, one can
be sure it is always to denounce others. Penitent judges."[33]

The main theme of *The Fall*, Camus's profoundly ironic and perhaps
greatest work of fiction, is easily recognizable. Its narrator-protagonist, a
former lawyer who describes himself as just such a judge-penitent, is a
duplicitous compulsive talker who entraps his silent interlocutor in an

endless, though not aimless monologue. The first-person narration, remi-
niscent of Dostoevsky's technique in *Notes from Underground*, posits an
unreliable narrator who moreover admits that it is hard to "disentangle
the true from the false" in what he is saying (119).[34] As in the case of
Dostoevsky's underground man, the confessional nature of *The Fall*'s discourse remains problematic and aggressive throughout. The very purpose
of a confession, supposedly prompted by sincerity and humility, is under-
mined in this narration. The narrator himself hints at an ulterior motive.
His words have a purpose ("mon discours est orienté"—131), he says; and
that purpose or strategy, as the reader gathers, is to create accomplices, to
spread shame and guilt like a deadly disease.

The title serves as a warning. The "fall" refers in part to the lawyer's
fallen professional state, to his comedown from the height of Parisian success, to his self-willed exile in the Jewish quarter of Amsterdam. It also
announces the episode of the young woman's suicide-fall from the Paris
bridge. But it is hard not to hear a deeper resonance in the title, namely
the memory of an earlier story about an original fall from innocence. And
this earlier story is not only the drama of a fall, but the plotting of a temptation carried out by an arch-tempter and arch-seducer.

It is not only the rhetoric of Camus's speaker that is ingratiating and
insinuating from the start; the substance of his discourse is seductive as
well. Can one fail to sympathize with him as he disarmingly reveals his
all too human foibles, or as he denounces the horrors of contemporary
history, and specifically the crime of silence in the face of Nazi deporta-
tions of Jewish families?

Other early signals, in addition to the title, help put the speaker's pretense at confession in perspective. A lawyer by training and profession,
proud of his courtroom theatrical talents, he is a master of rhetoric who
knows how to use language as both mask and weapon, if need be in the
service of a bad cause. Does one not speak of the devil's advocate? Far from
believing in justice, the presumption of innocence, and the defense of the
defenseless, Camus's cynical lawyer-protagonist proclaims a fiendish credo
based on the radical denial of innocence and the certainty of guilt. "Every
human being testifies to the crime of all the others—that is my faith and
my hope" (110). The perverse use of the words "faith" and "hope," which
are usually associated with religious beliefs, underscores the further perversity of his self-styled vocation as "judge-penitent." It is one thing for a
judge to discover his own guilt and unfitness to judge; it is quite another to
act out repentance in order to judge and condemn everyone. The implicit
inversion of the terms (judge-penitent/penitent-judge) reveals the depth
of the character's perversion.

The blasphemous assertion that even Christ was guilty and that he knew it (was he not responsible for the massacre of the Innocents?) is directly linked to the narrator's ironic choice of the name Jean-Baptiste Clamence. Jean-Baptiste brings to mind the prophet who announced and baptized Christ; Clamence alludes to the same prophet's voice crying out in the wilderness—"vox clamantis in deserto."[35] But the novel's Jean-Baptiste Clamence, as he himself puts it, is a "false prophet" rambling on in the modern wasteland (117, 147).

That wasteland—a desert of stones, stagnant waters, and soggy mists—takes on the symbolic aspect of contemporary hell. As Clamence points out to his listener, Amsterdam's concentric canals resemble the circles of Dante's hell. Installed in the sordid "Mexico City" bar that caters to sailors and shady characters of all nationalities, Clamence describes himself as waiting for forlorn travelers in the last and lowest of the circles. The image leaves no doubt as to the implicit association with the figure of Satan.

This narrator-devil bond is later confirmed by any number of details: references to a lost light, satanic laughter, exile, measureless pride, the power to enslave millions of subjects, the "bad angels" among whom he sits enthroned, dreams of playing at God. Placed in the ideological context of the 1950s, the devil motif as developed in *The Fall* closely relates to Camus's loathing for the moralizing arrogance of intellectuals exploiting the notion of collective guilt as a strategy of power and self-glorification.

Up to a point, Camus may have self-critically included himself (or his former self) among the intellectuals he condemns, thus adding to the complexity of the novel's confessional motifs. But he surely took his distance unambiguously in denouncing the radical immorality of pontificating and moralizing when these constitute a denial of goodness and love. Clamence refers bitterly to the virtuous Satanism of his "illustrious contemporaries" who climb up to their pulpit and curse humanity (134, 137). Speaking in his own name, Camus left little doubt as to whom he specifically had in mind. In an interview given to the *Gazette de Lausanne,* he openly stated his aversion to "those modern writers, among them the atheistic Existentialists, who have denied the existence of God but retained the idea of original sin."[36]

Camus's hostile reaction casts light on the strange story of violence and mutilation originally entitled "The Confused Mind," which he later published under the more pointed title "The Renegade." It is a parable of intellectual and moral aberration in the form of the hallucinatory interior monologue of a self-loathing missionary who sets out to convert the cruel "city of salt," and who, attracted to cruelty, adoringly submits to his tormentors. An allegory of moral masochism and a paean to evil, "The Renegade," through its incantatory rhythms and blinding images of pain, tells of the intellectual's self-betrayal in quest of the absolute.[37]

Between the Victim and the Executioner

Camus's distrust of any doctrinal moral stance goes to extremes. His distaste for the heroics of principles incites him to deplore the "madness of virtue" and its destructiveness. "Morality kills," he jotted down peremptorily, explaining in another entry the political context of his aversion. "I have given up a moral point of view. Morality leads to abstraction and injustice. It fathers fanaticism and blindness. Whoever is virtuous must cut off heads."[38] The political Terror remains a permanent danger.

Camus gradually evolved a refutation of the absolutism of all abstractions. Even before the polemics of the 1950s, he diagnosed the arrogance of what could be described as the Atlas complex of modern intellectuals, among whom at that stage he still included himself. "We have taken upon ourselves the misery of the entire world," he wrote, adding that there would be a heavy price to pay for such pride.[39] Evil becomes synonymous with abstraction, in the form of a theorem. "Démonstration. Que l'abstraction est le mal." This evil of abstraction bears the responsibility for wars, torture, violence. The heroic posturings of the practitioners of *littérature engagée* ultimately made Camus almost yearn for what he had always rejected: a literature of indifference. If such a literature of indifference was not compatible with Camus's temperament, it is certainly true that he became increasingly tempted by an ethics of abstention.

It was hard to maintain—as he does in "L'artiste et son temps"—that the artist must enter the arena and speak for those who are mute, yet at the same time yearn for the "divine freedom" that suffuses the music of Mozart. More pointedly still, Camus evokes the Chinese thinker Lao-Tzu as the exemplary "philosopher of indifference."[40] Camus likes to think that art always means both refusal and consent. The balance, however, is not an easy matter. Exasperated by the contradictory pressures of complex issues, Camus at times lay himself open—as during the Algerian war—to the charge that he had surrendered to the dubious moral imperative of abstention.

Camus's moral reticence should not be attributed to weakness or indifference. It is rooted in a visceral distaste for violence which takes on an extreme form in his reactions to capital punishment. The execution of a human being in the name of justice is a traumatizing motif in *The Stranger*, as well as in *The Plague*, linking the former in particular to Victor Hugo's pioneer novel *The Last Day of a Condemned Man*. Judges tend to be dealt with harshly in the work of Camus. Monsieur Othon sympathizes with the view that the plague is a deserved collective punishment. When the plague strikes Othon's own family, Tarrou sadly observes that one would like to help him, adding with infinite bitterness: "But how can you help a judge?" (242).[41] It is true that Tarrou has personal reasons. His father was a judge, and he rebelled against him when, as an adolescent, he heard him in court demand the death sentence for a wretched individual in the name of justice and society. As Tarrou explains, some elemental instinct swept him to the side of the victim of legalized murder (248).

The notebooks contain a curious anecdote that casts light on the theft, in *The Fall*, of the van Eyck altarpiece panel known as *The Just Judges*. In a brief entry, Camus records the story of the priest who confessed to having stolen that panel because he could not tolerate seeing any judges in the proximity of the Mystical Lamb.[42] The anecdote offers an implicit rejection of Tarrou's extreme position, of his utopian quest for an impossible purity. For Camus knew that there can be no moral struggle without dirtying one's hands. Camus's ambivalence is mirrored in the bond of friendship between Rieux and Tarrou. The latter dies, a victim of the plague he helped to fight, and Rieux remains to mourn him, aware that this death symbolizes an unavoidable defeat.

One might indeed speak of a "Tarrou complex." If the figure of Rambert corresponds to the message of solidarity, that of Tarrou relates to Camus's lasting dream of purity and revolt, and to the refusal to become in any way an accomplice of the plague. Tarrou puts it quite simply when he states his resolve to have no part in anything that, directly or indirectly, for good or bad reasons, brings death to anyone. And he adds, extending this conscientious objector credo to history itself: "I know I have no place in the world of today; once I'd definitely refused to kill, I doomed myself to an exile that can never end. I leave it to others to make history . . ." (253).

Nothing states more vividly Camus's proud but uncomfortable view of himself as increasingly caught between the victim and the executioner. Again the notebooks provide a lucid assessment: "We are in a world where one must choose between being a victim or an executioner—and nothing else." But can one really choose? And why is there "nothing else"? The truth is that the unheroic voice of moderation itself becomes a victim. Witnesses to freedom of thought are destined to be persecuted. But such witnesses, roused by moral scruples, do not give up the struggle, even though they know they cannot prevail. Over the centuries, the sacrifice of Socrates is reenacted over and over again.[43]

It is around the theme of the courageous weakness of the witness that we can best perceive Camus's personal voice. That voice can be heard with particular clarity in *The First Man*, which describes young Albert's childhood among the poor and uneducated in one of the disinherited quarters of Algiers. Camus himself writes that he never "recovered" from this childhood, suggesting that in order to make sense of his character and values, one must go back to the early setting of deprivation where he locates his most meaningful bonds. In his notebooks, he admits never to have had a clear vision of himself, complaining of the confusion and even "anarchy" in his personal makeup.[44] *The First Man* represents a pilgrimage to his youth in an effort to see himself more clearly, with all his contradictions. What appears is Camus's allegiance to the Algeria of his childhood and adolescence, as well as his profound attachment to his illiterate and largely deaf mother, whom he revered with a speechless love. Camus never wrenched himself away from what he depicts as the warm and innocent world of the poor.

The evidence of *The First Man* points not so much to temperamental "anarchy" as to the inner tensions of a *homo duplex*. Camus discovers in himself a split or ambivalent personality. There is the Parisian public figure, the author of well-known novels and plays, the former editor of *Combat*—a clandestine resistance paper during the Occupation. But there is also the other Camus, who feels most at home in a world of sand and wind, a world of wide open spaces. "The Mediterranean separates two worlds in me."[45] The split is psychological and moral as well. On the one hand, a fierce appetite for life, dark stirrings, and a poetic perception of things; on the other, a taste for lost causes and the will to courage.

Solidarity with the world of artisans, respect for the silent dignity of work, giving a voice to the voiceless—these are underlying motifs. Camus would always feel distant from the Parisian ideologues who merely theorized about the proletariat. But the deeper personal investment in *The First Man* lies elsewhere, principally in the search for his identity that is implicit in the title. The identity quest is linked to the search for the vanished father, a "dead stranger" as Camus put it. He tried to imagine this unknown father who died in the first few months of the great war, leaving him fatherless as an infant. When he visited his father's tomb in a military graveyard forty years later, he was struck by the realization that he was by then older than his father had been at the time he was hit by shrapnel near the Marne. Only one bond seemed to exist between himself and this dead stranger. As a boy, he had been lastingly impressed by the story of his father's experience of a public execution and his return filled with horror and nausea. For the rest, the father's legacy was a void.

But this void, this missing authority, is what made self-creation a necessity. Hence the metaphor of the "first man." The notion of the self-made person lends the book's title its full significance. The "first man" is young Albert Camus himself, compelled to bringing himself up alone, without the guidance and authority of a father, without a tradition handed down. As Camus explains, he had to work out his own moral values, and "create his own heritage."[46]

In no other text is Camus's voice more personal than in *The First Man*, though it is essentially the same voice that comes through in his other writings. It speaks of humble origins, the absence of a glorified model; refuses to become the accomplice of events and indulge in heroic strains; extols neither hero nor saint; proclaims repeatedly that there is no shame in happiness, and that—as Dr. Rieux realizes in *The Plague*—a loveless world is a dead world. Repulsed by sterile intellectualization and the quest for absolutes, Camus prefers instead to sing with restrained lyricism the beauty of the human experience and human vulnerability. His allegiance to the finite is well served by the quotation from Pindar's third Pythian Ode, which he chose as an epigraph for *Noces*. "Do not, o my soul, aspire to immortal life; rather exhaust the realm of the possible." It is the same fidelity to the human dimension that Camus reads into Odysseus's home-coming from the world of gods and monsters.

Two statements best sum up Camus's resistance to political and philo-sophical abstractions. The first comes from the preface to *L'envers et l'endroit*: "Poverty prevented me from judging that all was well under the sun and in history; the sun taught me that history was not all." The other, appearing in one of his notebooks, elaborates on a pronouncement by Dostoevsky: "One must love life before loving its meaning, says Dostoevsky. Yes, and when the love of life disappears, no meaning can console us." [47]

Camus knew that war, not peace, is normal; that Cain will always slay Abel—just as Dr. Rieux had no illusions about any radical disappearance of the killer bacillus. Lasting vigilance, rather than any heroic gest, was in order. There can be no truce in the struggle against suffering. The lesson Camus teaches is that we must learn to love that which is imperfect. This tragic humanism is both joyful and desperate.

PRIMO LEVI AND THE
CANTO OF ULYSSES

A Rescue Operation

The figure of Ulysses looms large in the work of Primo Levi. This may at first seem strange. Examining his intellectual development years after writing his book on Auschwitz, the death-camp survivor came to the conclusion that the experience of the Lager counted for less than the books he had read. Under the title *The Search for Roots* (*La ricerca delle radici*), Primo Levi published in 1981 a personal anthology of extracts from books that had really mattered in his life. This self-searching survey begins appropriately with the Book of Job, which, according to Levi, confronts the timeless question of suffering and evil, and challenges the apparent injustice of God, who crushes Job in an uneven contest.

More surprising is the preeminent place attributed to Homer, though not to his great war epic, the *Iliad,* which Levi finds intolerable with its endless heroic battles and the childish anger of Achilles. Levi's enthusiasm is exclusively about the *Odyssey,* the great "human" poem of the homecoming from the world of violence and monsters, a poem based on the hope that war and exile will come to an end, and that the world will be rebuilt in peace through justice.

Ulysses holds a special fascination for Levi. The second entry of *The Search for Roots,* entitled "A Man of Nothing" ("Un uomo da nulla"), is conceived as a song of praise for the victory of a weak mortal against the gigantic Cyclops—a victory due not to brute strength, but to wit, resourcefulness, and skill. Ulysses symbolizes a courage and pride that have more to do with survival and human values than with heroic deeds. Attracted to adventure, yet steadily nostalgic for Ithaca, Ulysses represents values most dear to Levi: keen curiosity, but also fidelity to memory and love of remembrance. The propensity to lament lost companions is bound to the urgency of telling (and hearing) the story, stressing the primacy of the narrative. For Ulysses, as Levi reminds his reader, is a storyteller who easily yields to the need to recite his epic travails and those of his friends.

Homeric echoes are unmistakable in Levi's own account of his return home to his Ithaca, Turin, after Auschwitz was liberated by Soviet troops in January 1945. This slow, circuitous journey is described in *La tregua* (*The Reawakening*), as a colorful railroad odyssey ("odissea ferroviaria"— It. 221)[1] that carries Levi and other freed camp inmates through extensive regions of Poland, Russia, Rumania, and Austria. Levi highlights epic comradeships and evokes occasionally relaxed moments when he and his comrades spent whole nights singing and telling each other their "stories," or, as some in their caravan were prone to do, ate and drank inordinately "like the companions of Ulysses" after pulling their boats ashore (215, 66).

The most striking reference to Ulysses occurs, however, in *If This Is a Man* (*Se questo è un uomo*), known to American readers as *Survival in Auschwitz*. The epic reference may at first seem out of place in a personal account of the death camp. The literariness of the reference is itself complex, for Homer's Ulysses is seen here in the perspective of Dante's *Inferno*. The title of Levi's chapter "The Canto of Ulysses" is indeed a clear allusion to the twenty-sixth canto of Dante's poem, in which the Italian poet, in the company of his guide and literary master, Virgil, visits the circles of hell.

The immediate context of the Ulysses episode in the book on Auschwitz is worth recalling. A young Alsatian inmate, known as Pikkolo, has asked Levi to teach him Italian. Levi, without at first understanding why, conjures up some lines by Dante to serve as the basis for the first lesson. This recourse to familiar poetry, once learned by heart, is both understandable and revealing. The lines retrieved by memory are associated with schooldays in Turin and, by extension, with his larger home, Italy. The joy of recalling and reconstructing, the excitement of shoring up fragments, can be intensely reassuring. Prisoners under the most distressing circumstances have testified to the keen joy of exercising their memory to reconstruct entire poems or musical compositions—a rescue operation that rescued more than music or poetry. Beyond the joy of remembering, beyond the sense of control and order, what is involved, it would seem, is a sense of personal freedom and survival. Levi clearly suggests a salvational motif when he claims to have "saved" ("salvato") a given line of Dante from oblivion.

It is significant that this salvation takes place under the sign of teaching. A link is established between the present reality and the poem of the past: Levi is teaching Pikkolo; Dante's Ulysses is teaching his men. The link is not merely thematic, but historical and transcultural: from Homer to Virgil, to Dante, to Primo Levi, to the future reader. The spanning of Greek and Roman antiquity, the Middle Ages, the modern period, suggests a reassuring permanence and continuity.

The teaching process is moreover embedded in the literary substance: Virgil, the Roman poet, had learned from his Greek master Homer, just as Dante had been inspired by his "maestro" Virgil. The notion of such a chain extending all the way to the present in itself transmits a message across time. The direct relevance of Levi's "Canto of Ulysses" chapter is thus not only the subject of hell—a hell on earth more hellish than anything Dante could have imagined; it is the theme of communication and of a lesson to be conveyed. For Dante's Ulysses, restless and eager to set out again on the open sea beyond the Pillars of Hercules, is a model of intellectual curiosity and courage. His burning desire, as he puts it, is to explore the ways of the world ("divenir del mondo esperto") and learn as much as possible about human vices and virtues.

The words with which Dante's Ulysses admonishes his men, as they sail on the ominous sea that threatens to engulf them, have an unmistakable bearing on Levi's own message from out of the abyss of the camp experience. It is a lesson in dignity and survival, yet also a reminder that sheer physical survival is not enough—that what defines a human being is the need and ability to pursue higher aims. Levi quotes the key lines of Ulysses' message:

> . . . for brutish ignorance
> Your mettle was not made; you were made men,
> To follow after knowledge and excellence. (113)

(The Italian is more specific: humans are not made to live like beasts, but to follow after *virtute* and *conoscenza:* virtue and knowledge.) A bitter reminder, in the context of the dehumanizing death camp, of the anguishing question raised by Levi's title: "If this is a man . . ."

Ultimately, the thrust of the Ulysses chapter is of a spiritual nature, ending as it does on an almost religious note. The recourse to Dante's poetry, in order to teach Italian to an Alsatian fellow inmate in a German camp deep inside Poland, where Yiddish is the common tongue, becomes a symbol of universality and of the possible survival of meaning. For Levi, the experience comes close to a revelation or epiphany. Reciting the well-known *terza rima*, Levi has the impression that he hears a trumpet blast sounding like the voice of God, that he sees "something gigantic" in a flash of intuition.

Bread and Language

Some readers have felt uneasy about the use of intertextual allusions and literary motifs to account for a historical experience in horror. It also seemed strange to them that a Jewish victim of Shoah should invoke a Christian medieval poem to bear witness to a collective atrocity that could not possibly be redeemed or justified in theological or aesthetic terms. Even more fundamental was the suspicion that the humanistic message of a reassuring cultural continuity might tame or even trivialize the horror of the events described. Levi himself had misgivings about the relationship between catastrophe and literariness. To what extent was it legitimate, he asked himself, to exploit violence for literary purposes.[2] Conversely, after rereading *Survival in Auschwitz* forty years after the camp experience, he wondered whether the "Canto of Ulysses" chapter was not too literary and whether he, the camp witness, was trustworthy when he affirmed that culture had "saved" him. But Levi quickly added that the Ulysses episode with Pikkolo was one whose authenticity he was able to verify. For Pikkolo, by his real name Jean Samuel, was another camp survivor, who, years later, confirmed the veracity of these pages. Levi was satisfied that where he had written that he would gladly "give today's soup to know how to connect" two isolated lines of Dante's canto, he had not lied or exaggerated. And, bread and soup, as he reminded his reader, were, under the circumstances, the equivalent of blood and life.[3] The connecting of these lines meant not only a retrieval of the poem, but a link with the past, and a means of saving one's identity and that of many others by a determined effort not to forget.

The "humanistic" motifs cannot, in all fairness, be attributed to self-indulgent aesthetization; they are vitally bound up with the multiple notions of communication and human solidarity. Two key images—bread and the Tower of Babel—carry the burden of complex thematic developments. Gian Paolo Biasin, in an essay entitled "Our Daily Bread," has convincingly shown how the multilingual words for bread (*pane-Brot-Broid-chleb-pain-lechem-kenyér*) convey at the same time the inmates' obsessive hunger and the chaos of languages in the camp.[4] In the grim chapter "Initiation," Levi recalls the frantic early morning rush to the latrines so as not to miss the daily distribution of the pitiful ration of bread. Hunger is the camp's permanent reality. Levi writes: "The Lager *is* hunger" (74).

The relentless obsession with food marks just the kind of dehumanization planned and gleefully observed by the SS. What indeed remains of human dignity when one steals bread from a dying neighbor or when one fights for a scrap of food thrown as to animals?

A world in which *fressen* (the animal way of devouring food) has replaced the human *essen* is a bitter reminder of the ancient significance of sharing bread as a yardstick of humanity, as a symbol of companionship and communion. When Levi refers to the pitiful daily portion of bread as "the holy gray slab" ("sacro blocchetto grigio"—It. 45), and to *essen* as a way of eating "seated in front of a table, religiously" (76) this is an implicit recall of the spiritual connotation of food, of its importance in prayer and thanksgiving. Significantly, the "rebirth" ("rinascita"—51), as the liberating army approaches, is marked by an elementary gesture of gratitude on the part of several deathly sick inmates who offer a slice of bread to thank their companions for a special act of devotion. This gift of bread was "the first human gesture that occurred among us," adds Levi (160).

The cries of hunger and pain in all the languages of Europe conjure up the other key image: the Tower of Babel. The harsh sounds of foreign words, coupled with the barking of orders by the guards, create a linguistic chaos that brings to mind God's confusing the language spoken in the land of Shinar so as to hinder the construction of the tower whose top was to reach heaven. The Biblical reference is clear enough, for the Carbide Tower in the Buna sector of Auschwitz, where the camp laborers were worked to death to help the German war production, was named the *Babelturm* by the inmates, who saw in it an insolent edifice erected by the Nazis "in defiance of heaven," to show their contempt for God and men (73).

Once again the negative is convertible into the positive: the linguistic chaos and the dreadful *Babelturm* are reminders, if not of a harmonious common language, at least of the need and yearning to communicate in the face of all that separates human beings. In *L'altrui mestiere,* a more lighthearted book describing the scientist's dilettantish excursion into literature, Levi evokes an ancient civilization "before the Tower of Babel," when the entire Mediterranean world spoke the same language (It. 207). What is at stake in *Survival at Auschwitz* is, however, more than harmony and nostalgia for a common culture: it is the very possibility of communication in a world gone mad, the urgency to tell the story, and thus to bear witness for all those who will never again be heard. It is language as survival—and this not only in the daily lifesaving communication within the camp, but in the ability to reach out to the world of the living and to posterity. The humanistic message of a sacred logos conceived in strictly human terms points to far more than physical survival, it concerns salvation. Hence the permanent fear, in the form of a recurrent nightmare, of speaking and not being heard.

The Lager as Expression

To speak for those who did not return was, as Levi reports, the deepest wish of all those who suspected that they would perish in the Lager. But Levi also knew that he was speaking for the few who did return, and who could not speak themselves because they had reached the bottom of abjection, had stared into the face of the Gorgon, and remained mute for life. It is a measure of Levi's honesty and modesty that he should acknowledge having been spared the worst (his training as a chemist saved him), and that as a relatively privileged witness, he also had the obligation to testify with "the humility of the good chronicler."[5] Writing about the camp was thus at the same time a duty, a liberating and exorcising act, and a recognition of the latent guilt of being a survivor. The book was written, Levi recalls, under a feverish compulsion. The largely autobiographical *The Periodic Table*, which describes this shame of having remained alive and the need to "tell," refers in a symbolic manner to the Ancient Mariner's narrative quest for purification (151). *The Drowned and the Saved*, written not long before his death, carries as an epigraph the pertinent lines from Coleridge's poem:

> . . . till my ghastly tale is told
> This heart within me burns.

But how to avoid vehemence, or at the other extreme, the coldness of a document? Levi finds his tone quite naturally. To convey the unspeakable, he combined a matter-of-fact sobriety of expression with a sense of form and structure that depended on literary conventions such as a suggestive title, a preliminary poem, and metaphorical chapter headings. Self-pity and heroic poses had no place in such a text. Discretion about his private anguish was the rule. It was only by allusion, and years later, that Levi referred to his personal tragedy, when he mentioned the woman with whom he "had gone down to the netherworld ("inferi") and who had not returned."[6] No pathos, no melodrama, no grand statements. The simplest means account for a radical defamiliarization, such as when he relates how, in an instant, upon the deportees' arrival in the camp, the women, the children, and the parents were taken away, never to be seen again—the first of the many "selections" for the gas chambers. "We saw them for a short while as a dark mass at the other end of the platform; then we saw nothing more" (20).

The banality of horror, the incomprehensible normalcy of madness experienced as though in a dream sequence, are communicated in ways that bring to mind the uncanny logic of Kafka's nightmares. Levi had read Kafka's *Metamorphosis,* and it is revealing that the word "metamorfosi" comes to his mind in the opening chapter of *Survival in Auschwitz,* in which he describes the transformation of human beings into hairless and nameless puppets dressed in filthy striped rags, walking in squads with their heads dangling—doomed men carrying a tattoo on their left arm until the hour of their death.

A stark and factual document, Levi's book describes the deportation, the first blows, the transport of the men, women, and children packed like cattle into goods wagons, the arrival in camp, where they were quickly stripped of their clothes, shoes, hair, and even their name. Meticulously, Levi goes over their daily existence in the camp: the gruesome work, the cold, hunger, filth, and illness—the merciless struggle for survival. He reports with precision on the cruel irony of the inscription over the camp gate ("Arbeit Macht Frei"—"Work Gives Freedom"); the Teutonic humor of the SS, who see to it that the labor squads march off and return to the tune of the sentimental song "Rosamunde"; the periodic "selections" for the gas chambers, when the deportees have to run naked in front of the SS, who decide at a glance whether they are still fit for work. The reign of brutality quickly imposes a hierarchy among the *Häftlinge,* the prisoners, engendering bestiality in the victims themselves. The worst offense is this "demolition of a man," for which, as Levi puts it, language has no words (26).

It is just this offense that is reflected in the multiple meanings of the Italian title, *Se questo è un uomo.* Is this still a man? Can one still recognize a human being in this debased creature reduced to utter nakedness and shame? The question implies that a basic image has been lost or destroyed. But it also suggests that it is essential to remember this precious image, and try to preserve, retrieve, or reconstitute it.

A world in which the image of humanity has disappeared is also a world "on this side of good and evil": the heading of one of the chapters. The twisted paraphrase of Nietzsche's famous title signals Levi's moral indignation at the satanic will to create conditions in which moral laws no longer apply or make sense, a world in which the notions of good and evil have vanished, where only the law of survival exists, where adapting in order to survive can only mean collaborating with the reign of violence.

Survival in Auschwitz stresses with factual objectivity the unheroic horror of the camp: the physical and mental debasement, the inhuman work, the blows, the utter shame of witnessing in abject silence the public execution of one who dared to rebel. But this objectivity is in reality the mask of a latent indignation announced by the invective tone of the preliminary poem, which echoes the Hebrew "sh'ma" (listen) and "zachor" (remember), laying a curse on the sin of forgetting or denying:

> Meditate that this came about:
> I commend these words to you
>
> .   .   .   .
>
> Repeat them to your children,
>   Or may your house fall apart.
>   May illness impede you,
>   May your children turn their faces from you.

If Levi, despite his harsh notion of bearing witness, never succumbs to pessimism about human nature, it is because of an underlying concern for meaning and values. He asks himself what good there is in retaining the memory of the camp. The answer, interestingly, is not at first moral but intellectual—even scientific. Levi is convinced that no "human experience is without meaning or unworthy of analysis," and that "fundamental values" can therefore be deduced from the world he describes (87). It is conceivable that Levi, the trained chemist, found a sense of order and security in a "scientific" way of looking at even the most horrendous reality, much as Levi the humanist found solace and salvation in Dante's poetry. It was a matter of holding on. The scientific tone was not merely a way of being precise and credible. On the same page where Levi maintains that fundamental values can be deduced from the camp experience, he also states that the Lager was "a gigantic biological and social experiment."

In that sense, Auschwitz was more than the destructive utopia, the "geometrical madness" of the master race (51). The organization of the camp, the ways in which the inmates reacted and adapted, involved a "social structure" that revealed fundamental truths about human nature and human laws (44). Toward the end of his life, in *The Drowned and the Saved*, going over the implications of his book on Auschwitz, and examining in depth some of the problems posed, Levi still believed that the camp had been a learning process, that it was a "cruel laboratory," and that one could speak of a "sociology of the camp." He eventually concluded (hoping his metaphor would not be misunderstood), that "the Lager was a University" where he and others opened their eyes and measured human beings. (95, 99, 141).

The combination of scientific curiosity and concern for literary expression, so typical of all of Levi's writings, casts light on the metaphorical texture of *Survival in Auschwitz*. Metaphor is certainly not meant here to call attention to the writer's cleverness. Poetic devices and literary references communicate the unfamiliar, while producing powerful effects of defamiliarization. If Levi highlights animal images (*fressen* opposed to *essen*, prisoners fighting for food and beaten as by cart drivers, human languages sounding like animal noises), it is to reveal the full extent of slavery and degradation. The prisoners' fascination with the steam shovel opening wide its surrealistic steel jaws, and snapping up "voraciously" the clayey soil, is obviously a measure of their obsession with food. The metaphor of the avid mouth hanging from its cables becomes an objective correlative of their chronic hunger (74). Other memories of a sensory nature (the whistle of the trains, the smells of the camp, the feel of the heavy loads to carry) create a network of associations that will continue to haunt the camp survivor.

The skillful use of the present indicative represents Levi's most effective narrative device. It conveys the immediacy of an endless present of toil and suffering. The death camp has separated its victims from their past as well as from any future. Theirs is the present eternity of punishment, the analogue of hell. "This is hell," writes Levi on the same page on which he describes the large gate with its bitterly ironic inscription: "Arbeit Macht Frei," the Nazi's sardonic version of the desperate words inscribed over the portals of Dante's inferno as a dire welcome to the damned: "Lasciate ogni speranza voi ch'entrate"—"Give up all hope, ye who enter."

Such literary devices and echoes (there are other allusions to the circles of Dante's hell, to the devils of Malabolge) also confirm the profound human need to tell, recite, sing, in order to commemorate the horror of events. Every night, Levi reports, the storyteller or "bard" ("cantastorie") secretly comes to their Block, sits himself on a fellow inmate's bunk and chants an "interminable Yiddish rhapsody" in rhymed quatrains—always the same one (58). In melancholic detail, it relates the life in the Lager. This self-mirroring, self-pitying compulsion to tell and listen is like an attempt to preserve at least the "skeleton" of civilization. In the face of this monstrous machine that reduces human beings to beasts, the thousands of individual stories are, as Levi puts it, like the stories of a "new Bible" (66). This notion of a *nuova Bibbia* suggests the obsoleteness of scriptures that fail to account for the atrocities and despair of the Lager. It also stresses, in the form of narratives that might be called "sacred," the mystery of hidden meanings, as well as the themes of survival and posterity.

The problem is not merely how to remain human at the edge of human endurance, but how to protect the form and fabric of human relations. This need to safeguard a skeleton of human institutions—even more than the need for a bartered object or service—underlies the importance Levi attributes to the internal economy, the so-called Market of the camp, complete with daily quotations and the spirit of speculation. Levi singles out the Greek Jews as the shrewdest, the most cunning. He does this with admiration: their sphinxlike demeanor and their transactions are the "repositories" of the worldly wisdom of all the "Mediterranean civilizations." Obliquely, in a radically nonheroic context, Levi harks back to the Ulysses motif. The central concerns are self-preservation, reconstruction, rebirth. Hence the recurrence of the mental image of saving: *salvare.*

The premium is on human ingenuity. In order to survive, even as manually ungifted an individual as Levi had to improvise tools, dig himself in, secrete a shell, create a defensive barrier. The image of Robinson Crusoe comes to mind as one reads about the apocalyptic last ten days of the camp. In a later book, unrelated to the camp experience, Robinson Crusoe is explicitly invoked as an example of human attachment to life.[7]

Motifs of hope and even of faith, whether as a memory of "biblical salvations" (158) or in the form of a "new Bible" made up of human stories of suffering, traverse *Survival in Auschwitz.* These motifs are, however, dialectically linked to a pervasive sense of despair. A central contradiction is thus embedded at the core of Levi's book. Symbolic images of bread, language, and rhapsodic recitation seem to suggest the presence of hope, the possibility of countering despair. Even at the very "bottom," these are a reminder of what human beings cling to: communication, communion, salvation. On the other hand, Levi makes it clear that after Auschwitz there is no room for faith or hope of a transcendental nature. Two statements are categorical on this matter. The first occurs when, after one of the periodic "selections" for the gas chamber, Levi watches a fellow prisoner, temporarily spared, pray and give thanks aloud to God.

> Does Kuhn not understand that what has happened today is an abomination which no propitiatory prayer, no forgiveness, no expiation by the guilty, nothing whatever in the power of man, can ever clean again.
>
> If I were God, I would spit out Kuhn's prayer. (130; It. 164.)

The other statement, even more absolute, appears in the final chapter: ". . . for no other reason than that Auschwitz existed, no one in our age should speak of Providence" (157–58). If there is neither Providence nor God, humans are tragically alone. More than ever, the act of witnessing and communicating becomes in itself an act of faith.

Redemptive Writing, or Levi the Witness

Love of language and clarity of expression are for Levi directly related to his horror of the ineffable. In *The Drowned and the Saved*, he objects to the notion that communication is impossible. On the contrary, to communicate is an imperative: "one can and must" (89). This compelling moral duty to reach the other is evidently related to the familiar fear of not being understood or even heard. The writer's vocation, largely developed in the camp, is linked to the nightmare of the closed ear. Ironically, this nightmare, which originally focused on the image of the sister, became a reality when his own teenage children, as soon as he tried to tell them about the camp experience, got red in the face, began to cry, and escaped to their rooms.[8] Yet silence, or noncommunication through willful obscurity, is a form of suicide. "To write means to transmit," Levi affirms apropos the hermetic German-Jewish poet, Paul Celan, who was ultimately driven to end his own life. Levi goes so far as to suggest that literary obscurity is a form of "pre-suicide."[9]

Levi's own obsession with language and his fascination with the image of the Tower of Babel were intensified in the camp by a linguistic barrier that imposed an additional sense of exile. As an Italian Jew, he did not know Yiddish. This further linguistic alienation in the Lager casts light on his determination to study Yiddish and to familiarize himself with the Ashkenazi tradition. The pursuit of such knowledge also became part of a rescue operation.

Whatever literary inclination Levi may have had before his deportation, it was the camp experience that led him to the notion of redemptive writing. In *The Periodic Table*, he refers to his "liberating book" on Auschwitz ("libro liberatore"), and evokes the immediate postwar period of compulsive writing through which he exorcised the memories that poisoned him. It was the act of writing, he recalls, that "purified" him of the shame of being and the guilt of survival. Telling and writing restored him to his dignity as a human being (159, 151).

The genesis of *Survival in Auschwitz* is therefore associated with a regenerative thrust. The homecoming sequel, *La tregua*, makes it clear moreover that writing, and even "writing well," is far more than a literary exercise. Levi might not have adopted Italo Svevo's art-conscious formula ("Outside the pen there is no salvation"); but it is certain that he came to view writing as a form of renewal, experiencing the "exaltation" of finding the right word (the "parola giusta") and discovering, somewhat to his surprise, that his store of atrocious memories was rich with life-giving seeds. He ultimately even adopted the old Italian adage about the "singing" manuscript: *carta canta*.[10]

Such notions seem to lead to "aestheticism," or the belief in survival through art. But Levi's love of language and literary form is not a substitute religion; it reaches beyond private redemption. Nor can his love for words be called sensuous. His philological passion implies a quest for a more meaningful survival. Hence his love for dictionaries and etymologies, his interest in Yiddish, in the resurrection of his family's Jewish-Piemontese idiom, and his conviction, as he put it in an article entitled "The Best Goods," that the Ashkenazis' linguistic tradition, hybrid and multilingual by nature, was their most precious possession, that the loss of the Yiddish culture that accompanied the dispersion of Eastern Jewry was an "irreparable loss" for humanity.[11]

Humanistic pride in the power of the word and the beauty of language informs Levi's ideal of communication and his residual idealism previously associated with science. The "word" ("parola") comes to have an almost sacred meaning. "We must learn how to make good use of the word, for the gift of language is what distinguishes us from animals" ("la parola ci differenzia dagli animali").[12] This reverence for language underlies the different facets of Levi as writer: the chronicler, the poet, the novelist, the essayist, the interlocutor, the listener, and always the witness. It is what enables the chronicler and the novelist to evoke smells and settings, to write in "technicolor" as Philip Roth reports, to mythologize.[13]

Verbal sensitivity and literary models suffuse his essays and articles. More than Rabelais, whom he liked to call his master, it is Montaigne who comes to mind in terms of the tone, rhythm, color, and sinewy prose. Levi prides himself on being a keen observer (he views his childhood yearning for a microscope as symptomatic) and a good listener to stories. "I am one to whom many things are told"—a trait Philip Roth confirms in his interview. "People are always telling him things."[14]

This disposition to be an attentive observer and a good listener is at the heart of Levi's modesty as a witness. The voice of the chronicler by its very nature is subdued: it is given to understatement rather than self-dramatization. Even though Levi deals with exceptional events, he does not indulge in what Sartre called a "literature of extreme situations."[15] Not having sunk to the bottom of abjection by collaborating with the brutality of the SS, as many others were forced to do, is not for him a matter of pride, but rather of humility. Suspicious of any rhetoric that might depict the victims as saints or heroes, Levi prefers to describe the psychological space where moral choices become almost impossible. In *The Drowned and the Saved*, he explores the "gray zone" that blends the victims and the tormentors. Unwilling to become judgmental, he refers to his *impotentia judicandi*. Levi recalls that Hans Meyer (alias Jean Améry), who never came to terms with the physical violence to which he was subjected, accused him of being "il perdonatore"—the great forgiver.[16]

Revisiting the camp experience, in *The Drowned and the Saved*, forty years after surviving its horrors, Levi thus continued to avoid the vehemence of the prosecutor, preferring the nuanced approaches of the *sciences humaines*. Claude Levi-Strauss thought that Primo Levi was, in his own way, "a great ethnographer." Levi did indeed refer to the Lager as a "ferocious sociological observatory."[17] His writings provide more than ordinary insight into the inner economy and social structure of the camp. They are studded with observations worthy of a political scientist addressing the question of power and authority, or dealing with individual and group behavior under the harshest conditions. Levi is particularly troubled by our ambiguity and fragility in the face of violence.

Some of Levi's most remarkable pages deal with the principle of moral contamination, the transfer of guilt and humiliation, the temptation to become an accomplice in atrocities. The worst crime of the Nazis, the "delitto demoniaco" that revealed the full abyss of evil, was their skill in transforming anyone's brother into a Cain. Levi imagines the satanic laughter of the SS at the thought of having created the infamous *Sonderkommandos*, the special squads of Jews forced to feed the gassed Jewish victims into the crematoriums—which they saw as proof that Jews were inferior beings, willing to accept every humiliation, including self-annihilation.[18]

The bitter humor conveys an indignation that is ultimately a form of judgment. Only Levi's judgment reaches beyond individuals, even beyond Nazi Germany. It points to the moral tragedy when civilized values collapse. And it contains a warning of our "essential fragility." For we are all ready to become the accomplices of power. We forget that we are all in a symbolic ghetto, that just outside its walls the Lords of Death are sealing our fate, and that the death trains stand ready to carry us away.[19] It could happen again.

"We Are Orphans": The Unheroic Note

This fragility makes immaculate virtue a hateful concept. Afraid of the tyranny of abstractions, Levi is ready to denounce the lie of any ideology. He claims, with some irony, that the Fascist racial laws, with their insistence on racial purity, developed in him the pride of being "impure."[20] As a chemist, he knew the reactive value of so-called impure elements. Increasingly, he came to see human beings as they are, warts and all, in their bare reality, echoing perhaps Lear's question: "Is man no more than this? Consider him well." Could not Levi's Italian title, repeated in the preliminary poem of the book, *Se questo è un uomo* (*If This Is a Man*) be read as a distant reminder of Lear's discovery on the heath, that "unaccommodated man" is but a "bare forked animal?" Levi loves Rabelais for describing unadorned, intestinal human nature, "tripes et boyaux" and all the rest. He praises the Renaissance humanist for having given shape to "modern man" in the figure of Panurge, whom he refers to as an antihero, an "eroe a rovescio."[21]

Discrediting the traditional notion of the "hero" is a permanent temptation for Levi. He is bothered by the untruths fostered when individuals or groups don the garb of heroes. Such posturings and fiction-making are, he feels, at the root of all mendacious rewritings of history. Hero worship not only runs counter to reality, voiding historical figures of their substance (the Italian cult of Garibaldi is given as an illustration); it is harmful in that it encourages a historical vacuum and moral irresponsibility in the face of the political present—not to mention simplistic and downright dangerous notions of courage.

Levi's hatred of militarism underlies this antiheroic perspective and explains why he considers Büchner's *Woyzeck* an immortal masterpiece.[22] But there are deeper reasons for his suspicion of the heroic mode. In an article entitled "Eclipse of the Prophets," he inveighed against the madness of delegation, denouncing the intellectual comfort of living by proxy, of revering great figures on pedestals who dispense us from making our own moral choices. Distant idols provide an excuse for our passivity. It is time we learn the bitter truth that prophets are false, that models are harmful, that we are all orphans who must construct our future without submitting to the deceptive inspiration of gilded "heroes," who have done enough harm in human history. It is hardly surprising that Levi found Nietzsche's oracular tone and his myth of the *superman* "profoundly repugnant."[23]

Which is not to say that the concept of heroic deeds or heroic behavior is altogether excluded—even in the unlikely conditions of the camp. But it is at best an adjectival, rather than a substantive concept. Levi observed on several occasions that the "political" prisoners, sustained by the meaning of their struggle, were tougher and better capable of putting up a lucid resistance. Open rebellion was, however, extremely rare; it was even unthinkable, except for very unusual individuals who had not yet been sapped physically. Even in Levi's one "heroic" novel, *Se non ora, quando?* (*If Not Now, When?*), a fictional account of the guerrilla struggle put up by Jewish partisans behind the German lines on the Eastern Front, it is taken for granted that a revolt inside a camp was practically impossible. Even suicide required an act of will that could no longer be summoned.

Rare heroic actions did of course occur, but to Levi they illustrated points not directly related to heroism. One such case, shrouded in uncertainty, is reported in one of the chapters in *Survival in Auschwitz*, entitled "The Last One": Levi and his fellow inmates were forced to attend the public hanging of a man accused of having had contact with rebels in a nearby camp and of plotting a simultaneous mutiny. The man's last cry before dying explains the title of the chapter: "Comrades, I am the last one!" The last one, *l'ultimo* in Italian, can mean that he is literally the last one of the group of rebels. But obviously the word has broader resonances: the last of the heroes, the vanishing of a certain image of man, the end of hope. The moment coincides with the deepest sense of shame and despair. Levi describes the abject silence of the inmates as they are made to watch the trap door open, and then file past the quivering body.

Shame is an important theme. It provides the title of a key chapter in *The Drowned and the Saved*. This individual and collective shame (not a murmur of defiance was heard at the public hanging!) marks the success of the Nazi assault on humanity. Beyond the shame felt at the thought of those few exceptional beings who found the strength to resist, there is the ignominy of contemplating the willful physical and moral destruction of a human being, because it is a crime in which, according to Levi, all humanity has a share.[24]

Levi's reluctance to extol heroic values must also be understood in the context of the nettling questions asked by those who listened to his camp stories when he first returned from Auschwitz. Levi was disturbed by their surprise that the camp inmates did not rebel, that they did not prefer a dignified death to being herded into the gas chambers. Other questions struck him as equally uncomprehending. Why did they not attempt to escape? Why did they not avoid capture and deportation in the first place? The romantic stereotypes implicit in such questions belong, Levi felt, to the world of Monte-Cristo, Papillon, and Hollywood escape fantasies. They had little to do with what is remotely conceivable inside a camp. Levi goes to some lengths to discredit the illusions fostered by literary and cinematographic conventions of heroism which leave no room for realities, such as camp latrines, body lice, and debilitation from hunger and disease.

The unadorned frankness of Levi's tone underscores how closely he links heroic rhetoric to falsehood. He prefers to take a modest view of human nature, reserving his sympathy for the limited and flawed *Mit-mensch*—the fellow human being of "flesh and blood."[25] This affection and even compassion for the human flaw is inscribed in the title of his collection of stories *Vizio di forma*, which explicitly refers to a fundamental defect.

Levi is honest enough to admit that he always lacked physical courage, specifically the ability to "hit back," *zurückschlagen*, as it was called in the camp.[26] Wistfully, he notes that he was not made for vengeance and vindictiveness, that there is nothing of the Count of Monte-Cristo in him (215). Fistfights, even in his schooldays, were not his forte. Though he briefly joined a partisan group in the Piedmont hills in 1943, where he was captured by the Fascist militia and later deported, he admits that he was not cut out to be a guerrilla fighter, that he would not have known how to use a pistol. In the autobiographical *The Periodic Table*, he again refers humorously to his private dreams of courage: the "heroic" struggle of the scientist.

With typical candor, Levi also speaks of his slow puberty and chronic timidity with women. But there is more to this than ordinary sexual self-consciousness. His sense of "unvirility" is admittedly bound up with his self-consciousness as a young Jew, and the belief fostered by schoolmates, at the time Italian fascism was entering its anti-Semitic phase, that circumcision was a sign of sexual inadequacy.

The Jew as Hero?

Jewishness turns into a metaphor. By extension, it applies to all young intellectual Italians in Levi's generation who, even though hostile to fascism, were politically passive. About his submissive generation Levi feels retrospective guilt. In *The Periodic Table*, he recalls how he and his friends were too ironic and too honest to accept fascism, but too skeptical to oppose it actively (63). Resistance took on a private form: the desire not to be contaminated. Theirs was a slow apprenticeship in political reality. The racial laws of 1938 caused a rude awakening; but even then they failed to grasp the full extent of the tragedy. Opposed to violence, they had not understood as yet that violence is often needed to combat the evil of violence, that not to fight back could be a form of complicity. But of course, as Levi remarks, "We are not all born heroes" (223).

The special condition of Italian Jews needs, moreover, to be mentioned. Not only did anti-Semitism appear late and as a foreign import in the history of Italian fascism, but it was endemic neither to the Italian character nor to Italian Fascist ideology. Unlike Jews in Eastern Europe, who lived in a hostile environment, Italian Jews felt very much at home in what they considered their country. Their patriotic zeal had been fostered ever since the unification of Italy under the house of Savoy, which actively promoted the cause of Jewish emancipation. Well-to-do Jewish families in Turin, Levi's hometown, were known to send their sons to military academies. Quite a few prominent Jewish families in fact supported fascism, especially in the early years. Levi's father had enrolled in the party, though having to put on the party uniform on special occasions struck him as a somber masquerade.[27]

Even Jews, however, cultivated nonheroic stereotypes about themselves. Discussing his Piemontese Jewish background under the symbolic title "Argon" (an inert gas) in the opening chapter of *The Periodic Table*, Levi stresses the sedentary, nonbelligerent virtues of his lineage: gentleness, meekness, studiousness, distaste for violence. He smiles at the unhandiness of his forefathers and their progeny. Unfamiliar with the hammer and the blade, what in fact were they able to do with their hands? Little or nothing, is the answer. Levi concludes that if man is *homo faber* or artificer, then Jews were not fully men in that sense. "We knew it, and we suffered from it." Yet there is also a measure of pride in this atrophy, as there is in the special bittersweet humor of the Diaspora, and generally speaking—as he confessed in an interview with Philip Roth—in belonging to a "minority."[28]

Such self-conscious views, Levi knows, are conditioned and exacerbated by popular prejudices. In *If Not Now, When?* (1982), Levi's prize-winning novel about Jewish partisan groups fighting in the forests of Byelorussia, the Russian soldiers who make contact with them cannot quite believe that Jews, whom they know as tailors, petty merchants, or benign patriarchs, can be warriors or even heroes. It is true that Mendel, the Jewish guerrilla fighter, has an instinctive horror of killing, and is weighed down by an atavistic sense of sadness and fatigue. But to the surprise of the Russians and the Poles, who think of Jews as resourceful but cowardly, Mendel the clock maker and his comrades are capable of singular feats of courage.

Unlike the book on Auschwitz, *If Not Now, When?* is fiction, not a personal testimony. But it does illustrate Levi's underlying dream of a heroic stance. He knows—as Mendel, the central character in the novel, knows—that a Jew has to be twice as brave as others to avoid being called a coward. Hence the special need for Jewish partisans. It is with epic pride that Gedaleh, the guerrilla leader, speaks of all those in the ghettoes of Warsaw and Vilna, in Treblinka and Sobibór, who have had the courage to resist—those few survivors who are now fighting in the woods.[29] Heroism, bearing witness, storytelling are all part of the same effort to retrieve dignity. It hardly matters if the action is doomed to failure. At one of the most desperate moments, in what may be a totally futile and self-destructive action, one of the partisans sums it up: "We're fighting for three lines in the history books" (98). Narrative is here part of the struggle against despair.

The story told has its epic as well as profoundly ironic side, including the bitter experience of having to kill despite the ancient awe of the Commandment: "Thou shalt not kill." According to the Polish officer Gedek, the Jewish saga of ghetto and guerrilla resistance inspired the Polish Resistance movement. Once again, heroism is related to the act of narration. The fight against all odds for just three lines in the history books is seen not to be in vain. It appears evident that Levi projects heroic fictional themes to fill what is perceived by him as an absence, a void. It is revealing that Schmulek, the Jew who crawls out of his underground hiding place, envies the band of partisans for having had the courage to take up arms. Levi's admitted sense of inadequacy as a would-be partisan casts light on the episode. Equally revealing is the figure of the Soviet intelligence officer who turns out to be a Jew and who, in his relatively safe function as a neatly uniformed interrogator, also experiences envious admiration as he confides that he would like to "write the story" of the Jewish partisans (269, 298). This "story" is of course exactly the one Levi felt impelled to tell or invent.

Fiction can be another form of witnessing. Levi reminisces that *If Not Now, When?* was born from the stories reported by a friend who was active as a volunteer worker in Milan immediately after the war, and who had knowledge of odd guerrilla bands who found their way to Italy together with countless other refugees and displaced persons. In a postface to the novel, Levi explained that his aim was not to write a "true" story, but rather to reconstruct the "plausible yet imaginary" itinerary of one such guerrilla group.

In describing their topographic and moral itinerary, Levi displays remarkable novelistic gifts, as he evokes landscapes and settings colored by his own homecoming odyssey: the scent of Russian and Polish forests, the music of the rain, the flight of migrating birds, the smell of mushrooms and musk. Against the somber and often frighteningly silent background, he offers glimpses of sharply etched portraits of individual types personifying moral attitudes and issues, invents dialogues that uncannily catch in the Italian idiom the rhythm and inflections of Yiddish sentences—all this against the fateful month-by-month progress of the war on the Eastern Front. Dramatic episodes acquire a subdued epic tonality as the self-doubting, long-suffering protagonists rise to the humble dignity of an *aristocrazia miseranda*—a nobility of woe (It. 104).

Yet courage is never the supreme value. The Germans may understand only force. The Jewish partisans, while accepting this raw reality and meeting the Germans on their own ground, consistently reject the notion that physical valor is the mark of superiority of one person or group over another. Committed to the belief that to kill is wrong, Mendel and his comrades indulge in typical Jewish humor about their own Biblical heroes. When one of the particularly religious women, teased by her comrades about Samson, expresses the view that to kill is always a sin, someone in the group suggests that perhaps Samson did not destroy the Philistines on the day of the Sabbath (228). Levi seems especially taken with a range of Yiddish expressions that undercut the heroic dimension: *nebech, meschugge, narishe bucher* ("pathetic," "crazy," "foolish fellow"). Gedaleh has no difficulty admitting that they are tired of war and heroism, that they all yearn for the constructive labors of peacetime. In one of the finest scenes of the book, after helping Ukrainian villagers reap, the Jewish partisans, sitting in what amounts to an archaic vigil next to the village elder, express their overwhelming fatigue of killing and destroying (207).

Gedaleh—fighter, dreamer, fiddler—is no doubt the most picturesque character in the novel. He seems to come straight out of a Chagall painting, set against the background of the war-torn landscape. His companions are aware of his "many faces" (229), his inner contradictions. Hard to predict, difficult to interpret, he is a creature of excess who throws himself into action with abandon and inventiveness. He has the temperament of a musician, the playfulness of a child, the theatrical instinct of an itinerant comedian, the vitality Levi associates with the Russian soil. The nonbelligerent guerrilla fighter Mendel, with his moral qualms and thirst for justice, may be the central consciousness of the novel, but it is Gedaleh, the cheerful avenger—singing, dancing, and laughing to the accompaniment of his violin—who remains the outstanding character of the book because of his colorful and enigmatic nature. Even his Biblical name stands in apparent contradiction to his exploits. For the Gedaleh of the Old Testament, whom Nebuchadnezzer had named governor of Judea, was in a sense a collaborator, and justly killed by Ishmael, who comes much closer to the image of a partisan. Levi's Gedaleh, on the other hand, lives by an epic honor code exemplified when he tells Mendel: "If your enemy falls, don't rejoice" (307). And in the end he leads his men and women to Palestine, their promised land.

Gedaleh's Chagallian postures are memorable, whether he plays the violin seated on a tree trunk near a river, with his feet in the water, or dances wildly to the tune of his own music, raising his feet high up in the air. It is he who sings the song about the surviving sheep of the ghetto who have been persecuted for a thousand years and are now set on vengeance, each

of them symbolically carrying the stone that crushed Goliath's skull. Gedaleh's song twice repeats the words that provide the title of the book: "If
not now, when?" But Gedaleh is more than a Chagallian figure echoing
rabbinical statements. Talkative, articulate, endowed with a narrator's
gifts, supremely inventive and even crafty in action, he is an Ashkenazi
Ulysses dedicated to the art of survival, to leading his comrades to safety,
and ultimately, after a long odyssey of exploits and perilous travels, back
to their true "homeland."

The Need for a New Courage

Survival is not all. Homecoming can be a bitter experience. The end of *La
tregua* (the accurate translation of the title is "The Respite," not "The
Reawakening") records how, after the camp liberation and the railway odyssey, after the early euphoria and illusion of resurrection, there followed
an incurable feeling of emptiness. "Tregua" suggests a temporary respite
before succumbing, now that hourly physical suffering was no longer all-
absorbing, to the lasting sense of powerlessness and nothingness ("nul-
lità") of existence (It. 211). After the poison of Auschwitz, how indeed was
one to find the strength and the joy to face daily life and daily struggles?
The end of *La tregua* describes the feeling of despondency that overcame
Levi upon his return to Turin, the sense of being weighted down by centuries of oppression. He could not forget the brutal kapo command at dawn:
Wstawać (Arise!), which continued to jar in his ear. The Polish *wstawać*,
like the German *aufstehen*, can of course be given several meanings. It
refers, literally, to the quotidian camp reality. But it could also connote
rising up for the survival struggle, and ultimately might suggest some
form of recovery or resurrection. The final paragraph of *La tregua* dispels,
however, any notion that the Lager experience has been overcome. "Nothing was true outside the Lager" is the terrible sentence that sums up the
overwhelming feeling that everything else—the liberation, the return to
the family, the return to work—was but a dream, a brief vacation, a mi-
rage of stability, marred by deep anguish and the steady fear of chaos and
disintegration.

   How, under these circumstances, was one to gather the strength to live,
to meet the demands of family and work? Levi was to find some stability
in his responsibilities as manager of a chemical plant, and later—but only
to some extent—as a fully committed professional writer. After Auschwitz, together with the shame of survival, came the difficulty of giving
battle when the enemy was now within. Levi's well-known smile covered
the unmedicable sadness of one who had understood that even our capac-

ity for unhappiness is limited. Afflicted by a sense of emptiness, Levi continued his daily existence aware of the constant presence of an abyss. But
what does it mean to be a Pascal without faith?

Where, after the experience of the camp, was one to find the will to
give battle ("dare battaglia") in everyday life? Levi speculated on various
forms of courage related to intellectual survival. *La ricerca delle radici*—
his personal anthology, *In Search of Roots*—is in large part a search for
answers. There was the nobility and heroism of science, even though Levi
himself could become ironic about the exploits of the research laboratory
as an escape from political engagement. But there were, undeniably, noble
achievements in the pursuit of knowledge. As a paradoxical example, Levi
extols Darwin, who denied the human species a privileged position in the
universe, yet through his intellectual courage reaffirmed "the dignity of
man" (It. 23). If Levi values *Moby Dick*, this is primarily because Mel-
ville's epic illustrates the search ("ricerca") for full human experience.
Such a perception of mankind's tragic drive once again recalls Dante's
Ulysses roaming the seas in quest of adventure and the broadest moral
consciousness.

On a less exalted plane, there is the dignity of one's craft or profession,
the ennobling relation between man and his tools. Levi never ceased mar-
veling at the adventures of technology. One of the books featured in his
personal anthology of seminal texts is a novel by Jean Vercel that happened to be the first book to fall into his hands during the last chaotic days
in Auschwitz, and which recounts a "technological adventure" confirming
that human beings can be heroic in peaceful endeavors. Levi's lasting admiration for *homo faber* is developed more fully in a book he published
more than thirty years later, *La chiave a stella* (*The Monkey Wrench*),
whose protagonist, Tino Faussone, is a constructor of cranes, pylons, and
offshore oil derricks, carrying out his work in distant and often dangerous
regions. Faussone's love of his craft, including victories and defeats, comes
close to epic pride. He himself compares his emblematic monkey wrench
to the knight's sword. Whether in Alaska, India, or Russia, he goes into
battle, sustained by the honor code of his profession.

The heroic struggle against nature and matter leads Levi to invest the
human mind with philosophical dignity. He takes pride in that, through
trial and error, the human race has over the centuries strived to master the
material world. Among the inspirational works of his private anthology,
Levi included S. Thorne's "The Search for Black Holes," which he considered both tragic and uplifting. Under the title "Siamo soli" ("We Are
Alone"), Levi explains in almost Pascalian terms that the ability to con-
ceive of black holes and the awareness that the violent and hostile universe

was not created for the human race (always crushed and defeated) are in themselves a victory of human intelligence over blind forces (It. 229).

The nobility of work, the nobility of the mind: it is not surprising that Levi should be led back to the power of words and the craft of writing. In his conversations with Faussone, the expert rigger with the symbolic monkey wrench, the narrator—Levi himself—makes the point that he too, as a writer, is a "rigger" of sorts, painfully assembling words, sentences, and thoughts, always with the risk they will shift or even fall apart. Levi's faith in the clarity of well-assembled words and thoughts suggests a fundamental humanistic optimism. Throughout his life, he believed, or liked to believe, that words were in the service of meaningful communication, that one must therefore write in a clear and orderly fashion. This belief at times verged on naive assumptions, surprising in a person who had stared into the face of irrational cruelty. In *The Drowned and the Saved*, Levi asserts that there are no problems that cannot be solved by good will and trust in a round-table discussion. He knew better, of course. Not even writing could be unequivocal in conveying meanings and giving courage. Narration was a struggle against despair, but did not protect against it.

It is moving to watch Levi's efforts to find new forms of courage. His condition of unbeliever—he calls it his "laicità"—did not make things easier. With subdued humor, Levi observed that you cannot change the rules of the game toward the end of the match. Conversion at the point of drowning seemed unworthy to him.[30] He knew, as he put it in one of his poems, that he had seen the full horror of the Medusa,[31] meaning that he knew there is no providence, no divine justice, no justification for suffering and evil. The scientific perspective only magnified human insignificance and exacerbated feelings of futility, the awareness that not only human beings, but culture and civilization itself were mortal.

This sobering view of the insignificance, if not the nothingness, of humanity in a scientific perspective casts light on what in Levi's work might be considered a marginal addiction to *fantascienza*, or science fiction, exemplified by texts collected in *Storie naturali* (1966). These stories convey, with bitter humor, the fear of a takeover by machines or natural forces of the supposed primacy of the human species. Levi's science-fiction exercises are far from innocuous. An imaginary technological miracle such as the Torec (the "Total Recorder"), an electronic device capable of transmitting sensations to the brain without the mediation of the senses, leaves the subject with the feeling of an utter void when the tape has been played out. Levi observed on the back cover of his book that his science-fiction inventions were not unrelated to the trauma of the Lager. Their Kafkalike humor indeed points to monstrous transgressions, like systematic genocide, engendered by the nightmare of rational planning.

Even the theme of survival is viewed in a somber perspective. In an ironic essay on coleoptera, reprinted in *L'altrui mestiere* (*Other People's Trades*), in which Kafka's hallucinatory vision is evoked, Levi imagines how, after a global nuclear catastrophe, the beetles will supplant humans as the new kings of the earth (It. 180). The logic of such black humor leads to images of self-destruction. One of the more disturbing stories in *Storie naturali* describes the effects of a newly discovered substance, versamina, which converts suffering into pleasure, so that the individual who ingests it, especially if the appetite for life has been lost, is no longer protected.

The theme of suicide, hidden and not so hidden, runs through Levi's entire work. The Torec involves a movement toward death. At the end of his chapter on intellectuals in Auschwitz (*The Drowned and the Saved*), Levi states that the aim of life is "the best defense against death," and that in the Lager the urgency of the survival instinct was such that there was literally no time to think about death. Repeatedly, Levi observed that suicide was a rarity in the camp. The very strength to carry it out was lacking. But things changed once out of the camp. Hence the importance of the closing paragraph of *La tregua*. Levi reports on numerous occasions that suicide became a recurrent temptation for those who survived, and that it was related in part to the shame or guilt of surviving. Between survival and suicide there was, it would seem, a dialectical link. Levi's ultimate act of April 11, 1987, when he let himself fall to his death, was evidently on his mind much earlier. In a self-revealing article about psychological tests in industry, Levi recalls how, shortly after the war, he was subjected to a questionnaire which contained the surprising question: "Do you sometimes think that suicide might solve your problems?" Levi remembers his silent answer: "Perhaps yes, perhaps no. In any case, it is not in you that I will confide."[32] The notion of such a personal secret is no doubt related to Levi's lifelong conviction that suicide itself remained a mystery. Recalling the self-inflicted death of the "suicidal philosopher" Hans Meyer (alias Jean Améry), Levi wrote in *The Drowned and the Saved* that every suicide gives rise to a galaxy of nebulous explanations ("nebulosa di spiegazioni"), but ultimately remains inexplicable.[33]

The word "drowned" ("sommersi"), which had already appeared in one of the chapter headings of *Survival in Auschwitz*, points to the metaphor of a shipwreck. Self-destruction as an act of will and a manifestation of freedom implies a tragic resolution. We return once again to the image of Dante's Ulysses, who, after all, in his tenacious quest for adventure and moral experience past the pillars of Hercules, finds a sea death.[34] But this shipwreck is associated with lucidity, dignity, and intellectual courage in pursuit of what Dante calls "virtude e conoscenza"—virtue and knowledge.

APPENDIX: SVEVO'S WITNESS

A Crypto-Jew

Italo Svevo seems to have been embarrassed by his Jewishness; he hardly ever mentions it in his writings. His fictional work simply elides the subject. In his self-promotional autobiographic essay, *Profilo autobiografico*, there is not a word about his Jewish family background.[1] He elusively refers to his foreign-born father as an *assimilato* in the city of Trieste, which itself is referred to as a "crogiolo assimilatore"—the Italian equivalent of melting pot. Although the *Profilo* opens with a reference to his provocative pen name ("Svevo-the Swabian bringing the Germanic into fraternal alliance with Italo-the Italian") not the slightest reference is made to his recognizably Jewish name, Ettore Aron Schmitz.

True, as Svevo's biographer John Gatt-Rutter reminds us, the *Profilo* was drafted in 1928, at the height of Fascist nationalist feelings, and understandably lays stress on Svevo's credentials as a lifelong Italian patriot.[2] Thus the *Profilo* hastens to state that both his grandfather and father married Italian women, but again there is not a word about the totally Jewish background of these wives. Svevo himself married into a family of converts, the prosperous Venezianis. His wife's mother was a Moravia—another recognizably Jewish name, indeed the very name of Svevo's own mother, for Svevo married a cousin once removed. Livia Veneziani had been raised as a Catholic, and to please her, at a time when she was ill, Svevo had himself baptized, though he remained hostile to all religion. His atheism is probably what Livia had in mind when, in her biography of Svevo, she referred to his "pessimistic vein."[3]

Following Svevo's lead, Livia in *My Husband's Life* (*Vita di mio marito*) remains altogether evasive about his Jewish origins and family atmosphere. It is the Italian background that she stresses. "The son of an Italian mother, he felt totally Italian." Although she covers Svevo's literary career in considerable detail, she fails to mention that his first published article, a unique concession to a Jewish theme, was quite revealingly on Shakespeare's Shylock. She refers at length to Svevo's friendship with Joyce, even evoking discussions between the two writers about the figure of Leopold Bloom, but she does not so much as hint at the fact that Joyce on these occasions consulted Svevo at length on matters Jewish. Rather, she underlines those aspects of Svevo that make him a "uomo europeo"—not once forgetting to insist that he was first and foremost Italian and Triestino.[4]

What is more striking still is that in his fictional writings Svevo seems to avoid all themes, subjects, or characters even remotely Jewish. H. Stuart Hughes in his survey of Jewish Italian writers, *Prisoners of Hope*, understandably asked himself: "How Jewish was he, if he seldom mentioned his origins and wrote novels devoid of Jewish characters?"[5] The answer is far from simple, and goes to the heart of Svevo's indirections, oblique strategies, ambivalences, and irony.

The hard fact is that Ettore Aron Schmitz's childhood and adolescence were steeped in Jewish-Triestino life, surrounded by relatives and family friends whose names ring like a directory of Trieste's Jewish community: Pincherle, Cohen, Weiss, Wertheimer, Ziffer, Levi—including also the more Italian-sounding Jewish names of Morpurgo, Finzi, Vivante, Ancona, Camerini. Moreover, it appears that his parents were observant, that he attended the Jewish elementary school directed by the chief rabbi of Trieste, and that when his practical-minded father decided to send him and his two brothers Elio and Adolfo to a German school (German was considered essential for a business career in Trieste), he chose the Brüssl'sche Handels-und Erziehungsinstut in Segnitz on the river Main, whose Jewish headmaster, Spier, catered in large part to a clientele of German-Jewish business families. Svevo's reluctance to deal openly with his Jewishness is all the more remarkable in that the Austro-Hungarian port of Trieste, which prided itself on its relatively independent status, was, unlike Austria, where anti-Semitism ran rampant, a city where Jews had known early emancipation, were respected, and enjoyed a leading role in the community.

Even in the private papers, notes, reminiscences, and correspondence, there are surprisingly few references. The few exceptions do not amount to much. About Kafka ("his last literary love" according to his wife Livia[6]), whose condition as a multiple outsider offers a number of parallels with his own, Svevo observed with typical understatement that to be a Jew was "not a comfortable position." Much earlier, in a letter to his wife, referring to a career possibility, he noted pessimistically: "I sense that, as we Jews say, the Messiah will not come from that direction." Elsewhere, he sallied in an almost Existentialist manner: "It isn't race which makes a Jew, it's life." In one of his last letters to Mme Benjamin Crémieux there is a playfully bitter allusion to those "blessed Rumanians, with all those anti-Semites." And in an article on Richard Wagner published in the same Trieste newspaper that had published his piece on Shylock he noted, with apparent objectivity, that the composer's anti-Semitism was of a cultural and critical nature, that it was based on the notion that Jews are cosmopolitan "mediators," therefore incapable of genuine artistic creativity.[7]

It is not surprising that H. Stuart Hughes found Svevo's rare references to his Jewish origins inconclusive and puzzling. In the wake of the critic Giacomo Debenedetti, who blamed Svevo for having repressed the Jewish element, Hughes even refers to a brand of Jewish anti-Semitism illustrated by Otto Weininger, who defined the Jewish psychology as one of "feminine passivity suffused with self-hatred." Hughes rejects this extreme view in favor of a more smiling notion of crypto-Jewish survival humor.[8]

Hughes's intuition of literary disguises and transfers of the Jewish theme is undoubtedly correct, and finds powerful support in a late, unfinished narrative published posthumously, *Corto viaggio sentimentale* (*Short Sentimental Journey*). In it, a wandering protagonist, Signor Aghios, is made thoroughly uncomfortable by a fellow traveler, the boisterously xenophobic insurance inspector Borlini, who expresses suspicion about Aghios's non-Italian (Greek) name, accusing him moreover in a Philistine manner of being a "poet in disguise" ("poeta travestito"). The hostile glance of the Fascist Borlini in the railroad compartment corresponds to Signor Aghios's multiple insecurity and disguises. For the Greek name—Aghios claims apologetically to have only a very "distant" Greek origin—is not only a recognizable pun (Aghios/Hagios, the saint), but brings to mind another traveler also away from his Penelope, and also carrying an ancient scar, Ulysses. But the ironic Ulysses theme is in itself a transparent transfer. Borlini's ostensibly Greek-directed xenophobia has all the earmarks of anti-Semitism. And Aghios, self-conscious about genetic determinism, experiences a characteristic blend of guilt, atavistic resignation, vulnerability, and pride in not belonging. Some of Aghios/Svevo's statements have an ironic confessional ring: "It's convenient to belong to another race. It is as though one were perpetually traveling; "If one is born in a certain way, one stays that way"; "I come from a more ancient race than the Celts." The reference to the Celts is a signal that even the link with Ulysses has a special meaning: the Greek and Jewish motifs are bonded in the literary friendship with Joyce. In a lecture on Joyce given late in his life, Svevo remarked that Joyce's Ulysses, a transplant in the

modern world, respects the gods and loves his family as does "the Jew
Bloom," and that there exists a singular affinity between the Jewish and
the Irish people, two races with dead languages ("... *i due popoli dalla
lingua morta*").[9]

Not surprisingly, Svevo's choice of pen name is more revealing than
would appear at first. His pseudonym provocatively and defensively
couples the Germanic and Italian elements in his background, referring
all at once to his German schooling, his Triestino irredentist allegiances,
and his ambitions as a writer whose native idiom, far removed from the
Tuscan literary language, condemns him to write in a foreign tongue. But
there is perhaps more in this contrived Italo-German name than a mere
allusion to the two national identities. The Italian-sounding Svevo (the
Swabian) refers to a region in Germany precisely in the manner in which
many names of Italian Jews (Morpurgo or Moravia, the name of his
mother, are good examples) refer to specific regions or towns. Such a sly,
imbedded "Jewish" signal becomes even more likely in view of the information his brother Elio gives concerning the paternal grandfather Abramo
Adolfo Schmitz, who was a native of Köpchen, a town in Transylvania
where the Germans spoke a Swabian dialect.[10]

Themes and Variations

The question of Svevo's Jewishness is not merely a matter of setting the
record straight, or of diagnosing a fairly well-known malaise of the cultur-
ally assimilated Jew. In the lifelong struggle between Schmitz and Svevo,
between the family/businessman and the artist, it may now seem that the
ultimate victory rests with Svevo the artist. But such a view fails to take
into account the distinctive Svevian shuttle between art and life, and his
thematic inspiration—whether the suicidal maladjustment of Alfonso
Nitti in *Una vita*, the premature sense of defeat of Emilio Brentani in *Senilità*, Zeno's painfully humorous and estranged insight into his own consciousness, or Aghios's wily development of survival values—always
rooted in a keen perception of family situation and experience.

The key document, one with which Svevo was intimately acquainted
and to which he even contributed, is his younger brother Elio's diary. Elio
Schmitz (1863–86), who revered his elder brother, died in his early twen-
ties of a chronic illness. The *Diario*, which gives detailed accounts of the
family atmosphere and of the brothers' common school experience, adolescence, and early efforts at entering into the world of adults in fin-de-siècle
Trieste, was carefully kept by the family, and was released for publication
in 1973 by Svevo's daughter, Letizia, almost a century after it was written.

From Svevo's wife, Livia, we know that Svevo, deeply affected by his brother's death, preserved the *Diario* "religiously" throughout his life "like a precious relic." [11]

Elio and Ettore were very close. Together they faced paternal dictates. They studied, wrote, practiced the violin in the same room. When it came to literary ambitions, Elio experienced them vicariously, and with pride. Unconditionally and touchingly, he accepted Ettore's intellectual superiority and pretended to do nothing more important than serve as his devoted chronicler. Elio's admiration and cult of memories provided Ettore with a mirrorlike referent. Many years later, he advised a budding English writer to look at himself daily in a textual "looking glass" by writing down an account of his day in order to achieve self-knowledge and "a great sincerity." [12] In a sense, Elio's *Diario* provides the basic example of such a private looking glass, and constitutes an oblique confession made even more personal by the several pages Svevo contributed in his own hand, which focus on derogatory self-assessments.

Objectively, Elio's *Diario* casts precious light on family values in the Jewish community of Trieste, and more generally on the social, political, and artistic life of the city at a time when *irredentismo*, the movement for unification with Italy, inspired many of the liberal elements of this thriving Adriatic port that was part of the Austro-Hungarian empire. We learn of the two brothers' deep attachment to their native city, of their conflicts with their father, of the pressures of the business ethos and careerism, of the young men's sense of servitude and humiliation in a bureaucratized society. Their common experience in the German boarding school in Segnitz, their artistic ambitions and projects, their procrastinations and uncertainties, are all vividly described and help us understand better some of the recurrent themes in Svevo's work. Svevo's own character traits are sharply delineated.

About the Jewish background, the brother's diary is particularly open and informative. Elio provides a genealogy of the large family; he talks candidly about prevailing opposition to intermarriage; he gives otherwise unavailable details about the festive Friday evening meals; the Jewish wedding of their sister Natalia under the traditional canopy; the celebration of Purim, which their father did not like; their father's election to Hatan Bereshit, an honor which entitled him to read the beginning of the Pentateuch during services in the synagogue. Repeated mention is made of anti-Semitism, especially of the Viennese variety. Of particular interest is the account of Ettore's humiliation when, after much time spent in the waiting room, he was refused an entry-level job for which his knowledge of four languages qualified him "because the candidate is a Jew." (202,

203, 221, 236–37, 256, 290.) Is it a simple coincidence if Svevo's first article, on Shylock, was written just a few weeks after this experience?[13]

As cultural background, the *Diario* of Elio Schmitz is also a precious document about the social, economic, and artistic climate of Trieste. This port city (Austria's only direct access to the Mediterranean), this bastion of Mitteleuropa business mentality, enjoyed a surprisingly rich theatrical life. A number of theatres offered first-rate performances of plays ranging from Alfieri to the most recent authors—Giacosa, Sardou, Dumas father and son, Strindberg, Ibsen—and invited such great stars as Eleanora Duse. The theatre life, which the two brothers followed keenly, was part of the *italianità* of Trieste.

For Ettore and Elio, the images of Trieste and of Italy tended to merge. As Triestine students in Germany, they felt entirely Italian. But in their case the notion of *patria* ("fatherland") was both abstract and concrete: abstract, because they were not Italian, but Austrian subjects; concrete, in that their notion of *patria* was focused not on a nation, but on their native city. One thing is clear: neither brother felt any allegiance to Austria, and the idea of compulsory military service in the Austrian army, with a possibility of having to fight for causes not their own, was repulsive to them.

Trieste was thus, for young Svevo, both a physical and a spiritual entity. Among the aspects of Svevo's work that Joyce later valued was his ability to use his native city as an integral part of his fiction's thematic structure. The admiration was mutual. As Schmitz's Berlitz School English teacher, Joyce read to his much older pupil a story from *Dubliners* which he had recently completed. Both writers, in different ways and contexts, mythologized their native cities, raising them to the level of poetic topos and protagonist.

Elio's *Diario* reveals how profound the two brothers' attachment to Trieste really was. Ever since their childhood, they referred lovingly and possessively to "la mia bella Trieste" (205). Exiled to school in Germany, they experienced a poignant nostalgia often associated with the image of trains, which, they felt, must all lead to Trieste. The sense of exile became particularly painful in later years, when Elio, for reasons of business and health, had to leave Trieste for Cairo, and wrote that he cried like a child, exactly as he did when he and Ettore left for Segnitz (297).

Yet that love was ambivalent. Elio repeatedly mourns over Trieste's comedown, over its subservience to material interests which brings its business needs into unavoidable conflict with its patriotic idealism. A rift between commercial aspirations and irredentist yearnings corresponded to a deeper political rift between the Austrian and the Italian side of the Triestine mentality. However, this crisis of conscience was not limited to

Trieste. It may not be exaggerated to say that Trieste, in Svevian terms, stood for a more pervasive malaise, or even sickness of the European bourgeois conscience, and that the diagnostic and prognostic aspects of his work point to a calamitous future.[14] *La coscienza di Zeno*, Svevo's novel about "consciousness" and "conscience" written in the wake of World War I, concludes revealingly with the image of an apocalyptic manmade explosion that marks the end of human life on this globe.

Though essentially private and centered on family matters, Elio's *Diario* provides a political *basso continuo*. Much of this still has to do with the home atmosphere, for his family, like many other Triestine business families, was divided over the question of irredentism. Uncle Vito felt committed to the Italian destiny of Trieste, while Elio's father had strong Austrian sympathies. Elio remembers arguments between these two over the outcome of the Franco-Prussian War. His father predictably took the side of the Prussians, asserting that they would soon be in Paris. Eighteen-seventy, the year of the Prussian victory, seems indeed to be a key date in Elio's political memory. This childhood point of reference is of particular interest if one considers that the opening page of *La conscienza di Zeno*, written some forty years later, associates the date of 1870 with Austria and the memory of the first cigarettes Zeno smoked—the beginning of a lifelong "vice" from which he would never free himself.

The family's division over allegiance to Austria or to Italy is not surprising. Many Triestine business people dealt primarily with Austria or were employed by Austrian firms. Business interests and family values were enmeshed. The business community prized solidity and solvency over idealistic rhetoric. Its symbol was the strongbox ("cassa forte"—263) and its measure of accomplishment the acquisition of wealth or, at the very least, gainful employment. Business metaphors informed everyday conversation, and even found their way, naturally though often humorously, into the style of Elio's diary. There is talk of a promissory note ("obligazione"—221) signed by Ettore, committing himself vis-à-vis his brother to complete his play *Ariosto governatore* by a given date. (The play never got beyond its initial stages.) A few weeks later, Ettore signed five bills of exchange ("cambiali"—231), engaging himself to complete the five acts of a new comedy with a deadline of twenty days each. The signed bills and promissory notes anticipate the motif of the repeatedly postponed last cigarette, and clearly indicate how early, in Svevo's case, the image of a transaction and the notion of a transgressed deadline are related to the act of writing.

Typically, the brothers also rebel against the business mentality associated with Trieste. Elio complains that money mania ("denaromania"—

295) clashes with lofty dreams. The conflict is not abstract for the two would-be artists. The ethos of commerce embodied by their father signified a Philistine hostility to any artistic activity that endangered the "seriousness" of purpose befitting young men. Elio aspires to be a musician and a composer. In a most interesting image of a parallel sacrifice involving politics, survival, and dreams of artistic creativity, the violin plays a symbolic role. "Trieste is going from bad to worse, which is precisely my situation. The city must sacrifice its nationality for the sake of commerce, just as I must sacrifice the violin to earning money" ("... io devo sagrificare [sic] il violino al guadagno"—264). The violin is not an empty image. It was one thing to have a subscription to the theater, and quite another to aim at an artistic career. Elio notes laconically that his father dismissed the violin teacher (252).

The Schmitz family, like most Jewish families, encouraged sentimental values. Elio and Ettore grew up with the cult of the living and the dead. Births and deaths were celebrated with great emotion. The deceased were not allowed to be forgotten. Month after month, year after year, the brothers evoke the memory of Uncle Vito and visit the grave of their sister Noemi. But the dominant values were Mitteleuropa "bourgeois": aversion to idleness ("ozio"—198), obsession with "health" both physical and social, preoccupation with illness as "disorder," addiction to cures and thermal resorts, respect for doctors, law and order. Typically again, even though Elio rebels against materialism, claiming that money desecrates all noble causes, he nonetheless subscribes on almost every page of his diary to the articles of faith of his milieu. Much like Svevo's later fictional work, the diary is constantly astride a critique and an apologia of the bourgeoisie. To be "healthy" ("essere uomo sano"—294) is of course a perfectly legitimate desire on the part of one afflicted with a severe form of nephritis, but the ambition is also symbolic and ironic (198, 294). The role of doctors appears as significantly ambivalent: enjoying a power and a prestige largely grounded in their patients' fears, they are also—to the extent that they constitute a guild protecting one another's ignorance— the butt of resentment and caricature.

Over this family world enfolded in the larger world of Triestino Jewish business families, the father looms as a heavy presence, both oppressive and repressive. Resenting his son's illness and the expenses it entailed, sacrificing everything to business concerns, increasingly depressed over money matters, Francesco Schmitz is moreover revealed to be commercially inept, a prisoner of outdated methods. Yet the son feels the constant need to justify himself in the eyes of his father, even within the privacy of his own thoughts. And what is true of Elio is also true of Svevo and of his fictional world. He will accept and internalize the very values he questions and denies. Schmitz/Svevo's life and fiction (hence the importance of the word *coscienza* in his most famous title) display a consciousness unresolvedly polarized between the exigencies of the "artist" and those of the "businessman."

Ettore: The Flaw

Reflecting or anticipating Ettore's way of thinking, the brother's diary provides a curious mirror image, though it is not always clear who the beholder of the mirror is.[15] Elio, age sixteen, writes: "Ettore is now 18 years old. He is something of a poet, and it seems that he has much talent. He writes verse" (215). Over the next few years, the diary reveals Ettore's basic character traits. He is moody, secretive, distracted, often apathetic in appearance, but these are deceptive signs hiding an intense inner life. He can be a prankster, but most often he is described by Elio in the act of reading or writing. He uses all his savings to buy books, and he resists his father's strict injunction not to read at night. (Elio even claims that if Ettore has one shoulder higher than the other, it is because of prolonged periods of reading.) At school, his predilection goes to German literature, and he proclaims the superiority of Schiller over all other literary geniuses. He reads Shakespeare in a German translation, knows *Hamlet* by heart, and is haunted by the famous lines about being or not being. But his greatest exaltation seems to have come earlier, from secretly reading all the French novels he could get hold of.

To achieve literary fame was Svevo's *idée fixe*, and in his dreams of literary glory he first turned to drama—a genre for which he had little talent. Much like Stendhal, he discovered in time that his mind was basically averse to theatrical structures, which left little room for ambivalences and elusive strategies. In quick succession, to the amazement and dismay of his brother, he began and abandoned a number of theatrical projects: *Ariosto governatore, Il primo amore, Le roi est mort, vive le roi, I due poeti*—these are just some of the titles. After a while, his admiring brother almost lost faith in him. The diary, at a certain point, is studded with remarks such as: "I don't know whether he'll complete it," "He won't finish this one either," "This one too will end up in the fire" (232, 235).

Elio's worries go beyond the immediate present; they point to fundamental problems of Svevo's literary temperament. Procrastination, changes in direction, and discouragement were to afflict him throughout the years. Yet there was also the stubborn will to write, even if resolutions, like Zeno's famous last cigarette, led from postponement to postponement.

The link between "smoke" ("il fumo") and literary determination is symptomatic as well as symbolic. Hence the promissory notes he cannot honor, and the further commitment that if he does not finish the play by a given day, he is to pay his brother over three whole months ten *soldi* for every cigarette he smokes. A chain of smoke firmly links Elio's portrait of young Ettore Schmitz to the antihero of Svevo's great novel written forty years later.

For Ettore's flaws lead to his literary *eureka*, after which point his weaknesses are transformed into artistic virtues. As we have seen, Elio reports that Ettore triumphantly announced one day that he had discovered his true subject, which was to be called *Difetto moderno*, or *The Modern Flaw*. There follows an entry in Svevo's hand dealing exclusively with his shortcomings as a would-be writer. He blushes at his misconceptions, abstruseness, ugly style, hackneyed sentences. This exercise in self-criticism and despondency corresponds to a "negative" moving force that will lead up to three novels whose titles are in themselves revealing: *L'inetto* (*The Inept One*—a title his publisher forced him to change to *Una vita*), *Senilità*, and *La coscienza di Zeno*.

If the *Diario* provides a mirror image for Elio's private use, it is also a mirror in which Ettore could observe himself. His own entries make clear that he read his brother's entries on a regular basis. After his brother died, he kept his diary as an intimate belonging. His wife Livia's testimonial is categorical. He not only treated it as a cherished relic, but more precisely "mirrored himself" ("si rispecchiava") in the consciousness of the irreplaceable witness who had been the confidant of his literary dreams, and had believed in his destiny as a writer.[16] This belief in his glorious future must have sustained Svevo, though he must also have been amused, to say the least, by Elio comparing himself to an admiring historian of Napoleon (295), especially since Napoleon stood as the very embodiment of careerism and decisive action. Allusions to Napoleon, in fact, appear repeatedly in Svevo's writings, usually as ironic signals of an impossible or undesirable heroic model.

The parodic and deflating mood so characteristic of Svevo's work already informs his own entries in the *Diario*, most particularly in the severe, self-deprecatory analyses in which he indulges. He makes fun of the "grandi destini" to which the diary seems dedicated (219). Even banal episodes are debunked. He mocks his glib flirtation with a young actress. But even this mockery, in dialogue form, remains characteristically incomplete, confirming Elio's complaint that he cannot ever finish anything.

Elio, or the Witness as Model

The mirror also functions in reverse, so to speak. As Ettore reads Elio's diary, he sharpens his perspective on his brother. This perspective has a triple dimension: what he knows from daily contact, what he gathers as reader-participant, what he understands posthumously as he remembers, or re-reads this personal record in conjunction with his own activities as novelist. It appears very likely indeed that Elio's character traits were an important literary inspiration for Svevo after his brother's death, and that he used his brother as a model for some of his most memorable characters: Alfonso Nitti, Emilio Brentani, and Zeno Cosini. Certain psychological tensions and themes dear to Svevo are clearly prefigured in Elio's account of himself: the permanent awareness of the conflict between the world of art and the world of commerce; a sense of frustration, melancholy, and self-doubt; the obsession with aging, disease, and death; the relationship between illness, irony, and renunciation; the refuge in illness and the corresponding fear of life; and above all, an underlying sense of destiny as failure.

In a sense, Elio welcomed his illness. It became an alibi for his dedication to art as well as a justification for failure. Seeking refuge in inertia, he radicalized his passivity. One is reminded of Sartre's diagnosis of young Flaubert adopting a posthumous stance. Hence the irony of the patient waiting for a cure in which he does not really want to believe. Svevo as novelist was to develop at length this sense of the great sweetness of defeat.[17] Zeno resists the cure in large part because he discovers that so-called health is the real disease.

In his brother's diary, Ettore could read contradictory signals. There was the guilt of self-blame that came from seeing his inadequacies with his father's eyes; he accepted his milieu's severe judgment of the "idler" and "good-for-nothing." He shudders at the thought of becoming a "vizioso" or a "uomo da nulla" (257). Writing was indeed seen by Elio as a form of death, associated with a morbid cult of memories and a disbelief in the future. Revealingly, he has the family carpenter build a "box" which is to become the coffin-like repository of his diary and his letters. Yet the act of writing is also seen as futile. Elio refers disparagingly to the silly scribblings ("sciocchezze") that fill his useless notebook ("inutile libraccio"— 278–79, 266).

As he re-read his brother's notebook, Svevo must surely have empathized with the steadily felt tension between unattainable idealism and despondency. Elio's diary plays variations on the themes of self-improvement, moral purpose, gratuitous love of art, elevation through creative effort. Yet concomitantly with the search of a secret dimension, rooted in the sense of precious selfhood, there is a conviction that things can only go from bad to worse, and a cruel capacity to see oneself as inferior to others. Filled with self-pity, Elio is moreover a constant reminder of the "unfairness" of life. Only Svevo, having reached maturity and become resigned to the unpredictable fluctuations of existence, will translate this "unfairness" into a paradoxical and ludic notion of the "originality" of life.[18]

Svevo must also have savored the bittersweet melancholy ("dolce malinconia"—253) that ironically sets Elio's inner fog against the sunny land- and seascape of Trieste. In his novels, but perhaps nowhere more masterfully than in *Senilità*, Svevo will continually exploit the ironic gap between the subjective reality of his protagonists and the objective reality of the city, associating sickness and pain with the poetic evocation of his native Trieste.

This sense of lucidity about one's powerlessness and blind spots, this immersion in passivity and conviction (or hope) that life chooses for us, this quest for that which one does not really desire, will take many shapes in the fictional work of Svevo. The uses of the brother's diary are revealing because the specific artistic elaboration, with its multiple instabilities, indirections, humorous obliquities, and self-defensive *Witz*, allows him to convey much that is not directly stated. To write, Svevo believed, is to try to get to the heart of one's complicated being. But he knew that only the "lies" of fiction could reach that heart, and that self-deceit was his truth. This may explain why his form of narrative remains so close to the confessional and autobiographic modes.

Elio's *Diario* makes explicit the many kinds of malaise that were to afflict Svevo during his life, among which his Jewishness was not the least disturbing to him. And related to it there was also the malaise of being a multiple outsider: as a Jew, as a Hapsburgian subject in an Adriatic city that yearned overwhelmingly to be united with Italy, as a writer whose native idiom was not Italian. This linguistic alienation ultimately became for Svevo the very condition of the writer. Zeno's observation that he was bound to lie with every word he spoke in the Tuscan tongue held for him a universal meaning. It illustrated the gap between spoken and literary language, and even more profoundly, the gap between any language and the constant mobility of our consciousness.

Much more than Proust, to whom his early critics compared him, it is Kafka who comes to mind. Like Kafka, who always anticipated the worst, Svevo had recourse to the humor of despair. For Svevo, too, writing was a form of nonliving: a necessity as well as a form of salvation. Only in writing is there salvation, he asserted in his private notes. Yet he was equally convinced that literature is a laughable, futile, and even harmful activity ("ridicola e dannosa").[19] All of this was to be played out, with variations, in the constant shuttle between his life and his work. But in the destiny of his brother, who died so young with so many unfulfilled hopes, he could read what he himself described as a "Schopenhauerian" affirmation of life intimately bound up with its negation.[20]

NOTES

Chapter One

1. Fyodor Dostoevsky, *Notes from Underground*, New York: Dutton, 1960, p. 114.

2. Raymond Giraud, *The Unheroic Hero*, New Brunswick: Rutgers University Press, 1957, p. 52. See also Allen H. Pasco, *Sick Heroes: French Society and Literature in the Romantic Age, 1750–1850*, Exeter: University of Exeter Press, 1997.

3. George Steiner, *The Death of Tragedy*, New York: Alfred Knopf, 1961.

4. See Bernard Knox, introductions to Sophocles, *The Three Theban Plays*, tr. Robert Fagles, Penguin, 1982, as well as his discussion of the Sophoclean hero in *The Heroic Temper*, Berkeley: University of California Press, 1964.

5. Aeschylus, *Prometheus Bound*, line 268; Sophocles, *Oedipus the King*, tr. Robert Fagles, New York: Penguin Classics, 1984, p. 241.

6. Maurice Blanchot, "Le Héros," *Nouvelle Revue Française* 25, 1965, p. 93. Quoted in Walter L. Reed, *Meditations on the Hero*, New Haven: Yale University Press, 1974, p. 133.

7. See in particular chapters 3 and 25 of Voltaire's *Candide*.

8. Primo Levi, *La ricerca delle radici*, Milan: Einaudi, 1981, p. 19; *I sommersi e i salvati*, Milan: Einaudi, 1986, p. 92.

9. For a thorough discussion of the notion of *mètis* see Marcel Detienne and Jean-Pierre Vernant, *Les ruses de l'intelligence: La mètis des Grecs*, Paris: Flammarion, 1992.

10. Yannis Ritsos, "Non-Hero" and "Penelope's Despair," in *Repetitions, Testimonies, Parentheses*, tr. Edmund Keeley, Princeton: Princeton University Press, 1991, pp. 33 and 91. See Edmund Keeley's useful introduction, in particular pp. xxi and xxv–xxvi.

11. See George Roche's interesting essay "Modern Unbelief and the Curious Faiths of the Antihero," in *The World and I*, February 1988, pp. 607–22. For a broader development, see the author's *A World without Heroes: The Modern Tragedy*, Hillsdale, Mich.: Hillsdale College Press, 1987.

12. Friedrich Schiller, "Über Bürgers Gedichte" (1789), Nationalausgabe, vol.

22, p. 253. See also *Briefe über die ästhetische Erziehung des Menschen* (1795). Thomas Carlyle, *On Heroes, Hero-Worship and the Heroic in History* (1840). Joseph Campbell, *The Hero with a Thousand Faces*, Princeton: Princeton University Press, 1972, p. 16.

13. Johan Huizinga, *Homo ludens*, Paris: Gallimard, 1951, pp. 76, 91, 156, 111, and 218. Sigmund Freud, *Moses and Monotheism*, New York: Vintage, 1967, pp. 9, 111.

14. Joseph Conrad, *Heart of Darkness*, New York: Norton, 1988, p. 69. See also Marlow's admiring statement, at the beginning of the novel, about the intrepid Romans who dared explore the northern regions of fog and death which at the time appeared like the very end of the world: "They were men enough to face the darkness" (p. 10).

15. Paul Valéry, "Tel Quel" in *Oeuvres*, Pléiade, Paris: Gallimard, 1966, II, p. 773. Victor Hugo, *Les misérables*, Le Club Français du Livre, 1969, pp. 262 and 287. The entire section on the battle of Waterloo is of specific relevance. See also the chapter on *Les misérables* in Victor Brombert, *Victor Hugo and The Visionary Novel*, Harvard University Press, 1984, in particular, pp. 90–101 on the death of the hero.

16. Herbert Lindenberger, *Georg Büchner*, Carbondale: Southern Illinois University Press, 1964, p. 47.

Chapter Two

1. See, for instance, Maurice B. Benn, *The Drama of Revolt. A Critical Study of Georg Büchner*, Cambridge: Cambridge University Press, 1976, p. 263.

2. George Steiner, *The Death of Tragedy*, New York: Alfred Knopf, 1961, pp. 273–74, 281.

3. G. W. F. Hegel, *The Philosophy of Fine Art*, London: G. Bell and Sons, 1920, I, pp. 246–63. Victor Brombert, *The Hero in Literature*, New York: Fawcett World Library, 1969, pp. 186–201. See also Jean Duvignaud, who mentions Hegel in relation to Büchner's techniques of caricature and derision (*Georg Büchner*, Paris: L'Arche Editeur, 1954, p. 110).

4. Georg Büchner, *Werke und Briefe*, Munich: Carl Hanser Verlag, 1988, pp. 157, 137.

5. Letter of January 1, 1836 (*Complete Works and Letters*, tr. Henry J. Schmidt, ed. Walter Hinderer and Henry J. Schmidt, New York: Continuum, 1986, p. 283).

6. *Complete Works and Letters*, op. cit., p. 276; *Werke und Briefe*, op. cit., p. 305. The expression "Tugendhelden" might be translated more literally as "heroes of virtue."

7. "Es fällt mir nicht mehr ein, vor den Paradegäulen und Eckstehern der Geschichte mich zu bücken" (*Werke und Briefe*, op. cit., p. 305). Henry J. Schmidt translates this metaphorical sentence as follows: "I no longer intend to bow down before the parade horses and pillars of history" (*Complete Works and Letters*, op. cit., p. 260).

8. The numbers in parentheses refer to the numbers of the acts and scenes of the play.

9. Herbert Lindenberger, *Georg Büchner*, Carbondale: Southern Illinois University Press, 1964, p. 27.

10. *Werke und Briefe*, op. cit., pp. 17–34. See the excellent notes provided in this edition, pp. 420–25, 426–34. See also Gerhard Schaub, "Der Rhetorikschüler Georg Büchner. Eine Analyse der Kato-Rede," in *Diskussion Deutsch 17*, 1986, H. 92, pp. 663–84.

11. *Werke und Briefe*, op. cit., p. 278.

12. Ibid., pp. 17, 27.

13. Walter Hinderer, Introduction to *Complete Works and Letters*, op. cit., p. 14.

14. *Werke und Briefe*, op. cit., pp. 145, 181.

15. Ibid., p. 33.

16. Ibid., pp. 144, 306, 284. See also Lindenberger, *Georg Büchner*, op. cit., pp. 23–24, with reference to parodistic effects; and Benn, *The Drama of Revolt*, op. cit., pp. 81–82, 97, concerning Büchner's aesthetic revolt against idealization, ennoblement, and his fundamental suspicion of "high" art.

17. *Werke und Briefe*, pp. 110–11, 88.

18. Ibid., p. 83.

19. Ibid., pp. 122, 110, 114, 84.

20. Lindenberger, op. cit., pp. 46–47.

21. *Werke und Briefe*, op. cit., pp. 92, 128.

22. Ibid., pp. 85–86, 98. Maurice B. Benn mentions Hamlet in connection with the "fatal consequences" of Danton's delays (*The Drama of Revolt*, op. cit., p. 113).

23. *Werke und Briefe*, op. cit., pp. 119, 129.

24. Ibid., pp. 168, 178, 172.

25. See Gutzkov's pun: "Von Ihren 'Ferkeldramen' erwarte ich mehr als Ferkelhaftes" (Letter of June 10, 1836, *Ibid.*, p. 350).

26. The image is quite explicit: "Er laüft ja wie ein offnes Rasiermesser durch die Welt . . ." (Ibid., p. 244).

27. See Benn, *The Drama of Revolt*, op. cit., p. 229.

28. *Werke und Briefe*, op. cit., pp. 238, 242.

29. Ibid., pp. 239, 242.

30. Ibid., p. 247; *King Lear*, IV, 6.

31. *Werke und Briefe*, op. cit., pp. 236–37, 245.

32. Ibid., pp. 249–50.

33. Ibid., p. 250, *King Lear*, IV, 6.

Chapter Three

1. Boris Eichenbaum speaks of Gogol's "phonic inscriptions" and "sound-semantics" in "How 'The Overcoat' Is Made," in *Gogol from the Twentieth Century*, ed. Robert A. Maguire, Princeton, N.J.: Princeton University Press, 1974, p. 280.

2. See John Schillinger, "Gogol's 'The Overcoat' as a Travesty of Hagiography," *Slavic and East European Journal* 16, no. 1 (Spring 1972): 36–41.

3. See Anthony Hippisley, "Gogol's 'The Overcoat': A further Interpretation," *Slavic and East European Journal* 20, no. 2 (Summer 1976): 121–29. Hippisley points out (p. 123) that Gogol, in his *Meditations on the Divine Liturgy*, quotes Psalms 132:9: "Let thy priests be clothed with righteousness . . ."

4. The expression is Charles Bernheimer's, in his fine essay "Cloaking the Self: The Literary Space of Gogol's 'Overcoat,'" *PMLA* 90, no. 1 (January 1975): 53–61.

5. Letter to Pogodin, quoted by Charles Bernheimer ("Cloaking the Self," op. cit., p. 53) and Donald Fanger, *The Creation of Nikolai Gogol*, Cambridge, Mass.: Harvard University Press, 1979, p. 146.

6. Dmitry Chizhevsky, who stresses the presence of the Devil in "The Overcoat," writes: "As someone who was well read in religious literature, as a connoisseur and collector of folklore materials—from popular songs and legends—Gogol of course knew about the Christian and folk tradition that the Devil is faceless." ("About Gogol's 'The Overcoat'," in *Gogol from the Twentieth Century*, op. cit., p. 320.

7. I am largely indebted to Dmitry Chizhevsky, who has shown how the repeated and incongruous use of the adverb "even" (*daje*) breaks up the logical train of thoughts, enlarges trivia, and frustrates the reader by making the insignificant seem significant, and vice versa. Such a narrative strategy is related by Chizhevsky to the semantic oscillations of the text. ("About Gogol's 'Overcoat'," in *Gogol from the Twentieth Century*, op. cit., pp. 295–322.

8. Boris Eichenbaum, op. cit.; Vladimir Nabokov, *Nikolai Gogol*, New York: New Directions, 1944; Victor Erlich, *Gogol*, New Haven: Yale University Press, 1969; Charles Bernheimer, op. cit.; Donald Fanger, op. cit.

9. Victor Erlich has very convincingly discussed Gogol's motif of the mask and tendency to "speak in somebody else's voice" in his chapter "The Great Impersonator" in *Gogol*, op. cit., pp. 210–23. Gogol himself writes: "If anyone had seen the monsters that issued from my pen, at first for my own purposes alone—he would certainly have shuddered" (quoted by Valery Bryusov in his essay "Burnt to Ashes" reproduced in *Gogol from the Twentieth Century*, op. cit., p. 111).

10. Vladimir Nabokov, *Nikolai Gogol*, op. cit., p. 143.

Chapter Four

1. The roman numerals in parentheses refer to the parts of the book; arabic numerals indicate the sections. I have based my discussion on the Russian text, but I have consulted the excellent translation by Ralph E. Matlaw, *Notes from Underground*, New York: Dutton, 1960.

2. According to Tzvetan Todorov's fine formula, we witness the "mise en scène" of an idea (Introduction to *Notes d'un souterrain*, Paris: Garnier-Flammarion, 1992, p. 12).

3. Saint Augustine, *Confessions,* Book II, 3.

4. Tzvetan Todorov, Introduction to *Notes d'un souterrain,* op. cit., p. 27.

5. See the excellent discussion in Joseph Frank, *Dostoevsky. The Stir of Liberation, 1860–1865,* Princeton, N.J.: Princeton University Press, 1986, pp. 331ff.

6. The relevant parts of this letter are reproduced in Ralph E. Matlaw's edition of *Notes from Underground,* op. cit., pp. 194–95.

7. Joseph Frank, *Dostoevsky,* op. cit., p. 315.

8. Jean-Paul Sartre, "Présentation des *Temps Modernes,*" in *Situations II,* Paris: Gallimard, 1948, pp. 20–21.

Chapter Five

1. The numbers in parentheses refer to the original French, *Trois contes,* Classiques Garnier, 1988. I have consulted Robert Baldick's translation, *Three Tales,* New York: Penguin Books, 1976.

2. Gustave Flaubert, *Correspondance,* Paris: Conard, 1926–33, VII, p. 307.

3. Flaubert, *Correspondance,* op. cit., VII, pp. 295–96; George Sand, *Correspondance,* Paris: Calmann-Lévy, 1892, VI, p. 376.

4. Flaubert, *Correspondance,* op. cit., VII, p. 307.

5. Ibid., VIII, p. 65.

6. Ibid., I, pp. 678–79.

7. Ibid., VII, pp. 295–96, 307.

8. Albert Thibaudet, *Gustave Flaubert,* Paris: Gallimard, 1935, p. 178.

9. *Correspondance entre George Sand et Gustave Flaubert,* Paris: Calmann-Lévy, 1904, p. 433.

10. Ezra Pound, *Letters,* New York, 1950, p. 89. Quoted by Harry Levin, *The Gates of Horn,* New York: Oxford University Press, 1963, p. 292.

11. Flaubert, *Correspondance,* op. cit., II, pp. 345–46; VII, p. 294.

12. Flaubert-Sand, *Correspondance,* op. cit., p. 513.

Chapter Six

1. For quotations in the original Italian, I have used the *Opera omnia,* Milan: dall'Oglio, 4 vols., 1966–69. All page numbers preceded by a roman numeral refer to that edition. All quotations in English from *Confessions of Zeno* refer to Beryl de Zoete's translation, New York: Vintage Books, 1989.

2. *Diario di Elio Schmitz,* ed. Bruno Maier, Milan: dall'Oglio, 1973, p. 295. For a more detailed discussion of the brother's diary, see my Appendix, "Svevo's Witness."

3. About this notion of the "failed" writer—the *fallito*—see Denis Ferraris, "L'invention du raté en littérature," *Chroniques Italiennes* 13/14 (1988): 99–119.

4. *Diario di Elio Schmitz,* op. cit., p. 244.

5. Gustave Flaubert, *Sentimental Education,* tr. Robert Baldick, Baltimore: Penguin Classics, 1964, p. 409.

Chapter Seven

1. Hašek's novel appeared over several years (1921–23). Cecil Parrot's translation, Penguin Books, 1973, which is the edition I use, contains an abundance of Lada's illustrations, including the cover page. The numbers in parentheses in my text refer to the pages of this edition. The quotes in Czech refer to *Osudy Dobrého Vojáka Švejka*, Prague: Československý Spisovatel, 4 vols., 1966.

2. See the interesting remarks of Radko Pytlík in *Jaroslav Hašek et le brave soldat Chvéïk*, tr. Marcel Garreau, Prague, 1983, pp. 25, 33, 37.

3. Czeslaw Milosz, *The Captive Mind* (1953), New York: Vintage, 1990. The text by Arthur de Gobineau to which Milosz refers is *Religions and Philosophies of Central Asia* (1865).

4. For a good discussion of this aspect of irony, see Harald Weinrich, *Linguistik der Lüge*, Heidelberg: Verlag Lambert Schneider, 1966.

Chapter Eight

1. Unless otherwise specified, the numbers in parentheses refer to the following English translations: *Sketchbook 1946–1949*, tr. Geoffrey Skelton, New York: Harcourt Brace Jovanovich, 1977; *Sketchbook 1966–1971*, tr. Geoffrey Skelton, New York: Harcourt Brace Jovanovich, 1974 (designated as *Sk.* 1 and *Sk.* 2). The German original *Tagebuch 1946–1949*, Frankfurt: Suhrkamp Taschenbuch, 1985 (1950) and *Tagebuch 1966–1971*, Frankfurt: Suhrkamp Taschenbuch, 1979 (1972), are referred to as *Tg.* 1 and *Tg.* 2.

The following German editions have been used for the other texts: *Die Chinesische Mauer*, Frankfurt: Suhrkamp, 1964; *Don Juan oder Die Liebe zur Geometrie*, Frankfurt: Suhrkamp, 1968 (1952); *Der Mensch erscheint im Holozän*, Frankfurt: Suhrkamp Taschenbuch 1981 (1979). Numerals preceded by the letter G. refer to these German editions. *Homo faber*, Frankfurt: Suhrkamp Taschenbuch, 1977 (1957); *Mein Name sei Gantenbein*, Frankfurt: Suhrkamp Taschenbuch, 1975 (1964); *Montauk*, Suhrkamp Taschenbuch 1981 (1975); *Stiller*, Frankfurt: Fischer Bücherei, 1965 (1954);

The English language editions used are as follows: *Gantenbein*, tr. Michael Bullock, New York: Harcourt Brace Jovanovich, 1982; *Homo Faber*, tr. Michael Bullock, New York: Harcourt Brace Jovanovich, 1987; *I'm Not Stiller*, tr. Michael Bullock, New York: Vintage Books.

2. For a further development of Frisch's notion of language as void, see Werner Stauffacher's interesting essay "Sprache und Geheimnis. Über die letzten Romane von Max Frisch," in *Materialen zu Max Frisch "Stiller*," ed. Walter Schmitz, Frankfurt: Suhrkamp, 2 vols., 1978, I, pp. 53–68.

3. "Öffentlichkeit als Partner," in *Forderungen des Tages*, ed. Walter Schmitz, Frankfurt: Suhrkamp, 1983, p. 300.

4. See the 1971 interview quoted in Rolf Kieser, *Max Frisch, Das literarische Tagebuch*, Frauenfeld and Stuttgart: Huber, 1975, pp. 121–22.

5. The connotations of the prison motif in *Stiller* were originally developed, in a different context, in my article "Frisch, Cheever, the Prison Cell," *Rivista di Letterature Moderne e Comparate* XL, no. 1 (1987): 59–64.

6. Friedrich Dürrenmatt, "'Stiller', Roman von Max Frisch," in *Materialen zu Max Frisch, "Stiller,"* op. cit., I, p. 81. Dürrenmatt states that the reader has to "play along with." The suggestive substantive for this kind of participation is *Mitmachen.*

7. For a developed treatment of this mythological theme in Frisch's novel, see Ronda L. Blair, "'Homo Faber,' 'Homo ludens,' and the Demeter-Kore motif," *Germanic Review* 56 (1981): 140–50. Reprinted in translation in *Frisch's Homo faber,* ed. Walter Schmitz, Frankfurt: Suhrkamp, 1983, pp. 142–70.

8. On this opposition of cyclical and linear time in the modern consciousness, see Mircea Eliade's invaluable *The Myth of the Eternal Return,* tr. W. R. Trask, New York: Pantheon, 1954. Reprinted, Princeton: Princeton University Press, 1971.

9. Werner Stauffacher speaks of the systematic destruction of myths in *Stiller* ("Sprache und Geheimnis," in *Materialen zu Max Frisch "Stiller,"* op. cit., I, 59).

Chapter Nine

1. Albert Camus, *The Plague,* New York: Vintage, 1991, p. 255. (*La peste,* Folio, Paris: Gallimard, 1995, p. 230.)

2. Camus, *Carnets II,* Paris: Gallimard, 1964, pp. 31, 172. *Le mythe de Sisyphe,* Gallimard, Collection Idées, 1963, p. 165.

3. *Noces,* Paris: Gallimard, 1950, pp. 41, 48, 80. *L'envers et l'endroit,* Paris: Gallimard, 1958, p. 125.

4. *Carnets II,* op. cit., p. 87.

5. *The Plague,* op. cit., p. 133.

6. *Ibid.,* pp. 137–38, 209, 162. (*La peste,* op. cit., p. 129.)

7. *The Plague,* op. cit., pp. 127, 253, 6.

8. *Carnets II,* op. cit., p. 175.

9. Pascal, *Pensées,* Baltimore: Penguin, 1968, p. 165.

10. *Le mythe de Sisyphe,* op. cit., p. 181. *Noces,* op. cit., p. 15. André Malraux, *Saturne,* Paris: La Galérie de la Pléiade, 1950, p. 113.

11. *Carnets III,* Paris: Gallimard, 1989, p. 277.

12. "L'artiste et son temps," in *Albert Camus,* ed. Germaine Brée, New York: Dell, p. 204.

13. *The Plague,* op. cit., p. 12. (*La peste,* op. cit., p. 19.)

14. Camus, *The First Man,* New York: Knopf, 1995, pp. 244, 155.

15. *The Plague,* op. cit., pp. 128–29.

16. *Noces,* op. cit., p. 43.

17. *Carnets III,* op. cit., p. 21. *Noces,* op. cit., p. 48.

18. *Noces,* op. cit., p. 98.

19. *Le mythe de Sisyphe,* op. cit., p. 118.

20. "Je suis de ceux que Pascal bouleverse et ne convertit pas." (*Carnets III,* op. cit., p. 177.)

21. *Les Justes,* in, *Théâtre, Récits, Nouvelles,* Paris: Gallimard, 1962, p. 375. *L'envers et l'endroit,* op. cit., p. 123. *L'étranger,* Poche, 1957, p. 175.

22. *Le mythe de Sisyphe,* op. cit., pp. 88, 119.

23. *Carnets II,* op. cit., pp. 21–22.

24. *The First Man,* op. cit., p. 318. (*Le premier homme,* Paris: Gallimard, 1994, p. 318.)

25. *Noces,* op. cit., p. 96.

26. *Ibid.,* pp. 15, 101.

27. *Le mythe de Sisyphe,* op. cit., pp. 70, 18.

28. *The Fall,* New York: Vintage, 1991, p. 97.

29. *Carnets II,* op. cit., pp. 240, 317. *Carnets III,* op. cit., p. 171.

30. See in particular Jean-Paul Sartre, *Situations 2,* Paris: Gallimard, 1948, pp. 12–13, 246–50.

31. *Carnets III,* op. cit., p. 63. *Carnets II,* op. cit., p. 180.

32. "L'artiste et son temps," in *Albert Camus,* op. cit., p. 188.

33. *Carnets III,* op. cit., pp. 63, 147.

34. Numbers in parentheses refer to page numbers in *The Fall,* op. cit.

35. See Matthew 3:3.

36. Quoted in Jean Onimus, *Camus,* Paris: Desclée de Brouwer, 1965, pp. 88–89.

37. For a closer analysis of "The Renegade," see Victor Brombert, *The Intellectual Hero,* Philadelphia: Lippincott, 1961, pp. 227–31.

38. *Carnets II,* op. cit., pp. 250, 254. *Carnets III,* op. cit., p. 269.

39. *Carnets II,* op. cit., p. 209.

40. "L'artiste et son temps," in *Albert Camus,* op. cit., pp. 186–87.

41. Numbers in parentheses from here on refer to pages in *The Plague,* op. cit.

42. *Carnets III,* op. cit., p. 189.

43. *Carnets II,* op. cit., pp. 141–42.

44. *Ibid.,* p. 303.

45. *The First Man,* op. cit., p. 196.

46. *Ibid.,* p. 278.

47. *Carnets II,* op. cit., p. 276.

Chapter Ten

1. *La tregua,* Turin: Einaudi, 1963.

The numbers in parentheses refer to pages of the English language translation in the following editions: *The Drowned and The Saved,* tr. Raymond Rosenthal, New York: Vintage Books, 1989; *If Not Now, When?,* tr. William Weaver, New York: Penguin Books, 1986; *The Periodic Table,* tr. Raymond Rosenthal, New York: Schocken Books, 1984; *Survival in Auschwitz,* tr. Stuart Woolf, New York: Collier Books, 1993.

The numbers preceded by the abbreviation "It." refer to pages in Primo Levi's works in the Einaudi Tascabili editions.

2. *La ricerca delle radici. Antologia personale*, Turin: Einaudi, 1981, p. 145.

3. *I sommersi e i salvati*, Turin: Einaudi, 1986, pp. 112–13.

4. "Our Daily Bread—Pane-Brot-Broid-Chleb-Pain-Lechem-Kenyér: Primo Levi, *Se questo è un uomo*," in *The Flavors of Modernity: Food and the Novel*, Princeton, N.J.: Princeton University Press, 1993, pp. 128–42.

5. *I sommersi e i salvati*, op. cit., pp. 64, 9.

6. *Il sistema periodico*, Einaudi, 1975, p. 157.

7. *Vizio di forma*, Einaudi, 1971, p. 85. The figure of Robinson Crusoe also comes up in Philip Roth's "A Conversation with Primo Levi," in *Survival in Auschwitz*, New York: Collier Books, 1993, pp. 179–80.

8. Massimo Dini and Stefano Jesurum, *Primo Levi. Le opere e i giorni*, Milan: Rizzoli, 1992, p. 51.

9. *La ricerca delle radici*, op. cit., p. 211. "On Obscure Writing," in *Other People's Trades*, New York: Summit Books, 1989, p. 173.

10. *Il sistema periodico*, op. cit., p. 90. The original Italian for "the written word speaks out" is "La carta canta," *L'altrui mestiere*, Einaudi, 1985, p. 233.

11. *Other People's Trades*, op. cit., p. 85.

12. "I padroni del destino," in *L'altrui mestiere*, op. cit., p. 171.

13. "A Conversation with Primo Levi," op. cit., p. 182.

14. *Il sistema periodico*, op. cit., p. 72; Roth, "A Conversation with Primo Levi," op. cit., p. 176.

15. Jean-Paul Sartre, "Qu'est-ce que la littérature?", in *Situations* II, Paris: Gallimard, 1948, p. 250.

16. *I sommersi e i salvati*, op. cit., p. 110.

17. Claude Lévi-Strauss is quoted in Dini and Jesurum, *Primo Levi*, op. cit., p. 181. *Other People's Trades*, op. cit., pp. 103–4.

18. *I sommersi e i salvati*, op. cit., pp. 40–41.

19. *Ibid.*, p. 52.

20. *Il sistema periodico*, op. cit., p. 37.

21. *Other People's Trades*, op. cit., p. 135.

22. *I sommersi e i salvati*, op. cit., p. 92. (*The Drowned and the Saved*, op. cit., p. 116.)

23. Ibid., p. 84.

24. Ibid., p. 66.

25. Ibid., p. 42.

26. Ibid., p. 109.

27. On some Jewish families under fascism, see Alexander Stille, *Benevolence and Betrayal*, London: Cape, 1992. On Primo Levi's father, see Dini and Jesurum, *Primo Levi*, op. cit., pp. 20ff.

28. "A Conversation with Primo Levi," op. cit., p. 184.

29. The *New York Times* obituary page of August 23, 1995, reported the death of Alexander Z. Bielski, who had been a Jewish guerrilla leader during World

War II in the very region Levi describes. His group of some three hundred fighters was known as the Bielski Brigade, carrying out relentless guerrilla action against the Nazis. Levi's novel of Jewish heroism was grounded in reality, though the picturesque figure of Gedaleh belongs rather to the realm of invention.

30. *I sommersi e i salvati*, op. cit., p. 118.

31. The poem in question, "A Mario e a Nuto," is quoted in Dini and Jesurum, *Primo Levi*, op. cit., p. 200.

32. *L'altrui mestiere*, op. cit., p. 212.

33. *I sommersi e i salvati*, op. cit., p. 110.

34. Zwi Jagendorf makes the interesting point, relevant to Levi's predicament as survivor and witness, that Dante's account of Ulysses is a "story of disaster embedded in a narrative of salvation" ("Primo Levi Goes for Soup and Remembers Dante," *Raritan* XII, no. 4 (Spring 1993): p. 48.

Appendix

1. *Profilo autobiografico* in *Opera omnia*, Milan: dall'Oglio, 4 vols., 1966–1969, III, pp. 799–810.

2. John Gatt-Rutter, *Italo Svevo. A Double Life*, Oxford: Clarendon Press, 1988, pp. 16–17.

3. Livia Veneziani Svevo, *Vita di mio marito*, Milan: dall'Oglio, 1976, p. 80.

4. Ibid., pp. 14, 85–86, 72, 90–91.

5. H. Stuart Hughes, *Prisoners of Hope. The Silver Age of the Italian Jews, 1924–1974*, Cambridge, Mass.: Harvard University Press, 1983, p. 38.

6. Livia Svevo, *Vita di mio marito*, op. cit., p. 145.

7. *Opera omnia*, op. cit., I, pp. 115, 867; III, p. 598. The comments on Kafka and "life" making the Jew are quoted in Hughes, *Prisoners of Hope*, op. cit., p. 39.

8. Hughes, *Prisoners of Hope, op. cit.*, pp. 42–45; Giacomo Debenedetti, "Svevo e Schmitz," in *Saggi critici*, Milan: Il Saggiatore, 1971, pp. 47–113. The developments on the feminine passivity of the Jewish anthropological type are to found in Otto Weininger, *Sex and Character*, London: W. Heinemann, 1906.

9. *Opera omnia*, op. cit., III, pp. 192, 176. On "Corto viaggio sentimentale," see Victor Brombert, "Svevo's Trains of Thought," *2PLUS2, A Collection of International Writing*, Lausanne, 1985. The text of the Joyce lecture appeared as one of the "Saggi" in *Opera omnia*, op. cit., III. See in particular pp. 717–18.

10. *Diario di Elio Schmitz*, ed. Bruno Maier, Milan: dall'Oglio, 1973, pp. 195, 212. See also John Gatt-Rutter, *Italo Svevo*, op. cit., p. 17. From here on all page references to the *Diario di Elio Schmitz* will be given in parentheses in the text.

11. Livia Svevo, *Vita di mio marito*, op. cit., p. 16.

12. Letter to Cyril Drucker, in *Opera omnia*, I, pp. 836–37.

13. By a touching coincidence, of which both brothers were well aware, the article was printed on the eve of their parents' twenty-fifth wedding anniversary (*Diario*, op. cit., pp. 238–39).

14. Thus Gabriella Contini, in *Il romanzo inevitabile*, Milan: Mondadori, 1983,

p. 117, speaks of the Triestine "space" as the figuration of a "historical disease" ("La città appare ulteriore figura di malattia storica").

15. The mirror image is quite explicit. At the age of seventeen, Elio Schmitz asks himself why he is keeping this diary, and concludes that he wants to keep for his old age a "mirror" ("specchio") of all he did day by day. Ironically, it is Svevo who kept this diary as a mirror-relic.

16. Livia Svevo, *Vita di mio marito,* op. cit., pp. 16, 26.

17. Svevo comments on this sweetness that comes with the "inertia of the vanquished" ("inerzia del vinto") in "Pagine di Diario e Sparse," *Opera omnia,* op. cit., III, p. 841.

18. To his brother-in-law and business associate who complains that life is unfair and hard, Zeno replies, as we have seen: "Life is neither good nor bad; it is original" (*Confessions of Zeno,* New York: Vintage Books, 1989, p. 312.)

19. *Opera omnia,* op. cit., III, pp. 816–18.

20. "Profile autobiografico," *Opera omnia,* op. cit., p. 801.

INDEX OF NAMES

Note: Numbers in parentheses refer to the text page on which the note number appears.